Worker-Mothers on the Margins of Europe

Worker-Mothers on the Margins of Europe

Gender and Migration between Moldova and Istanbul

Leyla J. Keough

Washington, D.C.
Woodrow Wilson Center Press

Bloomington
Indiana University Press

EDITORIAL OFFICES

Woodrow Wilson Center Press
Woodrow Wilson International Center for Scholars
One Woodrow Wilson Plaza
1300 Pennsylvania Avenue NW
Washington, DC 20004-3027
www.wilsoncenter.org

ORDER FROM

Indiana University Press
Office of Scholarly Publishing
Herman B. Wells Library 350
1320 East 10th Street
Bloomington, IN 47405-3907
Telephone 812-855-8817
iupress.indiana.edu

© 2015 by Leyla J. Keough

All rights reserved
Printed in the United States of America

2 4 6 8 9 7 5 3 1

Library of Congress Cataloging-in-Publication data has been applied for.

ISBN 978-0-253-02088-8 (cloth)
ISBN 978-0-253-02093-2 (paper)
ISBN 978-0-253-02101-4 (ebook)

Woodrow Wilson International Center for Scholars

The Wilson Center, chartered by Congress as the official memorial to President Woodrow Wilson, is the nation's key nonpartisan policy forum for tackling global issues through independent research and open dialogue to inform actionable ideas for Congress, the Administration, and the broader policy community.

Conclusions or opinions expressed in Center publications and programs are those of the authors and speakers and do not necessarily reflect the views of the Center staff, fellows, trustees, advisory groups, or any individuals or organizations that provide financial support to the Center.

Please visit us online at www.wilsoncenter.org.

Jane Harman, Director, President, and CEO

Board of Trustees
Thomas R. Nides, Chair

Public members: William Adams, Chairman of the National Endowment for the Humanities; James H. Billington, Librarian of Congress; Sylvia Mathews Burwell, Secretary of Health and Human Services; Arne Duncan, Secretary of Education; David Ferriero, Archivist of the United States; John F. Kerry, Secretary of State; David J. Skorton, Secretary of the Smithsonian Institution. Designated appointee of the president from within the federal government: Fred P. Hochberg, Chairman and President, Export-Import Bank of the United States

Private citizen members: Peter Beshar, John T. Casteen III, Thelma Duggin, Lt. Gen. Susan Helms, USAF (Ret.), Barry S. Jackson, Nathalie Rayes, Earl W. Stafford, Jane Watson Stetson

Wilson National Cabinet
Ambassador Joseph B. Gildenhorn & Alma Gildenhorn, *Co-Chairs*
Eddie & Sylvia Brown, Melva Bucksbaum & Raymond Learsy, Paul & Rose Carter, Armeane & Mary Choksi, Ambassadors Sue & Chuck Cobb, Lester Crown, Thelma Duggin, Judi Flom, Sander R. Gerber, Harman Family Foundation, Susan Hutchison, Frank F. Islam, Willem Kooyker, Linda B. & Tobia G. Mercuro, Dr. Alexander V. Mirtchev, Thomas R. Nides, Nathalie Rayes, Wayne Rogers, B. Francis Saul II, Ginny & L. E. Simmons, Diana Davis Spencer, Jane Watson Stetson, Leo Zickler

For anneanne, mom, and Sinan.

Contents

Maps and Figures	xi
Acknowledgments	xiii
Introduction	1
1. The Returns on Mobile Mothers' Work	35
2. Uplift in Gagauz Yeri	75
3. Desiring a New Domestic	99
4. Working in Istanbul	135
5. Managing Migration	175
6. Conclusion: "Driven" Women	207
Bibliography	215
Index	231

Maps and Figures

Maps

I.1.	Map of Moldova.	xix
I.2.	Map of the Black Sea Region.	xx

Figures

1.1.	Congaz Church, Gagauz Yeri, Moldova, 2004.	52
1.2.	Congaz Elementary School, Gagauz Yeri, Moldova, 2004.	54
2.1.	Statue of Lenin in Comrat, capital of Gagauz Yeri, Moldova, 2004.	80

2.2.	Gagauz- and Russian-language signs, Museum of History and Society, Comrat, Moldova, 2004.	81
3.1.	Bosphorus Strait and bridge connecting the Asian and European parts of Istanbul, 2004.	108
3.2.	The Mosque of Suleyman, seen from the Golden Horn in Istanbul, 2009.	109
4.1.	View of the village of Beşalma, 2004.	163
4.2.	View exiting Beşalma, 2004.	164
5.1.	Branding image, IOM "You Are Not a Commodity" campaign, 2002.	185
5.2.	Branding image, IOM "Smart Migration" campaign, 2004.	188
5.3.	Cover of the pamphlet *Yes or No,* IOM "Smart Migration" campaign, 2004.	190

Acknowledgments

This book was made possible through the generosity of many individuals and institutions. Its first iteration emerged from a phenomenal nine months in 2007–8 as a Title VIII Research Scholar at the Kennan Institute of the Woodrow Wilson International Center for Scholars in Washington, D.C. My fellow scholars and friends at the Kennan Institute, and at the Wilson Center more widely, helped me develop my arguments and find the right pitch so that a broader public could hear them. I am also indebted to critical engagement with this work by two anonymous reviewers, Jennifer Patico, and the editorial staff at the Woodrow Wilson Center Press. The last's meticulous work has made the book ring with a clarity that I could not have accomplished alone. That said, I take full responsibility for any notes that remain off-key.

The research on which the book is based was funded by IREX, the Institute of Turkish Studies, and the University of Massachusetts Amherst European Field Studies Program. I would like to thank the UMass Anthropology Department and particularly my advisors, Jackie Urla, Julie Hemment, Joya Misra, and Andrew Lass, for their intellectual guidance, enthusiastic encouragement, and insightful suggestions on my research, writing, and career over the years. For their suggestions on this work and their collegial rigor, I would also like to extend my gratitude to the group of scholars represented at the "Bessarabia Conference" at the Max Planck Institute in 2005, New York University's Gender and Transition Workshop in December 2005, the Social Science Research Council's Dissertation Development Workshop in 2006, and the Five College Women's Studies Center where I was a resident scholar in 2006. I would also like to thank my fellow members of SOYUZ (the Postsocialist Cultural Studies Working Group) and the Graduate Association for the Anthropology of Europe at the University of Massachusetts-Amherst Anthropology Department. Dmitry Tartakovsky, Elizabeth Anderson, and Corey Patterson helped get me through fieldwork in Moldova. Dr. Hülya Demirdirek and Dr. Luba Chimpoesh provided many contacts and advice on Gagauz Yeri, which proved crucial to my research and for which I am deeply grateful. I would also like to extend my appreciation to the staff at the International Organization for Migration in Moldova and Turkey for their interest in my research and the time and assistance they gave me, especially Tatiana Jardan for her careful translations from Russian into English.

I am lucky enough to have spent a good portion of 2005 doing research in Istanbul, and in 2008–9, I was graciously hosted as a visiting researcher and lecturer in Cultural Studies at Sabancı University in Istanbul. My time there allowed me to hold more extended conversations with scholars in Turkey—Ayşe Parla, Didem Danış, Ayşe Akalin, Deniz Yükseker, Levent Soysal, Selmin Kaşka, and Mine Eder, among them. I'm grateful for their continued insights into this area of study. I'd like to thank Riva Kantowitz, Esra Başak, and Işık Özel for making my stay at Sabancı not only fruitful, but fun. I extend warm appreciation to all my family in Istanbul—especially Ferruh Iskenderoglu and Beral Madra—for all their help while I lived there. My time in Turkey ended with my participation in the 2009 Hrant Dink Memorial Workshop, where Ayşe Gül Altınay, among other scholars and activists working on behalf of social justice and diversity in the region, showed me first-hand how a small group of people really could make the world a better place. Back in the United States in more recent years, I have been similarly inspired and motivated by Hampshire College's vibrant and dedicated community of concerned citizens and scholars.

I could never have completed the writing of this book without the encouragement of my dear friends back in the "happy valley" of western Massachusetts and in Washington, D.C. They have been there through thick and thin, helping me keep it all in perspective: Kate Wellspring, Sanjiv Gupta, Emily West, Kevin Anderson, Amel Ahmed, Chris Golden, Kenan Ercel, Ceyda Oner, and especially Yahya Madra. A special shout-out to Elizabeth Heath, Lisa Modenos, and Milena Marchesi for their continued friendship through the journey of graduate school and well beyond.

I want to thank my entire family—in the United States, in Turkey, and in Pakistan—for their love and support, but especially my mother, Birsan Iskenderoğlu Clark, for always being there for me and for the transnational family life she created for us between the United States and Turkey; my *anneanne* (grandmother), Leyla Iskenderoğlu, who inspired my interest in this topic, and whose kind inner calm and limitless generosity I do my best to remember in the spirit of everything I do; and my father, Bill Keough, whose poetic instructions for me on life, love, and writing are ever-present.

My greatest thanks goes to the migrant women I write about in this book, whose fortitude I continue to find awe inspiring. More broadly, I am grateful for all the individuals in Istanbul and Moldova who patiently answered my questions and generously offered stories and opinions about their experiences, whether through outspoken objections or whispered confessions.

While completing this book, I began a journey of my own into novel transnational spaces and worker-motherhood, one that I realize is very privileged. Ultimately, it was the steady support and persuasive argument of my husband and best friend, Salman Hameed, that dreams really can be achieved, that convinced me that I could complete this book. I am so very grateful for our son, Sinan—the product of our Turkish, Irish, American, Pakistani conglomerate—whose own power of observation never ceases to amaze me. He teaches me new things every day about the meaning of being a working mom, and about joy.

Leyla J. Keough
Amherst, Massachusetts
July 2015

Worker-Mothers on the Margins of Europe

Map I.1. Map of Moldova.

Map I.2. Map of the Black Sea Region.

Introduction

It's the same with everyone, the same problem. . . . Nobody here, not even doctors—not even other educated and experienced people with stable jobs—can look after themselves on their salaries. US$50 a month is the highest salary here. You can't get by on that. It isn't even enough to pay the electricity and phone bills!

—Tatya, migrant worker, October 2004[1]

You can tell the people who have worked abroad: they hold themselves in a different way, they have self-respect now, they were drowning and now they are able to keep their heads above water.

—Tzina, daughter of a migrant worker, November 2004

There really *is* domestic work in Turkey?

—Iris, International Organization for Migration staff, October 2004

---

[1] All names used are pseudonyms. All translations are the author's own. Moldovan spellings have been used for places in Moldova, including locations in Gagauz Yeri.

It was early fall in 2004, and Tatya, Lana, and I were sitting at a white plastic table on the patio of a new market café. I had spent the day with Tatya in her home in the Gagauz Yeri region of the post-Soviet state of Moldova, interviewing women—teachers and administrators at a local elementary school—who had migrated illegally to Turkey for short periods to work as domestics. While walking through the center of town we had run into Lana, a friend of Tatya's who had also gone to Turkey to work, so we all decided to sit down and talk about her experiences as well. It was toward the end of this final interview of the day that Tatya, in a sad and exasperated manner, commented on the meager wages available even to professionals.

In conversations over the course of fourteen months of ethnographic research in the villages and cities of Moldova and in Istanbul, I listened to women from Gagauz Yeri, an autonomous region of Moldova, describe the effects of the end of socialism with the fall of the Soviet Union. The political and subsequent socioeconomic upheavals had left *everyone* unemployed, underpaid, and underserviced, and had changed long-familiar status distinctions—between white-collar and blue-collar workers, between doctors and farmers, between urban and rural populations. At the same time, neoliberal capitalist restructuring, which emphasizes the retraction of public services and the strengthening of the private sector, had prompted a need for money to pay for basic necessities that once had been taken care of by the state but now were the responsibility of individuals—and were very expensive.[2] As a result, up to one-third of Moldova's population, including half its working-age population, now labored—and labors—abroad (World Bank 2004, 2005; Lücke et al. 2007; Migration Policy Centre 2013).

Most of these migrant workers "commute" back and forth in the margins of Europe, working abroad for six to twelve months at a time to support their families. Many "shuttlers" from Moldova are men who travel to Russia or Italy to work in the construction industry. But women, especially mothers, make up more than 40 percent of these transnational migrants. Some go to Italy and Russia, but many go to Turkey. Known as a sender of *Gastarbeiter* (guest workers) to Germany, Turkey has become a recipient of migrant workers from the formerly socialist countries that surround it—especially

---

[2] By neoliberalism, I mean what is commonly known as "structural adjustment policies," which encourage state withdrawal from social welfare programs and fiscal conservativism and which put less pressure on the state to support populations and more pressure on individuals to support themselves (see Harvey 2005). For the ways in which these policies have variously affected different states in Europe, including examples of postsocialist states, see Joya Misra, Jonathan Woodring, and Sabine N. Merz (2006).

women, who come to work in the informal economy as small-scale traders, sex workers, and/or domestics.

Turkey is the prime destination for women like Tatya from Gagauz Yeri (also known as Gagauzia),[3] a region in southern Moldova (see map I.1) populated by Orthodox Christians who speak both Russian and the Turkic language, Gagauz. Sometimes up to half of the women from Gagauz villages make the difficult choice to leave their families to work in Turkey. They undertake these journeys because they can readily find jobs there as domestics. Doing so increases their monthly income from the $30 they might have earned at home to $300 or more. Tatya herself had been to Turkey four times in six years to work as a domestic for a household in Ankara. That work had provided well for her three children's education and had helped the family build a better home in their village. Tatya's and other women's stories in this ethnographic account incisively demonstrate that a mother's migrant remittances are vital to her children, family, and household.

This migrant work is not just a stopgap measure for families but a means to improve the circumstances of educated working women, their families, and their communities. It also expands notions about women's roles. Indeed, the women who migrate "hold themselves differently," as the daughter of a migrant put it. Nonetheless, their travels can be burdensome and stressful, as these women face accusations in Moldova of being bad mothers, emotionally difficult care work in Turkey, poor working conditions, and vulnerability to police harassment as undocumented migrant workers who are sometimes taken to be *natashas*—the infamous Soviet prostitutes. Time and again, women in these conditions justify their work abroad by appealing to their duty, as worker-mothers, to provide for their children. This repeated observation supports other social science evidence that women, even when seeking uplift and trying to overcome gendered norms, nevertheless point first and foremost to their roles as desperate mothers trying as best they can to provide for their children to justify their absence from home to work abroad.

Notably, these Moldovan women express socialist *worker*-mother values. Under socialism, women were expected to work as well as to care for their own

---

[3] About 170,000 people live in the Gagauz Yeri Autonomous Region in Moldova; another 50,000 to 80,000 Gagauz live in Bulgaria, and some live in Ukraine and the Balkans. Despite speaking a common Turkic language (Gagauz is closely related to Turkish), Gagauz identify themselves and are identified in Turkey as being generically Russian. They are predominantly Russian Orthodox, and Russian is their primary language. Of Moldova's population of 4.3 million, 35 percent speak Russian and 65 percent speak Moldovan.

families, somewhat different from the expectations of women who migrate from historically capitalist parts of the world. Ironically, the Moldovans' socialist values push them into the capitalist structure (and oppressions) of global domestic work. Nonetheless, these women do gain some freedoms, finding in Istanbul a form of worldliness and some respite from the physical exertions of village life. They therefore are forging new ideas about the roles and obligations of mothers and workers in this global neoliberal economy. I call this a new *gendered moral economy* to capture how both the changing political and economic conditions and shifting moralities regarding the appropriate responsibilities and obligations of women have transformed their lives.

These women's mobility and moralities are part of a new trend, one that is widely misunderstood. Since the late 1990s, the migration of women from throughout the former Soviet Union and Eastern Europe has grown exponentially. Although the media, nongovernmental organizations (NGOs), and governments have all publicized the alarming rise in trafficking in women in this region, much less attention has been paid to the growing phenomenon of undocumented migration by women like Tatya, who travel voluntarily for various types of jobs to help their families. The route from Moldova to Turkey has been identified as one of the easiest for trafficking in women, and as a result much effort has gone into preventing Moldovan women's migration. However, the route also leads to much-needed remittances from voluntary, if also illegal, migrant labor. Policymakers should recognize and address the needs of these working women as well.

The foremost institution dealing with migration in the region is the International Organization for Migration in Moldova (IOM-Moldova). It was the countertrafficking team member Iris, who I came to know during my research in Moldova in 2004, who exclaimed—eyes wide and mouth agape—"There really *is* domestic work in Turkey?" For the IOM, the idea of working as a domestic in Turkey was simply a ruse used by traffickers to lure unsuspecting young women from Moldova and then traffic them into sex work. Certainly, such sex-trafficking cases do exist, and the IOM countertrafficking team works hard to repatriate and rehabilitate victims and seek criminal prosecution. Yet, as Iris admitted, the IOM is struggling to find victims. Moreover, the problem of "retrafficking"—of women who, despite being repatriated and rehabilitated from trafficking by the IOM, choose to return to Turkey to find work—has made it clear that IOM projects are missing their mark.

Media, government, and organizations dealing with migration in the region cling to the story of the forced migration of women. They assume that all women who migrate to Turkey are very poor and are duped or forced into going there. The IOM in particular assumes that these women are driven to migrate by the tough economy, ignorance, and traffickers. The IOM's insistent focus on sex trafficking fits the story of trafficking seamlessly into a former socialist state narrative in Moldova, in which the "shock therapy" introduction of capitalism was accompanied by a high moral price—in this case, the so-called white slavery of beautiful Moldovan women. The panic over trafficking of women thus distills, for local Moldovans and global audiences, anxieties over the social costs of wider capitalist processes.

Such anxieties distort the picture of women's migration and misrepresent the effects of globalization on women in Moldova; they also fail to address the common socioeconomic causes and consequences of these migrations. As has been observed in ethnographic studies of migrant women more generally, in the Moldovan case too we find that women choose to work abroad after carefully weighing costs and benefits. Their reasons are complex, even if they primarily legitimate their journeys away from home by activating tropes of motherly sacrifice. The narrative of desperate women driven abroad, whether by traffickers or by the demands of capitalism, curtails our ability to hear the more common experience of gendered injustice and hardship in this former socialist state. When tracked more closely and carefully, we find that this is the experience of educated, resourceful working mothers who lost their jobs and welfare with the dissolution of socialism and who now regularly choose to pursue new work opportunities abroad to underwrite a better educate for their children, improve their own lot, and uplift their home communities.

To understand this migrant labor fully, it is important to look at the economic and social dynamics at the receiving end, in Turkey, as much as in Moldova. This book therefore offers a multisited, multisided ethnographic study in both countries. I offer a comprehensive picture of the supply and demand for this new type of back-and-forth, feminized migrant labor at both its source and destination, illustrated by the experiences and perspectives of the women who use informal networks to migrate for work, their families and communities in Gagauz Yeri, and their employers in Turkey. Discursive practices at these various sites create a social field (in Pierre Bourdieu's terminology) of women's transnational labor.⁴ I let individuals speak for themselves, as I describe the contexts in which these conversations took place, so we may better understand their reasoning.

Such a comprehensive and systematic approach to understanding women's migrant labor affords a unique perspective from which to assess policies that target mobile women in the region. To develop this perspective, my on-the-ground ethnographic research also extended to the IOM countertraffickers and migration managers in Moldova and Turkey, whose take on the situation stands in sharp contrast to what I learned about migration from those most intimately involved in it: the migrants, their families, and their employers. By expanding the scope and sites of study in this way, I was able to explore how ideas and practices regarding women, work, and upward mobility coincide and compete in Gagauz Yeri and Moldova, in Turkey, and at the IOM offices in both countries to influence this migration.

Although the IOM and other organizations might consider the plight of post-Soviet and postsocialist women to be special, this story is not unfamiliar to women the world over. Recent transformations in the global economy from socialist and welfare state models to neoliberal capitalist models centered on the private sector have increased burdens on women for family success and left them without employment at home, prompting them to seek work abroad. Saskia Sassen (1998, 2000) characterizes this phenomenon as a "feminization of survival," but those who have further studied the matter now agree that such migrations are not about the survival of the poor in the countries of origin, for only women with some resources and wealth are able to take advantage of opportunities to work abroad. And unlike the traditional patterns of migration—which brought families, initially men, from the global periphery to settle in urban western and northern centers—women's contemporary migrations are particularly telling of the new mobile and gendered form of transnational labor.⁵ Feminist ethnographers and

---

[4] The social field emerges both from practices of the employers, employment agents, and migrant domestics in Istanbul (among others) and from their discourses about their lives. I therefore sometimes use the term "discursive practices." I also use "discursive practices" because it refers to such "talk" as a practice (see Ries 1994).

[5] Roger Sanjek and Shellee Colen (1990); Thanh-Dam Truong (1996); Saskia Sassen (2000); Katie Willis and Brenda Yeoh (2000); Barbara Ehrenreich and Arlie Russell Hochschild (2002); Mary Beth Mills (2003); Sarah Mahler and Patricia Pessar (2006); and Mary Zimmerman, Jacqueline Litt and Christine Bose (2006) are among those who detail these new global trends in women's migration.

sociologists have examined this feminization of migration, relating narratives of migrant domestic workers who take routes from south to north, east to west, and third world to first world (see, e.g., Lutz and Koser 1998; Anderson 2000; Chang 2000; Hondagneu-Sotelo 2001; Parrenas 2001; Constable 2002; Lan 2006a, 2006b; Lutz 2007) and within Asia (Adams and Dickey 2000). These authors explain that women see their work abroad as a motherly sacrifice they undertake for their families.

The instance of women from formerly socialist Moldova working in Turkey contributes to this discussion of feminized labor a novel example of women commuting from west to east, within the formerly socialist margins of Europe. From this case, a unique perspective emerges: migrant work conducted in the context of thriving socialist ideals allows Gagauz women workers to continue to hold wage-earning and decision-making power in their households, instead of losing this power by becoming undervalued full-time housewives. The Gagauz migration thus provides a fascinating and important example of the new labor migrations in a changing global economy. And because it is occurring in a postsocialist country, where socialist ideals still strongly influence societal and personal expectations and decisions, the Gagauz migration sheds light on how migrant women workers and their families accommodate, negotiate, and resist shifts to the global neoliberal capitalism and conceptualize these shifts by reworking ideas about their obligations to their families and their role as workers.

Although economic conditions clearly play a decisive role in these migrations, so also do gendered stereotypes. The life of the women labor migrants I came to know was characterized by their being subject to various notions, some quite freighted, of gender roles. They spent a great deal of time and energy strategically positioning themselves within these representations of women. These gendered discursive practices, which regard women as "driven" in various ways, condition and affect the supply of this labor from Moldova and its consequences there, its demand in Turkey, and the IOM's response to it. Moreover, such *ideas* about the morality of women's labors and uplift work alongside the *structural political-economic conditions* of women. To capture how these two processes are linked, I call them gendered moral economies.

Ethnographers of the former socialist bloc countries have deployed the concept of moral economy to understand how transformations in the economy are accompanied by shifts in local understandings of what constitutes legitimate, moral decisions in work and in life.[6] Using this ethnographic work as a launching pad, I show how such understandings are gendered. In this book, "gendered moral economies" refers to the way in which ideas about the place of women are instilled in discursive practices of need, entitlement, desire, obligation, culpability, and responsibility in the economic processes of production (and reproduction), exchange, and consumption. In making this concept the underpinning of my analysis, I take my cue from feminist scholars, who argue that gender is a key cultural form through which shifts in the political economy of formerly socialist states can be understood and legitimated (Gal 1994a, 1994b; see also Berdahl 1999; Gal and Kligman 2000a, 2000b). Thus the social field of transnational labor migration is not only economic but also gendered, and controversies over migrant women are structured both by economic shifts and by changing views on the place of women in the economy. I also hold a feminist concern with the intersection of gender with other subjugations, such as those based on class, race, ethnicity, citizenship, nationality, and religion. These overlapping social and economic concerns inform Gagauz women's experiences and help us better compare them with the experiences of migrant domestic workers elsewhere.

The effects of a gendered moral economy on women are not stable or perseverant, and are highly likely to be influenced by local contexts. At times, such an economy may align women with patriarchal neoliberalism; at other times, women are able (if only momentarily) to resist gendered and capitalist systems of oppression. This book tracks the effects on women of the transformations from socialism to a private-sector economy, writ large, and also shows how moral ideas about workers' and mothers' roles inform this new economy and women's experience of it, and so become integral to the functioning of this undocumented transnational labor market.

Ideas about gendered work, furthermore, position women to participate in the global economy in certain ways. This book is concerned primarily with the ways in which gendered ideas shift in this changing postsocialist, neoliberal context and embed women in new economic practices that may offer new freedoms but also impose new limitations. Women resist such limitations in some ways, but are also complicit in demarcating them. Such

---

[6] See, for instance, the work of Yulian Konstantinov (1996), Ruth Mandel and Caroline Humphrey (2002), Deema Kaneff (2002), Jennifer Patico (2005), Catherine Wanner (2005), and Adrian Smith and Alison Stenning (2006). For a recent example of the use of "moral economies" in a migration context other than postsocialist, see Wise and Velayutham (2005).

gendered practices do not just negotiate contradictions; they also *authorize* the capitalist economy (Ong 1987; Gal 1994a, 1994b; Gal and Kligman 2000a; Mills 2003; Brennan 2004). For the Gagauz Yeri case, I trace how values placed on women's mobility—in terms of movement across geography, but also in terms of class and gender—play out in this social field of transnational labor.

A Social Field of Transnational Labor

Why map gendered moral economies as a social field of transnational labor? There are several reasons, but perhaps the most important one is to avoid bounding this analysis within nation-states conceived as ethnic entities in confined territories, which would restrict the study to methodological and philosophical nationalism.[7] Operationalizing Pierre Bourdieu's concept of a social field allows us to imagine our object of analysis—here, gendered moral economies—as multisited (Marcus 1995). This moves us away from anthropology's traditional, and problematic, objects of analysis—ethnicities, cultures, nations, or peoples—to an examination of competing *discourses* and *practices* of various actors in different places (Appadurai 1991; Gupta and Ferguson 1992; Marcus 1995).[8] Yet the concept of a social field goes beyond simply identifying multiple discourses and practices: it *relativizes* them, placing all of the actors and sites on a level playing field. In other words, it does not hierarchize discursive practices, placing some—those stemming from states or organizations, for instance—in an authoritative position "above" others, such as those stemming "below" from migrants themselves. Further, guided by the concept of a social field, we remain attuned to changes over time in different spaces. The concept of a social field assumes that political economies and discursive practices are always changing, simultaneously, in both home and host countries. This concept helps avoid the presumption that the movements of people over space from

---

[7] For more on a critique of methodological and philosophical nationalism in the study of migration, see Wimmer and Glick-Schiller (2003).
[8] Arjun Appadurai (1991), Akhil Gupta and James Ferguson (1992, 1997), and George Marcus (1995) ask us to rethink the idea of static cultures in bounded spaces as the objects of anthropological study. They call for us instead to position our studies in what Gupta and Ferguson term "multiple social-political sites and locations" (1997, 37) and to look more closely at the fluidity with which people, ideas, commodities, and objects move through geographic space. This is an argument to relinquish the idea of spatially and temporally immobile "cultures" because even if they ever did exist, they certainly do not anymore.

the former Soviet bloc countries to Turkey are also movements over time from a socialist past to an inevitable capitalist future.

Moreover, Bourdieu's notion of the social field of value also corresponds with the idea of a *moral* economy as used here. Questions about how and in which contexts gendered moral economies in this social field of transnational labor may help or hinder women's and workers' empowerment are the first set of concerns taken up in this book. Thus, as I use it here, the term *social field* is infused with power and agency. In all, the concept of social field is a way of accounting for the multiplicity of representations and practices, places and peoples, adding depth and breadth to our understanding of migration and gender. With it, we can see more closely the shifting value, over space and time, assigned to these women migrants, their labors, and their wealth (or lack thereof). We are then in a better position to understand their changing identities, practices, agency, and power. Before turning to the two primary concerns of this ethnography—how we understand the gendered nature of these moral economies and the value of socialist moralities to neoliberalizing women—it is important first to consider in what ways deploying a framework of the social field of transnational labor is fundamental to the argument of the book.

Bourdieu's social field provides a sophisticated means to get beyond nationality or ethnicity as a unit of analysis in studies of transnationalism.[9] This is especially important for studies of mobility within the former Soviet space. Initially, interest focused on returning, on movements motivated solely by ethnic belonging and the desire to undo the Soviet relocation policies of the past: the Germans of Kazakhstan returned to Germany, Tatars reclaimed Tatarstan. Today, there is a greater recognition that even though ethnic identity may drive these migrations in part, economic necessity can also play a significant role. At the very least, the interactions between feelings of ethnic belonging and the economic motives for migrations are complex (Buckley 1997, 14).

---

[9] The concept of a "transnational social field" forged by Nina Glick-Schiller, Linda Basch, and Cristina Szanton Blanc has helped migration scholars cross geographic, cultural, and political borders and move beyond familiar nationalist categories (1994, 7). The transnational analytical frame admits that despite being in different states, the political, social, and economic processes in which migrants engage "constitute a single field of social relations" (1994, 5). I use a somewhat different concept here, that of the social field of transnational labor, to illustrate this case. I do this because, while most studies of transnational social fields focus on the politics of transnationalism (or "transpolitics"; see Silverstein [2004] in particular), this ethnography speaks to the economics of transnationalism, a "commuter" (Gülçür and Ilkkaracan 2002) labor in the global neoliberal economy.

Surprisingly, in Gagauz Yeri, despite the professed Gagauz ethnic connection to Turkey, ethnicity turned out to have little to do with women's decision to work in Turkey. As someone who entered this project from Turkish studies, I was initially interested in the Gagauz position as Turkic speakers in Eastern Europe. Their language is similar to the Turkish spoken in Turkey and has remained so for generations, if not centuries.[10] Because of this language connection, I had expected that despite being Orthodox Christians, the people of Gagauz Yeri would be excited to connect to their Turkish brethren after decades of Soviet domination. Similarly, I had expected that Turks in Turkey, especially the upper-middle-class employers of migrant domestics from Gagauz Yeri—to whom secularism is important and Islam less so—would wholeheartedly embrace their Turkic (if Christian) cousins in Europe.

Contrary to my expectations, the language similarity played only a pragmatic role in these relationships; their common ethnic roots meant very little to either party. Gagauz identified closely with Russians as former Soviets and as Orthodox Christians, seeing Muslim Turks as others. For urban upper-class Turks, Gagauz are generic "Moldovans"—their citizenship in Eastern Europe and their class position in Turkey as workers trump any common Turkic connection. Thus, ideas regarding socialism and capitalism, men and women, rurality and urbanity, ethnicity and class, played a stronger role than ethnicity or nation in women's identifications, motivations, experiences, and understandings of the costs and benefits of their migrations. This is an example of the importance of drawing on the concept of the social field of transnational labor. It enables us to avoid regarding individuals in Gagauz Yeri and Turkey solely in nationalist terms based on ethnic belonging (whether Turkish, Moldovan, or Gagauz Turkic). Such terms only serve to essentialize these categories and are not necessarily relevant to migrant experiences.

By moving beyond these nationalist terms, the analytic of "social field" also allows us to recognize that individuals, even if they stay put in one nation, are always already transnational. It might be said that migrating just adds a new geography to existing transnationalisms. It is particularly clear in former Soviet bloc migrations that individuals enter this transnational field from contexts that are already multicultural. This social field of transnational labor thus involves exchanges not only between two nations and two peoples in host and home states, or between those who migrate and those who stay behind. It is instead a much more nuanced and complex situation,

---

[10] Gagauz is even more similar to Turkish than Azeri is.

one informed to a considerable degree by ideas and practices regarding the morality of women's labor in both home and host societies.

Istanbul is teeming with migrants from all parts of the former Soviet Union and Eastern Europe—a circumstance we might think of as a formerly socialist diaspora. Most studies of migration focus on the diversity of the host society.[11] To understand women's transnationalisms, however, we have to know whence the women came—and what kinds of transnationalism exist there.[12] As a result of the historical legacy of the Soviet-era simultaneous Russification of Moldova and support for Gagauz autonomy, the social field of transnational labor movement in Gagauz Yeri involves not only those who go to Turkey and those who stay behind, but also those who go to Russia. Women from Gagauz Yeri understand their migration as a decision among many possible migrant routes in an always already transnational Moldova—not just in the context of those who leave and those who stay behind but also of those who go elsewhere, or have been elsewhere, and those who have returned.

The experience of diverse transnationalisms in the former Soviet Union and Eastern Europe forces us to engage what Peggy Levitt and Sanjeev Khagram term a "philosophical transnationalism" that "starts from the metaphysical assumption that social worlds and lives are inherently transnational" (2007, 2). Levitt and Khagram propose that "transmigrants" are not necessarily following a pattern of settling in a new country, letting go of the old, and assimilating. Instead, they are integrating into new geographies and ideologies while simultaneously retaining or renewing ties to places of origin. Moreover, they write, "Our analytical lens must necessarily broaden and deepen because migrants are often embedded in multi-layered, multi-sited transnational social fields, encompassing those who move and those who stay behind" (Levitt and Khagram 2007, 284). In other words, an examination of both the sending and the receiving states is called for in a study of transnational labor movements.

However, it is still rare to find migration studies in which host and home are represented in one work, and in the case of migrant labor it is unusual to find both migrants and their employers represented.[13] Despite the early

---

[11] In the case of migrant domestic workers, see, for instance, Nicole Constable (1997a, 1997b), Christine Chin (1998), and Pei-Chia Lan (2006a).

[12] In the case of migrant domestic workers, works focusing on the "home society" include, for instance, Michele Gamburd (2000) and Nana Oishi (2005).

[13] David McMurray (2001) and Rachel Salazar Parrenas (2001) focus on migrants in the home and host community, but not on the home community's perspective on these migrants. Parrenas

insights of Nina Glick-Schiller, Linda Basch, and Cristina Szanton Blanc (1994) regarding the importance of transnational considerations, work on migration, especially migration in Europe, continues to be mired in nationalism. For example, such studies often analyze the settlement and integration of immigrants (and their descendants) in ethnic enclaves of "modern" cities in first-world nations. No doubt these issues continue to be important, but studies along these lines limit an understanding of migration to national dynamics, and more often than not focus solely on host nations (Nuhoğlu-Soysal 1994, Brettell 2003).

With increasing access to new communication technologies and in the context of trends toward globalization, migration is an experience that does not necessarily end in assimilation or acculturation into one nation-state and one citizenship. Individuals are continually moving around. Many people remain what Glick-Schiller, Basch, and Szanton Blanc call "transmigrants" throughout their lives, and their home countries continue to be important points of reference and wellsprings of cultural associations and

---

(2005) and Paul Silverstein (2004) look at the effects of migration at home. Notable anthropological works on migrations in Europe continue to cover "classic" cases: South Asians in Britain (Modood and Werbner 1997, Werbner 2002), Berbers and Arabs in France (Silverstein 2004), and Turks in Germany (Nuhoğlu-Soysal 1994; Çağlar 1995; Soysal 2003, 2004). For work on women migrants to Europe, see Morokvasic (1991, 1993), Koffman (1999) and Koffman et al. (2000). The topic of migration to southern Europe (Anthias and Lazaridis 2000) and to Italy in particular (Cole 1997; Carter 1997; Andall 2003) is increasingly represented as well. The topic of migration to the Middle East, with particular attention to labor and trafficking, has been taken up in a number of recent ethnographies (Gardner 2010; Mahdavi 2011), but the focus is firmly on the host society (Bahrain and Dubai, respectively). In the formerly socialist world, aside from the work of Patico (2010), there is no research that takes place at both source and destination, with employers and employees or host and home perspectives. Nonetheless, there is a burgeoning literature on transnational migration in this region, including Yulian Konstantinov (1996); Konstantinov, Gideon Kressel, and Trond Thuen (1998); Deniz Yükseker (2000, 2004); Blair Ruble and Nancy Popson (2000); Gülçür and Ilkkaracan (2002); Mine Eder et al. (2002); Alexia Bloch (2003); Hulya Demirdirek and Judy Whitehead (2004); Uygun (2004); Ruble (2005); Sebnem Koser Akçapar (2006); Didem Danış (2006); Ahmet İçduygu (2006); Selmin Kaşka (2006); Ayşe Akalin (2007); Ayşe Parla (2007); Ruble and Cynthia Buckley (2008); Danış and Parla (2009); and Eder and Özlem Öz (2010). An interesting study of Georgia's borderland with Turkey can be found in Mathijs Pelkmanns (2006). A study on the effects of migrant displacement on masculinity in Georgia can be found in Kabachnik et al. (2013). In cases outside the former socialist context, a few works deploy transnational research: see Ayşe Çağlar (1995) and Roger Rouse (1996); see also Jennifer Hirsch (2003), Nina Glick-Schiller, Ayşe Çağlar, and Thaddeus Buldbransen (2006), Lieba Faier (2009), and Patico (2010). Interestingly, Caroline Brettell's ethnography, which provides narratives of the lives of three rural Portuguese women working in France (1982), is an early exceptional example of a work that disrupts conceptualizations of migration in terms of gender and conceptions of core versus periphery.

moral understanding (1994). This is certainly the case with the women of Gagauz Yeri, who do not seek to settle in Turkey but only to commute there for work. Their primary frame of reference remains their homes in Moldova, though these homes are already transnational in some ways. I move forward theoretically and empirically with this case of migrant women workers who informally shuttle in Europe's margins with fieldwork that offers a view from both home and host societies. Assuming that Gagauz Yeri, Moldova, and Turkey are already transnational, this book—the result of multisited ethnographic research—documents transnationalism empirically, in contrast to the methodological nationalism that has prevailed in some spheres of effort. It also supports, in the conceptualization of a social field of transnational labor, a movement toward a philosophical transnationalism.

In the pages that follow, therefore, I focus on gendered moral economies not as products of national ideologies based on ethnic belonging in Moldova and Turkey but rather as discursive practices engaged in and embodied by individuals at particular times in specific places. Many people are constructing this social field of transnational labor: women migrants from Gagauz Yeri; family and friends who stay in Moldova (or those who go to Russia to work); Turkish male and female employers and their charges; other foreign and postsocialist women in Turkey; Turkish domestics; Gagauz women who have married Turkish men; Turkish male friends, lovers, boyfriends, or husbands; service providers for the commuters, such as the informal travel and employment agents and the minibus drivers who take consumer goods from Turkey back to Moldova; Turkish police and government officers; the IOM staff in Turkey and Moldova; and scholars of this region and of gender and migration. We hear from all of them.

The discursive practices of all these actors, whether manifested in their movements, work, discipline, caring, protection, gossip, flirtations, harassment, generosity, policy agendas, or publications, create the gendered moral economies in this social field of transnational labor. I investigate ideas about why women migrate and work in Turkey from many different perspectives located in various places: in whitewashed homes off muddy lanes in Gagauz villages; in the sleek, fast-paced offices of the IOM in the state capitals of Moldova and Turkey; in upper-class households in sanitized Istanbul *sités*, or apartment blocks;[14] in the commercial and red-light district of Laleli near the shores of the Bosphorus, where many former Soviets gather; in the dusty and bureaucratic offices of the Turkish and Moldovan governments; in

---

[14] *Sité* is a Turkish word taken from the French word *sité*, which means an apartment complex.

employment offices for domestic workers; in Orthodox churches tucked into old Istanbul neighborhoods; in local and international media, from newspapers to daily television talk shows; and in scholarly treatises.

I do not privilege one set of these narratives or sites over another. Placing all discursive practices regarding women's labor in one social field avoids the presumption, for instance, that researching IOM organizations is a form of "studying up" and that this is a privileged site for the construction of meaning, which is then disseminated "downward." Neither does it presume to separate the global context from the local context, or privilege the construction of knowledge in the center over the periphery. Rather, applying the social field concept places all of these actors and gendered moral economies on the same plane. I conceptualize this move as a "flattening" of these sites, that is, relativizing them before presuming the power they may hold in this social field. I see this as part of my work's radical act, its own "cosmopolitan ethnographic practice," in the words of Lila Abu-Lughod (1991, 1999a).

This relativizing is particularly helpful to understanding the Gagauz women migrants because even though migrant domestic work is informal, it is nonetheless systematic. The actions of employment agents, employers, and employees that constitute the system and help it endure are not condoned by the respective states, and these economies are not officially regulated. Thus, in this case it is particularly clear that the primary means for accomplishing systematization is not laws handed down from above but the discursive practices of morality followed by individuals on the ground.

As their narratives in the following chapters indicate, what determines the risk, security, and trust between Gagauz women, their employers, and other actors is the small, daily interactions among networks of people on the ground in Moldova and Turkey. These interactions build an understanding for those involved in migrant labor of how the system should or should not work. In some sense, the narratives and interactions and the common ideas and practices built through them—or discursive practices—are prompted by economic changes, but they also reflect what value is assigned to the type of labor women choose to do, where they work, what they buy with their wages, and their presumed agency, as well as notions of civilization, ethnicity, religion, citizenship, and race.

This brings me to the final reason why Bourdieu's concept of the social field is appropriate for this study: its focus on social fields of value coincides with my concern with *moral* economies. A social field, as conceived by Bourdieu, consists of fields of action; that action is to value, and valuations can be monetary or moral. A social field comprises subfields of competing and contradictory valuing activity by actors in various contexts. Bourdieu's "field of cultural production," for instance, delineates the various players in a field, the values they hold and are held to, the positions available and individual position-takings, and the strategic maneuverings that occur within the field. Actors compete not only, or even primarily, for economic benefit but also for social or cultural capital (Bourdieu 1993).[15] Capital, for Bourdieu, is another way of marking various forms of value; thus he uses the phrase "social field of value" to describe a field that encompasses these various forms of capital—wealth, education, social networks, and recognition. Moral economies are a particular type of social field of value. Bourdieu's analysis is sensitive to the unexpected nature of the distribution of value and the changing nature of various forms of values—to how a field such as education, in his example, that might otherwise be seen as based mostly in cultural capital (knowledge) might be as much about economic capital (wealth).[16]

This book is concerned with the maneuverings of moral values in a field of women's transnational labor that might otherwise be viewed as determined only by economic need or survival strategies. As much as it has to do with simply putting food on the table, Gagauz women's work abroad fulfills their longing for social prestige in their communities and their desire to be seen as a good mother. Both of these goals are moving targets. The social field of transnational labor is a particularly apt framework to link various discursive practices with which Gagauz migrant women, among other actors, strategize for moral as well as economic ground. People in Gagauz Yeri deploy complex ideological justifications for women's labor, switching between reasons involving economy and identity (gendered identities, but also ethnic, religious, and class identities) to decide where to work, to legitimate this decision morally, to understand its costs and benefits, and to articulate what it means to them. Paying attention to these gendered moral economies forces us to see women migrants and their female employers as agents who construct this social field of transnational labor. Through them, we also see how this migrant labor helps—or hinders—women, workers, and ideas about them in the new economy.

---

[15] For Bourdieu, cultural capital includes values like those of education, whereas social capital refers to social networks of people one knows.
[16] For more on social field, see Ladwig (1994), who analyzes education policy as a social field.

Gendered Moral Economies

The migration of women from Gagauz Yeri for work is part of a global trend, in which more than 50 percent of migrants are now women. Thus, women constitute this social field of transnational labor not primarily (as in the past) as migrants following their migrant husbands or left behind by them but as migrant laborers themselves (Brettell 2003; Pessar and Mahler 2003). As women have begun to migrate alone, concerns have arisen in both public and scholarly dialogue over their role as breadwinners of the family, located in the public realm, and their relative absence from the private realm of the household. In their new role of migrant working mothers, women from Gagauz Yeri transform their roles and their ideas of what it means to be workers and mothers in unexpected ways. They gain from their participation in the rapidly privatizing global economy, and also face new limits, some of which are self-imposed.

To understand fully the costs and benefits to women of migrant labor, we must consider agency and power.[17] Drawing on feminist works, in this book I examine how processes of patriarchy and capitalism are contradictory and reinforcing through foucauldian notions of discursive power—the kind of power that constructs subjectivities (ideas and practices about identity and notions of the self) and multiple subjugations (Foucault 1980; Butler 1992; Ong 1987; Grewal and Kaplan 1992; Kaplan, Alarcon, and Moallem 1999; Constable 2002). These processes are evident in gendered moral economies and the resistances to them at various locations: at home in Moldova, among the women's employers in Turkey, and at the IOM-Moldova, but, most important, among migrant domestic workers themselves. Indeed, gendered moral economies are transformed not by political-economic shifts of globalization alone, or solely by the actions of women.[18] The multiple workings of power subject these women to certain roles, identities, and statuses in their home and host societies. Migrant women are both subjects of gendered moral economies and themselves also constructing them. Through their

---

[17] For more the importance of agency to social fields, see Sherry Ortner (1996) and Terry Lovell (2003).

[18] Sherry Ortner uses the term "gender hegemonies" to define the various subjugations of individuals according to gender as a result of both economic and ideological structures (1996). By using "hegemony," she acknowledges that power is as much discursive as it is economic. I also use this term, along with gendered moral economies, to represent both discursive and political economic types of power. Gendered moral economies are not yet gender hegemonies. They may be emergent gender hegemonies, but they may also be simply coopted by existing gender hegemonies.

own practices of undocumented transnational labor and their narratives about it, women may accept or resist conventional values and representations, but they also seek to manipulate them for economic or moral ground, and so, whether intentionally or not, they often accommodate and confirm these constructions.

Tracking this transnational labor and the discursive practices surrounding it thus shows that structures and traditional notions about women, workers, and migrants are reproduced in some instances, even as opportunities and power for migrant women laborers are gained in certain contexts. Women's migrant labor and their own understanding of it can prompt productive slippages that rupture conventional gendered hegemonies. Yet such hegemonies shift in complex ways, changing while they seem to stay the same or appearing to change when in fact they are staying put. Women hold agency in these processes, if only sometimes, in their meaningful reinterpretations of their lives. In their accounts, we find that these migrant women are not simply pawns driven by economic forces beyond their control and are not just mothers seeking the survival of themselves and their offspring. Quite the opposite: these women have and express agency, and they are "driven" to uphold particular moral and cultural ideals. This book is thus an ethnography of women's agency and power and an analysis of the possibility of women's agency in a postsocialist setting.

The migrant women from Gagauz Yeri provide a different twist on familiar themes in the literature on the power and agency of migrant domestic workers. Like others, they legitimate and understand their work abroad through their gendered moralities, asserting that they are good mothers seeking to lift up their families. And, as in other cases, they seek various kinds of upward mobility, depending on their particular background, socioeconomic status, and identities. In other words, their urbanity, ethnicity, class, education, work experience, and notions of civilization all affect their power and agency. This perspective illuminates how these women are not, or not only, driven by some universal maternal instinct for survival. Like many other women in similar situations, they transform their gender roles in the process of pursuing uplift, arguing that mothers should be providers as well as nurturers. But a key difference is that for the women of Gagauz Yeri, this morality represents a *continuation* of the socialist worker-mother ideology, with both its benefits and its drawbacks.

The worker-mother discourse holds some similar consequences for Gagauz women as for women in other contexts, but certain effects are distinctive. In Gagauz Yeri, migrant domestic work creates some freedoms (working for wages and abroad) for women, but it also precipitates new consumer desires. Moreover, migrant work enmeshes these women in a kind of economic self-reliance that has become the oppressive mark of neoliberal capitalism. As in other cases, here too migrant domestic work has become instrumental in the reproduction of difference and social inequality (Rollins 1985; Romero [1992] 2002; Lan 2002), prompting contradictory movements in class and gender identities (Ong 1999; Parrenas 2001). Ultimately, that domestic work, whether waged or not, is still considered "women's work" in Gagauz Yeri exemplifies how migrating for domestic work helps reinforce gendered roles in the household and contributes to an undervaluing of this work in both home and host societies (Parrenas 2001). This case thus provides more fodder for Nancy Fraser's insistence that capitalism and patriarchy are in lockstep with each other (2006, 2009).

What makes the Gagauz case so interesting is that these former socialist women's relationship to capitalism is different from other women's experiences. In most feminist accounts of migrant domestic work (e.g., Ong 1987; Parrenas 2001; Constable 2002; Mills 2003), traditional capitalist gendered hegemonies are the baseline against which changes in women's status and gendered ideas are measured. The postsocialist difference is revealed in the gendered moral economies used alternately to criticize or to legitimate this labor abroad. Unlike in other cases, migrant women workers from Gagauz Yeri see themselves as *already* modern women workers. By and large, they get what they want from these transactions of labor for money, and are willing to continue to work abroad for it. They are highly valued as "modern" and "Western" in Turkey, even if there are some negative consequences to these attributions. In Moldova, however, their participation in capitalist labors in Turkey is not considered a morally legitimate path to modernity, progress, or uplift, but rather a *fall* from modernity and civilization. This dichotomy complicates Gagauz women's justifications of their new capitalist desires and their work to people at home and in Turkey, informs their recourse to discourses of motherhood to legitimate this work abroad, and affects the returns on their labors.

Postsocialism/Neoliberalism

One question persistently emerges in the case of Gagauz women migrant workers: Just what *is* the difference that the postsocialist experience makes? How do we best conceptualize and represent the experience of women who lived under socialism and went through its dramatic collapse? How do we compare this case with that of migrant domestics in capitalist contexts? Do their socialist roots define them to the extent that we must—still—refer to them as postsocialist? Or have they all become capitalists now? In this case, although their socialist pasts are clearly important to these women and help render their difference from others, the postsocialist label can obscure more than it illuminates. In the past, the term "postsocialism" was useful to describe the former Soviet Union and Eastern Europe in a period of transformation to an uncertain future (Bridger and Pine 1998; Burawoy and Verdery 1999; Hann 2002). More than twenty years on from that dramatic moment, we now can answer Katherine Verdery's (1996) question, "What comes next?" What came next was global neoliberal capitalism.

In this book, I have chosen to unhinge the postsocialism appellation from its limited geography (Eastern Europe and the former Soviet Union) and narrow time frame, and from its definition as a purely economic category. Instead, I use it to describe a broader moment of global economic and moral transformation from socialist and welfare states to neoliberal ones. The case of migrant domestic workers from Moldova demonstrates the coincidence of post-Soviet and post-welfare-state processes globally. The transformations associated with the state's rescission from social welfare, not only in the West and on its margins but also globally, prompted Nancy Fraser to posit that the world's condition is less postmodern than collectively postsocialist (1997). Following Fraser's gesture, I use "postsocialism" to refer not only to the loss of state-sponsored socialism in formerly socialist states but also to the decline of social programs in capitalist welfare states. I conceptualize postsocialism as one extreme of post-welfare-state neoliberalism—a new global economic process that shifts responsibility for the welfare of populations from the state or the public sector to the individual (Harvey 2005). Thus, this book positions the postsocialist transition in Eastern Europe as part of a geographically wider and historically deeper set of global transformations.[19] Postsocialism is an economic but also moral condition marked by new discursive practices.

In this framing, both Moldova and Turkey are postsocialist. In the case of Moldova, the collapse of government-sponsored employment and services placed women in a dire situation, lacking jobs, money, child care, and health

---

[19] Precedents for this kind of study include Alaina Lemon (1998), Andrew Lass (1999), Gal and Kligman (2000a, 2000b), Douglas Rogers (2009), and Verdery and Chari (2009). For more on the politics of knowledge production of this region, see Carl Pletsch (1981).

care. Fiscal reforms institutionalized these retractions to some degree. The Turkish economy was never socialist, but it was a mostly closed economy until trade liberalization in the 1980s, and similar fiscal dictates required similar state retractions (see Buğra and Keyder 2003). Such retractions have become a mark of the rise in neoliberal governance worldwide (Harvey 2005). These changes have helped create the demand among middle- and upper-class women in Turkey for live-in household workers. Turkish women increasingly must work outside the home to help their families sustain and improve their economic and social status, and they do not receive any state assistance for their duties at home. Fiscal reforms have meant a continued lack of social welfare and services that could have helped women in Turkey fulfill their household care needs instead of relying on migrant domestic work. Coinciding with these shifts in the Moldovan and Turkish economies is a heightened consumerism (characteristic of neoliberal processes) that has also structured both the supply of and the demand for migrant domestic work.

For these reasons, I consider Turkey and Moldova to be experiencing certain postsocialist, postwelfare, neoliberal commonalities that prompt the need for this kind of gendered labor migration. This approach moves away from a narrow focus on postsocialism in this region and on the "postsocialist woman" as a special case of migrant women. Instead, I point to problems and processes of globalization that hold wider significance, putting into question the categorizations of states and women as postsocialist, postwelfare, third world, global south, or postcolonial. This broad conceptualization of postsocialism takes very seriously Douglas Rogers's call to "unbind postsocialism" from its geographic shackles (2009) and also considers comparisons with postcolonialism (Verdery and Chari 2009). Here I place socialism, colonialism, and their aftermath into the wider comparative framework of transformations to neoliberalism. In this, I aim to free Eastern Europe from its "incarceration" in socialism/postsocialism as its dominant paradigm, or the assumption that this system is these states' and people's ultimate defining moment, and to move toward what Arjun Appadurai has called a "polythetical" approach (1988).[20]

---

[20] In this, I am inspired by Appadurai's insistence on bringing new theories to the study of India. As he has written, "In the discourse of anthropology, hierarchy is what is most true of India and it is truer of India than of any other place" (1988, 40). He suggests that we move from "incarcerating" regions in certain theories (giving as an example India being "incarcerated" in theories of hierarchy) and move to more "polythetical" approaches.

Conceiving of postsocialism in a broader context should help us better compare and contrast migrant women. Placing *all* migrant women in the same global context helps us view the gendered political economies and discourses on women, as well as their own practices and narratives, in one neoliberalizing social field of transnational labor. Analyses that categorize women migrants by their origins as postsocialist rather than postcolonial or third world tend to position postsocialist women migrants as different because of their whiteness, assumed beauty, educational status, and work experience. It is precisely this type of categorization that prompts the IOM, among others, to assume that all white Eastern European women working in Turkey must be sex-trafficking victims. In such conventional analyses, postsocialist women do not migrate as domestics. Migrant domestics are from the postcolonial third world. They are women of color from South and Southeast Asia, Central and South America, and Africa who are laboring voluntarily for first-world white women. Yet, as the Gagauz case illustrates, migrant domestics are now also a common export of Eastern Europe and the former Soviet Union.

Moreover, recasting postsocialism as a broader analytic helps us rethink the gendered labors and exploitations women face. Saskia Sassen (2000), Barbara Ehrenreich and Arlie Russell Hochschild (2002), Mary Beth Mills (2003), Denise Brennan (2004), and Banu Nilgün Uygun (2004) point to the continuities in women's labors—domestic, caring, and sexual—as a productive point of departure for thinking about the new global economy. Women use all of these types of migrant labor (sometimes exclusively and sometimes alternately) as strategies for survival and advancement. Indeed, whatever migrants' race, ethnicity, or nationality, and whatever types of labor they engage in, female informal laborers from all parts of the globe are equal products of neoliberal economic restructuring.

As an ethnography of the experiences of women from a postsocialist state working as domestics in Turkey, this book seeks to counter misrepresentations like those of the IOM that Moldovan women do not work in Turkey voluntarily as domestics, and must be sex-trafficking victims. I "write against" (Abu-Lughod 1991) the typecasting of postsocialist women in order to critique local, academic, and policy representations of trafficking victims and migrant domestic workers. And I plumb the data regarding the experiences of migrant women workers in other parts of the world to understand this moment of neoliberal transformation and its effects on women in the marginalized regions of Moldova and Turkey.

There are risks to seeing the case of these postsocialist women as one extreme of the neoliberal lot of migrant women. As insightfully argued by Rogers, the framework of neoliberalism could lead to further overgeneralization and could endanger our understanding of the specificities of former socialist states. Yet overemphasizing the importance of the socialist past to the present is an equally slippery slope. It overdetermines these women's experiences as former socialists, when many other features of their identities are also important. I address these challenges by focusing on the particularities of the socialist history of Moldova and its transition to neoliberalism. Differences between socialist and capitalist, as well as comparisons of postsocialist to third-world, postcolonial, or other global women, are undercut—and "diversified" (Abu-Lughod 1991)—in this ethnography, on the one hand by placing them all in one global neoliberal context, and on the other by highlighting the particularities of the transition from socialism to neoliberalism in Moldova and of migrant women's identities and experiences. I describe a deep and precise experience of migration for particular women, one complicated in this case by the Gagauz positionality in terms of being of an ethnic minority (the only Turkic-speaking Orthodox Christian population) with a strong rural history and a strong identification as Russophile post-Soviets.

Indeed, it is important to remember that the ability of women themselves to use or resist gendered moral economies depends on their positionalities not only as women generally but as women in a particular place and time, and on their specific experiences of education, work, wealth, urbanity, citizenship, religion, and ethnicity (see also Haraway 1988; Grewal and Kaplan 1992; McClintock, Mufti, and Shohat 1997; Mohanty 2003). As Abu-Lughod (1999a) reminds us, women's subjectivities are multidimensional. She conceptualizes particular configurations and intersections of these identities as contrasting forms of "cosmopolitanisms" and "overlapping subjugations" (1990). The Gagauz women whom I came to know—their backgrounds, their labors, and their migrant experiences—varied a great deal. Even though these women were all Gagauz who worked as domestics, they differed in their backgrounds (i.e., wealth, education, urbanity) and in the precise locations of their work. It is not surprising, then, that this diversity emerges in their narratives of their transnational commuter labor experiences. This ethnography pays close attention to these differences. Following Abu-Lughod, the term I use here to describe these variable subject positions is "particularities" (1991). Looking at these particularities allows us to "diversify" and specify difference and continue to move away from nations and cultures, East versus West, south or north, and capitalist or socialist as the main units of analysis.

This book is distinctly not, then, an anthropological study of a generalized culture clash: some form of static "former postsocialist woman" meets an equally timeless Western capitalism, or even Gagauz meets Turk. Such a project is simply not tenable. Not only is the Soviet and post-Soviet experience of Moldovans particular, but the Gagauz experience is unique within Moldova, the Orthodox Christian, and the Turkic-speaking world. This is not even to mention that in the formulation "former Soviets meet the West," the West here is represented by Turkey, a country that for centuries has been a geographically, politically, and culturally ambivalent part of the West at best, and is mostly seen as Europe's other. The families in Turkey for whom these women from Moldova work are also diverse. Turkish women employers also occupy specific locations in terms of wealth, education, work experience, ethnicity, religion, and age, and interactions with them offer particular experiences of capitalism and civilization.

A cautionary note on positioning both sets of women, employers and employees, as experiencing similar conditions is in order, however. A similar neoliberal structuring of the economy does not have the same effects for middle- to upper-class women in Turkey as it does for the lower to middle classes in Moldova. As employers and citizens of Turkey, the former have more power politically, economically, and socially; at worst, they are subject to fines because of their employment of illegal domestics. The latter risk much more: they could be thrown in jail, lose their life's savings, or suffer any number of other exploitations, with little ability to redress these injustices (Brennan 2004).

Identifying migrant women as particular while recognizing that Turkey and Gagauz Yeri are undergoing similar neoliberal processes also helps us move beyond envisioning migrants' lives as a unilineal movement from Gagauz Yeri to Turkey or from socialism to capitalism—from one way of life to another.[21] Instead, it places these spaces in the same transnational field and assumes both are constantly changing. Although Gagauz migrants are greeted in Istanbul by particular forms of capitalism, in the meantime, their own families, villages, and nation-state have been in the midst of a

---

[21] As Douglas Rogers interestingly notes, it also represents a different "vector" for studies of transnationalism in the region, one that looks to movements outward from the post-Soviet space instead of only movements into this space by development and democracy projects (2009).

political and economic transformation from state socialism for more than twenty years. This is not to deny that Moldovan women's understandings are affected by their Soviet socialist pasts, or that they are experiencing new capitalist forms, or that their location matters. Yet it would be equally an oversimplification to say they are now all fully neoliberal capitalists. In fact, as we hear in their stories, these notions of socialism and capitalism, of Gagauz Yeri and Turkey, are an important frame of reference. These women cannot be taken to be representative of typical postsocialist or capitalist subjects, nor can their experiences be seen as typically Moldovan or even Gagauz or Turkish. The situation is both more particular and more general than that.

As we find in their conversations in Istanbul and Moldovan homes, the gendered moral economies that migrant women themselves engage in are a form of poetics that sometimes support older, Soviet values and sometimes look forward to new capitalist, neoliberal ones (Konstantinov 1996; Herzfeld 2004). Yet these ideas and positionalities are not necessarily anomalies or signs of transitory growing pains of people making a simple shift from socialism to market capitalism, from past to future. This is an important point for the case of the former Soviet Union and Eastern Europe, where too often a drastic difference is mapped onto a linear path from socialist past to capitalist future (Verdery 1996; see also Smith and Stenning 2006). This book writes against positioning women's informal economic activities, including networking or undocumented work, as simply transitory survival strategies or a residue of the "backward" socialist times. These informal economic practices should not be envisioned as outside official economies, whether socialist or capitalist, but rather as part and parcel of what Adrian Smith and Alison Stenning call "diverse . . . economies of postsocialism."[22] What I do instead is track the complex articulations of gendered economic practices and ideas about them and their connections to earlier socialist moral economies and to current configurations of neoliberal capitalism.

In sum, postsocialism and neoliberalism, East and West, are not just categories referring to economies and locations in the world but moral concepts. And although we must avoid presuming national or ethnic belonging according to place, location—especially in relation to Europe and the West—still plays an important role in the gendered moral economies detailed here. Places

---

[22] As Smith and Stenning note, informal economic practices are too often negatively valued as the "defensive survival strategies" of rural poor in the periphery as opposed to "entrepreneurial" opportunities taken by proactive urbanites (2006, 207). They point out that neither economic practice necessarily alleviates poverty or offers emancipation.

can emerge as objects of discourse in the social field of transnational labor. In both Moldova and Turkey, located spatially and ideologically on Europe's periphery, the *idea* of Europe as "civilized" is an influential interlocutor. Turkey has long hovered in the European (especially Eastern European) imagination as the Muslim other. Yet, in the configuration of events since World War II, Turkey was a beneficiary of the Marshall Plan, a key NATO ally, and a modern military and capitalist bulwark against Soviet communism. This role gained it respect, if not membership, in Europe. Further, it was Turkish *Gastarbeiter* who helped to rebuild postwar Germany. Yet with the fall of communism and the perceived problems with the assimilation of three million Turkish citizens in Germany and xenophobia in Europe more broadly, not to mention recent wars in the Middle East, Turkey's potential membership in Europe is now more precarious.

By contrast, Moldova, as part of Eastern Europe (even if a former Soviet republic), is more secure even in Gagauz Yeri in its cultural ties to Europe conceived as a Christian entity. The region was a battleground between Christian and Muslim forces in Ottoman times, and as demonstrated in the crisis over Ukraine in 2013, it continues to be a region of contention between Europe and the United States on the one hand and Russia on the other. In many ways, Eastern Europe is still represented as the antithesis to a democratic Western Europe. Although the fall of the Berlin Wall in 1989 marked a turning point that drew the area more within the realm of the capitalist West, the unfulfilled promise of the transition from socialism to capitalism has left many people there, especially women, in dire conditions, and thus candidates for a potential new pool of cheap migrant laborers for Europe. Fears of the onslaught of Eastern Europeans have prompted the European Union (EU) to build in safeguards in accession agreements against the mobility of labor. Moldova, like Ukraine and Belarus, was an integral part of the Soviet Union. It is thus even more peripheral than formerly socialist states such as Bulgaria and Romania, which entered the EU in 2007. Thus, it represents another symbolically marginal area of Europe.

These ideas about Moldova's and Turkey's geographic and civilizational marginality are very much in play in the reasons for and understandings of women's migrant labor. In Eastern Europe, Turkey is not seen as a space of modernity and civilization but of barbarism and the Muslim other. From the perspective of the former Soviet bloc countries, Turkey's standing as a successful capitalist state does not mitigate its low value in their eyes. Western Europe and, for the Gagauz in particular, Russia are seen as sites of civilization. In Turkey, Moldova is associated with the highly valued secular

European civilization, but also with a more suspect morality. These ideas condition the supply and demand for migrant domestics, how employer and employee experience this migrant labor, and the exploitations involved. Women are trafficked here—as symbols in these discourses. And such discourses hold real consequences for women workers.

Whether because of the acrobatic moral poetics about socialism and capitalism, their shifting geographic contexts, or particularities, gendered moral economies in this social field of transnational labor demonstrate "slippages," or "moments of disorder," in the process of social reproduction and change. The analysis in chapter 1 focuses on these dynamics, on the discursive practices as performances of morality and how they may initiate moments of rupture with, as well as reproduction of, gendered hegemonies. The narratives of the women informants thereby create apertures in the socialist gendered ideology that these women grew up with, while also in some ways critiquing the neoliberal capitalist hegemony in which they are becoming complicit. This labor migration and women's legitimations of it through discourses of worker-motherhood cannot be seen as having improved or worsened women's status in any simple way. Instead, we might envision women's labor commutes and the discursive practices involved as creating certain spaces for the continuation but also change of conventional gendered moral economies, even if later these are coopted by or aligned with more global neoliberal structures of oppression.

Shifts and ruptures in gendered hegemonies are complicated by particularities and also by the transnational context. Considering the cultural and economic conditions and narratives in *both* home and host societies allows us to fully grasp the new vulnerabilities or freedoms women face both in Moldova and in Turkey. Thus, women from Gagauz Yeri are seen as "backward" villagers and "old-fashioned" Russophile communists in Moldova, but are taken to be "modern," "civilized," and "educated" "White Russian" women in Istanbul. Movements between these values affect slippages in these women's status back in Moldova and their lives in Istanbul. Women's migrations both provoke transformations and enforce continuities in social and economic stratification and gendered moral economies in Moldova, and move both Moldova and Turkey toward neoliberalism.

Looking at their lives in both host and home, and at these gendered moral economies in a social field, affords a deep contextual understanding of this commuter labor as well as a broader picture of these women's lives, the mobilities they experience, and the gendered moralities which they summon and to which they are subject. It also allows for an understanding of the gendered workings of structures and agencies in both host and home societies as well as globally, and a more complete picture of the commonalities and differences that span these societies and the lives of women. Migrant domestic workers in the former Soviet space and Eastern Europe share with the more familiar cases of migrant domestic workers in capitalist contexts, such as Filipina migrants (Parrenas 2001) and Mexican or Central American migrants in the United States (Hondagneu-Sotelo and Avila 1997), the gendered discourses of obligation and responsibility of mothers, workers, and consumers. In all these cases, the structural conditions that women experience and effect are prompted by the transformation to neoliberal capitalism. Yet this case of former Soviet migrant domestics is distinctive and alerts us to the significant problems in the ways that scholars and activists alike have conceptualized migration. It provides an opportunity for us to better address the variety of exploitations women migrants confront.

Sherry Ortner once challenged us to "tilt" our analyses toward the instabilities and incompleteness of gender hegemonies (1996, 18–20). The key to doing so is not only showing how structural economic contradictions are responsible for both positive and negative dislocations or slippages in gender hegemonies but also acknowledging the decisive and (per)formative role that complex discursive practices play in particular contexts. This kind of cultural and ethnographic analysis allows for a thick understanding of ideological processes and a conception of human meaning that is complex and open. This book is a testament to the fact that although individuals may act in line with a particular gendered moral economy (i.e., neoliberal, socialist), it is just as likely that this alignment is coincidental and is governed *also* by local logics and not only determined by a grand narrative or the economy of neoliberalism. It is within this complex and complicit form of agency that we might find moments of instability in gendered moral economies, inconsistencies in the making of gender hierarchies, or unintended effects that provide openings for freedom for women and workers.

My intention here is not to revel in narrative as a form of agency as opposed to an activism that consciously targets structural economic change (Žižek 2002; Fraser 2009). The former and the latter have to work together. It is important to understand that women's narratives are complicit in the political economy that structures neoliberalism. Certainly women's ability to question authority, voice their discontent, and resist unfair treatment is curtailed because this work is undocumented; their narratives relate these injustices consciously, without actually changing their structural conditions. Moreover, patriarchal structures clearly work with capitalist ones to oppress these women (Fraser 2009). Yet I cannot concede that the meaning they give their lives in these narratives functions only to further capitalism and patriarchy. Even if we do not yet see any on-the-ground activism by these women migrants, their new self-imaginings create a space for them to think about themselves differently and to change their lives. These acts hold revolutionary potential.

Ethnography and Ethics

The ethnographic method is particularly good at tracking slippages in gender hegemonies because it has the tools to examine the day-to-day experience and subjective understandings otherwise inaccessible to researchers of an underground transnational economy. Moreover, participant observation is an especially appropriate method for the study of populations such as undocumented migrant women, whose involvement in illegal activities makes their experiences otherwise inaccessible. In fact, qualitative, in-depth research with individuals in their homes and where they work may be our only route to understanding their practices. Using this method, I was able to build up my knowledge of individual lives and communities in fourteen months of research. My direct experiences with the women migrants began during a three-month research trip to Turkey in the spring of 2002, with one week spent in Moldova. I returned to Turkey for three months in the summer of 2004, moved to Moldova until the end of 2004, and then returned to Turkey in January 2005 and remained there until May. In Moldova I lived in a small apartment in the capital, Chişinău, and made six trips of about a week each to Gagauz Yeri, where I stayed with families I had come to know. In Turkey, I lived in Istanbul and alternated my time between employers and migrant domestics. As an invited scholar at Sabancı University in Istanbul in 2008–9, I conducted follow-up research as well.

During this extended period, I lived in the communities in question, slowly becoming incorporated into people's lives and networks, and had the opportunity to experience firsthand the practical conditions of their lives in both Moldova and Turkey. Through this intensive contact, I gained the trust of people, families, and communities. I supported this experiential knowledge with focused interviews, both formal (and taped) and informal, and with detailed descriptions of discursive practices. Interviews were conducted with IOM officials (project managers, psychologist, interns) and teens targeted for their information campaign, officials from the Bulgarian embassy in

Moldova, the US embassy in Moldova, a Moldovan Migration Department official, IREX (project manager for trafficking), Turkish police (those who deal with foreigners' residency and employment, and trafficking), Turkish NGOs (in particular the Human Resources Development Foundation, which runs a women's shelter for trafficking victims), the Turkish Ministry of Labour and Social Security, and the US consulate in Istanbul. I also interviewed people who run domestic work employment agencies (three in particular) and a Turkey-to-Moldova minibus driver. I spoke with many migrant domestics and others who had been to Turkey to work as tourists or for education. These individuals were from Gagauz Yeri and other parts of Moldova, and from other former Soviet Union and formerly socialist states. I completed thirty formal taped interviews of migrant domestics and spoke with seventy others informally in both Moldova and Istanbul. I taped formal interviews with six Turkish employers and spoke informally with fifteen others. My research also involved tracking media and other representations of migrant women. Research was conducted in Turkish and English predominantly, and to a much lesser degree in Gagauz and Russian.

Through this research and these methods, I acquired intimate knowledge of the multidimensional lives that people lead and the complex motivations for and the impact of this migration. As an ethnographer, I am only able to get to know well a few handfuls of people in one fieldwork stay; yet this knowledge is rich in detail, presenting a full picture of a limited number of lives. Such qualitative information on these vulnerable populations is not accessible through formal surveys and quantitative studies, and it helps deepen of our knowledge of undocumented migration in this region, the condition of women and laborers, and policies regarding them. I also offer a comprehensive view of this transnational migration from different sites throughout the research.

To some extent, being Turkish American with extensive personal and professional contacts and experience in Istanbul and native fluency in the language gave me an advantage for conducting this multisited research. Yet my positionality as Turkish American also structured many obstacles I faced in the field. Until I began doing research there in the mid-1990s on "new veiling" among Islamist women, my personal experiences in Turkey were mostly with my upper-middle-class, urban Istanbul, Turkish, and on the whole secular Muslim family and friends. My earliest experiences there took place almost entirely within the safe and warm embrace of the women of that family, especially my grandmother and her generation.

My family employed domestic workers to clean, cook, and caretake. This is not a rarity among the middle and upper classes in Turkey. These "girls" (*kizlar*) were an integral part of our family and were loved and cared for genuinely, and the attachment was often demonstrably reciprocal. Growing up, I witnessed many women employers, including my own grandmother, work alongside domestics, and just as hard, in a struggle to keep the household running smoothly. Yet I also remember my astonishment when some of these elder Turkish *hatuns* (ladies), otherwise so generous, kind, and composed, scolded or put down the domestic workers of their households in various ways. This rarely ended the working relationship but instead seemed an integral part of it. This perplexing and disturbing behavior drew me to try to better understand the situation from both perspectives. Why did these Turkish women only seem to assert such power here? And why did the employees not simply leave? What structures determined this situation? How did love and caring mix with power and agency in the labor-for-money exchange here?

When I returned one summer while in graduate school in 2001, my grandmother, who had had a stroke in 1994 that left her an invalid, had hired a Gagauz woman, Lidya, to take care of her. Lidya was a replacement for a working-class Turkish woman who had cared for my grandmother since 1994 but who had become old and infirm herself, and no longer worked. Many women from the former socialist bloc in the 2000s were employed as domestics. Some of the same power conflicts in the household continued between employer and employee, but I noticed that women from formerly socialist states were valued differently than Turkish workers, and that these conflicts were framed in new ways. For instance, my grandmother would say to Lidya, "We were so afraid of you ["Russians" or "Communists"] and now look—you are working for us!" And Lidya would reply smartly: "And us, too—we were afraid of Turks—but now you are under *our* care!" This pithy exchange indexes the continued problematics of power and gender in the Turkish household, but also new frames of meaning—issues of communist versus capitalist, Turk versus Russian, and Muslim versus Christian.

I came to this topic quite personally, from a deep appreciation of the dependency of such families in Turkey on migrant caretakers and, more particularly, from my location in a family that hired domestic workers in Turkey. Also, I myself acted as a caretaker for my grandmother for several months when she initially sustained a stroke in 1994. This obligation, I should note, was structured by the effect of gender hierarchies with respect to my own subject position as a Turkish-American woman. This experience gave me some idea of how difficult the job of a caretaker is. Over the years, as caretakers came and went from the household, I witnessed how dependent a family becomes on migrant domestics, and their lack of options with no extended family to rely on, in a state that does not provide any good care for the elderly, and with no affordable private care available. It is a situation ripe with resentment. Nonetheless, when I learned more about Gagauz Yeri from Lidya, I became fascinated by her former socialist experience; her Turkic language; and the fate of these Russophile, Orthodox Christian, but Turkic-speaking women from post-Soviet Moldova working in Turkey.

The issue of my own biases during my research and the question of whether individuals would be compromised by my connections with them were important for both parties and for my own ethics. I thus structured my research so that I was not interviewing both employer and employee from the same household. However, this decision made it difficult to conduct participant observation at these households, since it could only take place with the employer's permission and thus would immediately position me on the employer's side. Maneuvering between my family responsibilities and research aims, between employers and employees, I alternated my time in Istanbul between perspectives and spaces. My family members not only accommodated my interest in this topic but helped me whenever they could, especially with contacting employers and employees. And as they saw how I struggled with these tensions, I noticed that Gagauz women and their families gained respect for me, and I saw how it built trust between us. Interestingly, in the end, I found that it was not my Turkish identity but my American one that most determined my relationship to the people in Moldova and in Turkey whom I came to know in connection with my research. It structured my access, or lack thereof, to their perspectives and also conditioned the narratives I collected. The stories in this book incorporate my own positionality as appropriate to better understand the context of these conversations, as I am an actor in this social field and a guide to the journeys of the women represented here.

I have structured this ethnography of women's migrant labor as a whole story of neoliberal transformations in gendered moral economies that recaptures these migrant women's mobility in physical and social terms. It begins, in chapters 1 and 2, in newly transnational Moldova, moves to transnational Turkey in chapters 3 and 4; then looks at IOM activities in both places in chapter 5. From analyzing the supply-side gendered moral economies of this migrant labor and its effects on women, family, and communities in

Moldova, I move to the demand side of employers' and migrants' lives in Turkey, then explore the response to this migration at the IOM. I lead the reader through my experiences of fieldwork as an anthropologist entering Gagauz public spaces (workplaces in schools, hospitals, and museums) and private homes in chapters 1 and 2, and I try to provide a feel for the textures of Gagauz Yeri as a geographic and human landscape—something I also attempt in describing Istanbul in chapters 3 and 4 and for the high-paced offices of the IOM in chapter 5. I chose not to structure this book by alternating ethnographic vignettes and analyses but instead, with the theoretical framework outlined in this introduction in mind, to weave the stories into my analysis. I also embed these stories in the actual contexts in which I collected them, placing myself, and reactions to me by those I interviewed, as part of the context of what they reveal to me. I do this on purpose so that the reader can judge the meaning of a particular exchange and the ethnographic product, and understand how these particular contexts can affect the performance and meaning of these narratives. This is in recognition of the fact that our knowledge is always constructed dialogically and intersubjectively (Borneman 2009).

Although gendered moral economies may take a number of different forms and stem from various localities, for the Gagauz migrant women and their communities at home, the Istanbul employers, and the IOM staff, migrant women are *driven*, in several valences of that word, whether passively driven by traffickers, desperation, and poverty or actively driven by ambition and desiring too much. At all of these sites and from all of these perspectives, there is a common tendency to focus the blame for social disorder on migrant women. In different ways, all of these scenarios ideologically legitimate the policing of women's bodies, limit women to their nurturing role in the private realm of the household, and refuse to acknowledge their role as providers for their families. This situation contributes to what scholars have identified as the "feminization of the private realm" in the formerly socialist states, states where official ideology, however uneven or a failure in practice, used to uphold women as both mothers and workers. The migrant women's narratives in this book counter these representations in some instances but also show them being used to the women's advantage in other ways. Thus, whether women, or families, are better off as a result of this migration is a tricky question to answer. Economically, their remittances help their families not only to survive but, in many cases, to thrive. In terms of its social impact, new "transnational families" are difficult formations but are managed relatively successfully in most of the cases I describe here. What is clear is that moral notions about gender and labor are transforming along with the economy as it moves from socialism to neoliberal capitalism, and that women workers gain power in some contexts but are being restricted in others.

Globalization and the political-economic transformations in Moldova and Turkey have prompted new ways of living transnationally and new expectations for women's lives. Their emerging lives and identities are not easily characterized by models of the local effects of postsocialism or local assimilation to global neoliberalism. I characterize them instead as living out—and even helping to construct—neoliberalism in a transnational context. Indeed, their "globality" is always in a state of becoming, and always informed by the contexts they leave behind and those to which they return. Moreover, the processes of global neoliberalism that affect these women have also transformed the ways in which states and organizations seek to address their populations' vulnerabilities, whether economic or physical. Alongside the changes in women's lives and their responses to these changes, I speculate about the political-economic effects of such discursive practices and interventions on behalf of women migrants in Moldova, in Turkey, and at the IOM.

The migrant women from Gagauz Yeri face considerable conflict in their families and communities, are anxious about their family's upward mobility, and exhibit a defensiveness marked by the shame of working as a domestic in Turkey. As Luba Chimpoesh, an ethnographer and poet in Gagauz Yeri, put it to me, "You've chosen a very painful topic." I hope that my unpacking of this pain in this book does not make it more acute for the women involved in this migration and labor but rather helps to account for the structural and ideological roots of their choices and of the negative stereotypes of this migrant labor. By identifying their strategies and maneuverings as active attempts to negotiate their positions, and by highlighting some of the positive effects of their migrant labor, I hope that my analysis can lessen the stigma associated with their choice to work in Turkey and help to open up spaces for more progressive notions of gender, labor, and agency. Moreover, by deconstructing the IOM policy discourse on migrant women in the region, I hope to uncover how these projects may often contribute, however unintentionally, to women's subjugation, and suggest some ways to amend them.

Chapter 1

The Returns on Mobile Mothers' Work

> I look around my house and I see my first trip to Turkey: the washing machine; the second: the gas line; the third: the kids' new furnishings and the new entryway. The following trip was my first daughter's university education. The next one will be for the kitchen.
>
> —Tatya, October 2004

In many ways, the situation of women in Gagauz Yeri is structured by the same economic conditions that have affected poor women worldwide. According to the sociologist Saskia Sassen, women work abroad because they are poor and desperate, and as mothers under conditions of neoliberalism they will go to any length for their family's survival (1998, 2000). Gagauz women's explanations for their migrant labor generally uphold this "survivalist" theory. Without exception, all the women with whom I spoke said they worked abroad because they could not find work in the economic

---

This chapter incorporates and expands on material first published in Keough (2006).

circumstances of post-Soviet Moldova, and they felt obligated as mothers to take care of their families, particularly their children. In the women's narratives that make up the main substance of this chapter, joblessness, the lack of an income, and the relatively new need for cash for their children's benefit caused migration to Turkey. These gendered explanations are clearly genuine and may even help women and children cope with separation (Parrenas 2005).

However, such explanations for migrant work are also performances of particular values in specific contexts. As Tatya noted in the epigraph to this chapter, there is more to the story than simply getting by or providing basic necessities for children. Migrant working mothers want a better education for their children, and redecorated homes. They want upward mobility, not just survival. The agency these women exercise by migrating for work causes conflicts with the traditional expectations of women in their communities. Women resist these gendered expectations in some ways. In others, they reinforce them, especially when they legitimate their work abroad by asserting that they are carrying out their role as mothers above all else. Although they clearly express sincere feelings about a mother's obligation, their recourse to discourses of motherhood—in this case, that of the transnational worker-mother—shows that they are maneuvering in a context that is not only economic but also moral and cultural. Social conventions dictate that women's role is first and foremost to be mothers, in the private realm. As a result, women's migrant labor is often deemed legitimate only in cases of desperation and by appeal to their duties as the nurturers of the family. Men, by contrast, can legitimate seeking work abroad by claiming it as necessary to their role as providers. They may seek *opportunity* abroad, and not only out of desperation. These discourses of motherhood, then, even if they legitimate women's waged work abroad and provide upward mobility for families, can also limit women's agency and power through an ongoing gendered hegemony (Keough 2006).

What these women's stories offer us are an understanding not only of how women are experiencing neoliberal shifts in the global economy but also of how deeply embedded beliefs about gender, agency, and labor drive this economy.[1] Characterizing migrant women simply as pawns of economic forces, driven by some inherent maternal instinct to secure the survival of

---

[1] This claim is supported by other on-the-ground studies of migrant women in their countries of origin (Parrenas 2001, 2005; Lan 2006a).

their young, constrains our an understanding of their complex motivations and of the gendered and exploitative conditions of global neoliberalism to which they are responding. To fully understand the global economy and migrant women, we must move beyond such accounts of poor women's victimization and survival narratives.

For Gagauz women, informal and undocumented migrant labor represents an extension of their previous roles and ideas about worker-mothers under socialism. What is new for these migrant domestics is an upwelling of capitalist desires and the opportunity to fulfill them through domestic work in Turkey. Because of this context, the debate over migrant women in Moldova typically focuses on issues of motherhood and work, but its greater significance pivots on what uplift means, and how and where it might morally be achieved through engaging in neoliberal capitalism. This gendered moral economy holds consequences for the returns on women's migrant labor: whether it helps (or is perceived to help) women and families, or expands roles for women and ideas about gender. My analysis underscores the importance of considering both the global conditions and the local particularities in notions of motherhood and uplift to understand the benefits and drawbacks of women's migrant labor in a neoliberalizing global economy increasingly reliant on the private sector (Collins 1990; Zimmerman, Litt, and Bose 2006).

To understand these women's gendered justifications for migrant domestic work, as well as their experiences in Turkey, it is important to grasp both the conditions of economic instability to which they refer and their effects on women in the former Soviet Union and their migration opportunities, as well as their identities as worker-mothers in Moldova. I begin here by describing the political and economic conditions in Moldova. I then evaluate the reasonings of different sets of migrant women globally—both daughters and mothers—as detailed in various ethnographic works. Finally, the heart of this chapter consists of the accounts that women from Gagauz Yeri themselves relate. To provide context for the ethnographic data, I try to give some sense of the textures, sounds, sights, tastes, and smells of Gagauz Yeri, the pace of days there, the rhythm of movement, the tenor of lives, and how I first met the individuals whose stories we hear. I conclude with an analysis of how shifting gendered moral economies—ideas and practices about women, labor, and uplift—affect women and families and work with the neoliberalizing economy in this context, compared with other migrant domestic workers worldwide.

Gendered "Survival Circuits"?

In a general sense, women from Moldova can be viewed as part of a contingent of women worldwide who have turned to migrant work to support their families. The workings of the global economy prompt their reliance on circuits of remittances and migrant labor in many states (Sassen 2000; Misra, Woodring, and Merz 2006). In Moldova, the economic collapse of the Moldovan Soviet Socialist Republic (an integral part of the Soviet Union until the country's dissolution in 1989) and the demise of subsequent projects to develop the Moldovan economy prompted women to go abroad to find work. With the dissolution of the Soviet Union and the gradual formation of the Republic of Moldova throughout the 1990s came political and economic instability. Yet it was not until the Russian economic crisis of 1998–99 that this dynamic seems to have been fully felt by families in Gagauz Yeri. Like other places in post-Soviet Moldova, Gagauz Yeri was severely affected by the currency crisis at this time. As the economic collapse in Russia reverberated through the former Soviet sphere, the value of the Moldovan currency declined precipitously, the republic's main export market in the former Soviet Union disappeared, and the Moldovan state found itself no longer able to pay salaries or provide social services to its citizens.[2]

The state's collapse also coincided with the global spread of neoliberal development strategies. Specifically, international development efforts by organizations such as the International Monetary Fund and the World Bank prioritize making loans to struggling economies that agree to privatize, develop a market-based economy, and support certain imports and exports. To obtain these loans, states like Moldova instituted structural adjustment policies that encouraged a retraction of the state-sponsored social and economic welfare. This provided justification for the Moldovan state to not rebuild job-creation and social service programs. The new policies required populations to take more responsibility, and allowed the state less responsibility, for health and welfare. Such a change in the political and economic dynamics marks the state as neoliberal (Harvey 2005; Smith 2010).

As Nancy Fraser points out, the considerable downsizing of the welfare state in favor of neoliberal economic policies coincided with the end of the Cold War and the dissolution of the threat to twentieth-century capitalism

---

[2] The Moldovan wine industry was supported by the state in Soviet times, but since 1989 it has been difficult to find an international market for the country's wine. This has also served to undermine the Moldovan economy.

of an alternative vision of development through state-sponsored socialism. Fraser dubs this state of affairs the "postsocialist condition" (Fraser 1997; see also Verdery 1996; Gal and Kligman 2000a; Smith 2010).[3] The implementation of the new policies has brought widespread unemployment of those formerly employed by the state, a widening gap between rich and poor, and a lack of social services once provided by the state. Alongside these deficits, consumerism has risen in importance.

Such transformations disproportionately affect poor women in developing countries (Gal and Kligman 2000a; Sassen 2000; Ehrenreich and Hochschild 2002; Mills 2003). In her review of the topic, Mary Beth Mills argues that the "gender and labor inequalities of structural adjustment" policies around the world have decreased formal wage employment and the security associated with it and have "increase[d the] dependence [of women] on informal employment," such as "prostitution, domestic work, hawking/vending, craft production" (2003, 46–47; see also Babb 2005). In the absence of waged work in their home countries, women try to ensure the survival and success of their households by using combinations of legal and illegal methods to find work abroad, often for the short term. In so doing, they fulfill demands in other countries for sex or entertainment workers, traders, or domestic laborers. In economically more developed regions, the retraction of the state and the simultaneous creation of a new capitalist elite increases the demand for such low-wage service laborers (Sassen 2000; Parrenas 2001, 2005). Yet labor immigration policies remain restricted, so migration is increasingly undocumented and characterized by the use of illegal networks. The upshot is that women turn to migrant labor to make a living. In this way, the feminization of poverty has become paired with the feminization of often undocumented migration (Sassen 2000). Barbara

---

[3] Most relevant for the current case is the third feature of the postsocialist condition that Nancy Fraser identifies: increasing economic liberalism and capitalism marked by rising inequality. There are three features of this condition. First, with the decline of socialism there is no new comprehensive, progressive alternative vision to the present social order. Fraser argues that multiculturalism, radical democracy, political liberalism, and communitarianism are deficient because they do not address the political economy. Second, she notices that claims of justice for the recognition of group differences often elide claims of justice for social equality and redistribution. As a result, cultural politics and social politics, difference and equality, identity and class have become alternative choices. Fraser maintains that these are "false antitheses" (1997, 3). She sees these concerns as diverging along the lines of economism and culturalism instead of taking up what she sees as the crucial postsocialist tasks: "first, interrogating the distinction between culture and economy; second, understanding how both work together to produce injustices; and third, figuring out how, as a prerequisite for remedying injustices, claims for recognition can be integrated with claims for redistribution in a comprehensive political project" (1997, 3).

Ehrenreich and Arlie Russell Hochschild conceptualize the migrant domestics, mail-order brides, and sex workers who make up this new international labor force as "global women" (2002).

What formerly socialist women in Gagauz Yeri and Moldova face and how they respond to structural changes are similar in many points to the experiences and responses of Ehrenreich and Hochschild's global women, but there are also differences specific to the post-Soviet state context. For instance, when I asked in Gagauz Yeri to meet women who had commuted to work in Turkey, I was introduced to women currently working in professional positions at Moldovan state schools and hospitals as administrators and bookkeepers, teachers and professors, nurses and doctors. Despite training and experience, they had faced lengthy periods without wages and had had to devise alternative means of covering the shortfall. That women with professional credentials should have found themselves in such a situation is not surprising, in light of what we know about the effects on women of the fall of the socialist state. As in other socialist states, women in Gagauz Yeri during the Soviet era worked primarily in these professions. Although these women have in common the experience of working for the state, they held positions at different ranks within the centralized economy. Yet women on different steps of the professional ladder and in different professions all ended up in the same situation of losing their jobs and benefits.

These women had earlier benefited from socialist state policies that provided social welfare services such as health and child care and that secured employment, political representation, and reproductive rights for women.[4] In fact, one result of policies explicitly targeting women was that women were perceived as being in league with the socialist state.[5] Yet whether or not women worked for the state directly, the collapse of such state-sponsored programs increased their burden of both work and child care. The "shock therapy" capitalism instituted in the formerly Soviet space beginning in 1991 economically and morally devastated the populations of the newly independent states. Today, under neoliberal capitalism, the rights that were available under socialism carry a high price tag for the individual and are increasingly unaffordable. Having been a particular target of

---

[4] One notable exception of the latter is Romania (see Kligman 1998).
[5] See discussion in Julie Hemment (2007, 5). For more on contemporary women's activism in different postsocialist contexts, see Sarah Phillips (2008) for Ukraine and Katya Guenther (2010) for Germany.

these rights, women arguably lost most from their absence. The configuration that the market transformation has taken in the former Soviet states has resulted in a disproportionate downsizing of the "feminized" labor sectors (see Bruno 1997; Gal 1994b; Gal and Kligman 2000a; Berdahl 1999; see also Ghodsee 2005; Patico 2005). Coinciding conveniently with the lack of employment, the pro-birth policies adopted in many formerly socialist states have created an environment in which women are encouraged to forgo their public roles in work and politics for their roles as mothers and wives in the private sphere of the home. Susan Gal and Gail Kligman call this process the "feminization of the private sphere" (2000a). Yet, with the rescission of the state from social services and the increase in consumerism, families needed money to get by more than ever before; women could not afford to stay home and out of waged labor. It is not surprising to learn that, just as in the socialist era, women have *not* stayed home; their work in the public realm and also in the informal economy continues (see, e.g., Patico 2005; Ghodsee 2005; Hemment 2007; Onica 2008).

In critiquing the post-Soviet conditions of women, I do not seek to valorize their lot during socialist times or to exonerate the Soviet state of its role in producing women's currently poor conditions. The Soviet Union did not always come through on its promises for women (see, e.g., Ries 1994; du Plessix Gray 1989; Gal and Kligman 2000a). Moreover, the state failed to provide for the populace on several levels. Where the state fell short, informal economic activities took over. These activities were so common that they were structured into the workings of the socialist state and, according to Katherine Verdery, led to its disintegration (1996; see also Smith and Stenning 2006). Women in socialist states played a particularly prominent role in the informal economy, and this situation continues today. The household in the Soviet era relied on women's productive and reproductive activities. As many insightful ethnographic and sociological accounts have detailed, these activities involved women's strategies of networking and bartering (*blat*) in an informal economy to secure goods and services scarce under socialism (Bruno 1997; Ledeneva 1998; Pesmen 2000; Yükseker 2000). Although many of these goods are now available, they are no less difficult to obtain—and they cost more. As a result, women still use their informal networks to gain a livelihood. According to a number of scholars, a natural extension of women's entrepreneurial skills under socialism and of their roles in the gendered division of labor is small-scale transnational trading, or shuttle trading (*chelnok*) (Yükseker 2000; see also

Bruno 1997). Women also have increasingly turned to new transnational, informal, flexible work abroad, such as migrant domestic and sex work (see Demirdirek and Whitehead 2004).

With this neoliberalizing political economic background in place, we are in a better position to understand why women globally migrate abroad for informal work. Yet, as Adrian Smith and Alison Stenning warn, we should be careful about how any analysis of structural economic trends represents and values such informal economic strategies undertaken by women (2006). The picture painted in many analyses slips into overgeneralization, depicting destitute women who would not go abroad to work, or perhaps even work at all, unless they were desperate to survive. Ethnographic analyses that attend to women's agency and power reveal a much more complicated situation. They show not only how changes in economic structure affect women but also how neoliberalism is constituted through gender. It is to such analyses that we turn next.

Mobile Women

Ethnographers have transcribed women's own voices expressing a desire to migrate in order to secure social mobility for their families and for themselves. Such migrant working women usually are not from the poorest of countries but are instead from the global "middle" (Lan 2006a; Parrenas 2008), and in their home states they are not the most destitute. Pei-Chia Lan points out that most migrant domestics, for instance, hold intermediate status in the multitiered "international division of reproductive labor" or the "global care circuit" initially identified by Rachel Salazar Parrenas (2000; see also Parrenas 2008). This division of labor separates women from the middle or upper class in advanced economies both from the migrant domestics from second-tier countries whom they hire to meet their domestic labor needs, and from the poorest of poor women in the third world.[6] Migrant domestics, those who populate the middle of Lan's range, often have just enough education, contacts, and financial resources to take advantage of opportunities to work abroad and fulfill their own desires for upward mobility.[7]

---

[6] For a recent critique of the global care circuit framework, see Shirlena Huang, Leng Leng Thang, and Mika Toyota (2012), Parrenas (2012) and Parvati Raghuram (2012).
[7] Because of their absence from their households, some migrant women hire local women to fulfill their domestic duties (Lan 2006b). Yet it is important to remember that even those who do stay put are affected by globalization as local jobs such as domestic work open up to them in the absence of

In the context of neoliberal capitalism, this higher status inevitably entails acquiring the trappings of new lifestyles through the consumption of an ever-shifting supply of new commodities. Seeking uplift through work away from their homes and communities, often work of an informal and undocumented kind, takes courage, perseverance, and a sense of adventure: it takes considerable agency on the part of these mobile workers. However, in seeking uplift through work abroad, these women, especially the mothers, travel a thorny path beset by traditional gendered hegemonies that hold them back. And the women themselves may be complicit in upholding such limitations.

In case after case, ethnographers have found that women and their families legitimate their desire to work abroad through gendered ideas of a woman's duty to her family. Sometimes this dynamic takes the form of rural families sending their unmarried daughters to work in urban factories. The Malay girls described in Aihwa Ong's classic *Spirits of Resistance* were sent by their families to work in factories to provide a better life for their families at home (1987). Similarly, Mary Beth Mills found that the desire for modernity and new commodities drives the continued migration of young unmarried Thai women from rural communities to Bangkok (1999). Of course, these goals of betterment are a moving target. As Mills points out, the narratives of Thai migrant women "reflected an ongoing redefinition of both basic subsistence needs and local understandings of what constituted a desired quality of life" (1999, 73). Both of these ethnographic studies make clear that girls and their families legitimate these migrations for a better life through moral appeals to a daughter's obligation. Indeed, most of the wages of young migrants are sent home to improve their family's status.

Even as they dutifully undertake obligations to their family, however, these young migrant women and girls are also breaking down gendered ideas about activities appropriate for daughters in their communities. Daughters are traditionally expected to be nurturing helpers in the domestic realm of the household until they are married. By working outside the home to provide wages for their families, they show that a woman's obligation is not confined to traditional nurturing. Young women argue that they can nurture and provide only if they work away from home. Young migrant women also often use these opportunities away from home and their new wages to gain power within their families and independence from them. According to

---

transnationally working mothers. This can also be seen in the cases that Denise Brennan details, in which rural-to-urban migrant women in the Dominican Republic turn to local prostitution and strategic dating to find a ticket off the island on the arm of a European man (2004).

Ong (1987), Malay women who work in factories at a younger age, and so gain some independence from traditional expectations, postpone marriage decisions, evade male domination, and assert their individuality. They have newfound control over their wedding ceremonies and room to fulfill personal wishes. In such contexts, consumption can be a form of agency: Mills suggests that it is an "avenue by which many labor migrants hope to express their new sense of autonomy and agency, and to construct socially satisfying and valued identities" (1999, 128). Even if they are "doing it for the family," by working in urban factories, living in the city, and acquiring new consumption habits, women also have adventures and gain personal independence, thereby showing themselves to be "modern," Mills and Ong both suggest. This modernity is a goal they share with their families, who also believe that urban women workers represent progress, even "glamour" (Mills 1999). In this way, young migrant women's work in urban factories is a legitimate means for their families to obtain modernity.

Although they are helping their families, and are often pushed by them to work in the city, freedom of movement and decision making for these young migrant unmarried women comes with a degree of suspicion of their new desires and sexual mores. Having to negotiate these traditional gender hegemonies compromises women's freedoms in some ways. As Ong explains, the press, politicians, administrators, educators, and Islamic groups, among others in Malaysia, "raise key moral issues in a cacophony of critical commentaries" about migrant working women (1987, 179), who are charged with "being too social," implying that they are "looking for illicit sexual activities" (191). Ong describes young women whose movements and sexuality are under surveillance in the factory itself, which replaces the family as the source of patriarchal oppression in their lives.

Young women become complicit in this discipline by being docile workers. Some even become more overtly religious, taking the veil and identifying with a "cult of purity and self-sacrifice" to construct their gender identities (Ong 1987, 191). Mostly, young women respond to accusations of selfishness and suspicions of illicit desires by arguing even more forcefully that their duty to help their family is what drives them to work in cities. These assertions of new gendered moral economies are at odds with local gender hegemonies. This conflict compromises women's ability to work outside the home, constrains their options, and limits their freedoms. Moreover, these ethnographers argue that the debate over the capitalist exploitation of women in factories is cut short by the inordinate focus on women's sexuality and gendered obligations.

These dynamics take on a specific context in the case of migrant *mothers* who work abroad as domestics. Traditional gendered notions more tightly bind a migrant mother's (as opposed to a daughter's) desires for uplift, modernity, and a better life through work away from home. Compared to daughters, mothers are both more responsible for their family's welfare and less able to legitimate their work abroad through discourses of modernity. Because mothers traditionally have more obligations than daughters at home, their absence is especially problematic for the management of the house, as well as for sustaining gendered notions that a woman's place is at home. Thus, there is even more pressure on migrant mothers to legitimate their work abroad as a duty to their families and not necessarily as a means for themselves to advance. Even so, migrant mothers, like migrant daughters, introduce elasticity into gendered conceptions of appropriate activity for females by enlarging the scope of what counts as being a "good mother." In their seminal work, Pierrette Hondagneu-Sotelo and Ernestine Avila explain the ways in which the Latina migrant domestics they interviewed were helping to shape a new kind of "transnational mothering":

> Rather than replacing caregiving with breadwinning definitions of motherhood, they appear to be expanding their definitions of motherhood to encompass breadwinning that may require long-term physical separations. For these women, a core belief is that they can best fulfill traditional caregiving responsibilities through income earning in the US while their children remain "back home." (1997, 562)

Hondagneu-Sotelo and Avila found that mothers see their work abroad not as an abandonment of their duties as mothers but instead as an extension of caring for their children. Working abroad, for them, is a motherly self-sacrifice to provide "milk, shoes, and schooling" (562) and, no doubt, many new commodities for their children. Moreover, these migrant workers hold that their physical absence does not translate into emotional absence from their children, and that they actively engage in their children's lives through regular communication from abroad.

In reformulating definitions of motherhood, Hondagneu-Sotelo and Avila write, these women "blaz[e] new terrain" in a "brave odyssey, . . . improvising new mothering arrangements . . . to provide the best future for themselves and their children" (1997, 567). This amounts to a new gendered moral economy, one that pushes the limits of traditional gendered ideas and structures by reasoning that mothering has as much to do with providing for one's children through working for wages (even if abroad) as it does with nurturing them in the home. In this way, just as migrant daughters' waged work gives them new authority and expectations, mothers' wages from working abroad provide increased status at home, greater consumption power, and the ability to make decisions independently of their family and communities.

Like migrant working daughters, migrant working mothers push for new forms of gendered responsibility, but their increased power and agency come at significant costs. By leaving at all, mothers, more so than daughters, are suspected of shirking their obligations to home and family. Parrenas details the moral panic occasioned by Filipina mothers working as domestics abroad: they are accused of splitting up families, abandoning children, and jeopardizing their future (2005). In the protests over a mother's absence from home, we hear a discourse of blame similar to that directed against migrant daughters, yet there are some differences in emphasis. In the Philippines, a mother's duty is even more strongly tied to her family by means of local gendered expectations. Because she is older, a mother, and often a wife, she is perceived as more responsible than daughters for the decisions she makes and more culpable for the social consequences. Moreover, even though it is less commonly noted in the literature on migrant mothers, their desire to work abroad, like their daughters', brings down on them accusations of sexual indiscretion (even if the concern is not about loss of virginity and thus of marriageability) (Parrenas 2008). And these accusations are laid against them even though the migrant mothers' work in the domestic realm is less likely to bring them into association with single men. What is more, migrant mothers' desire for uplift through work outside their communities is not viewed as being as morally legitimate as it is for younger, unmarried women seeking a brighter future. Thus, ethnographers find that migrant mothers tend to focus less on uplift or the seeking out of modernity than on their roles as good mothers—doing whatever they can to help their children—to justify their trips abroad (Hondagneu-Sotelo and Avila 1997; Parrenas 2001, 2005, 2008).

Migrant mothers are also blamed more for local social disorder than fathers at home or abroad, even though there is evidence that transnational families function quite well with either parent working abroad (Parrenas 2005). This occurs in several ways. First, in the situation detailed by Parrenas (2005), when Filipina mothers work abroad, their husbands left behind in the Philippines are excused if they become "absentee fathers." Second, Parrenas shows that Filipino fathers' work abroad is perceived as legitimate by their children because it is seen as the man's role to provide for the family or advance his career. Mothers' work abroad, by contrast, is perceived by children as legitimate only if they are desperate to escape poverty or have no access to work at home. Furthermore, when mothers migrate for work, they are expected to overcompensate for their absence with intensive mothering from abroad or during their visits home.

According to Parrenas, mothers play into these tropes by asserting that they are "martyrs," pointing to the many personal sacrifices they make to do this difficult work in a foreign land for their children's economic welfare. As we will also see in the case of migrant domestics from Gagauz Yeri, migrant working women's legitimation of their work in terms of motherhood over and above other kinds of arguments is a performance of the gendered moral economies of their communities. Parrenas's work on Filipina migrant domestics demonstrates how this discourse reinforces gendered notions that a woman's place is in the home and that her most valued (now even commodified) ability is her maternal, caretaking nature (2008). Although the modernity of factory work distinguishes the migrant daughters in Mills's and Ong's studies from migrant domestics in some ways, both factory workers and domestic workers working away from home make similar compromises to their freedoms. Just as the factory reproduces patriarchal hierarchies, so too, and more predictably, does working as a domestic in the private realm. That women and not men are expected to do domestic work limits their advancement. Few men are expanding their understanding of fatherhood to include nurturing and caretaking in the private realm. Parrenas conceptualizes this dynamic as the maintenance of women's "domesticity" (2008). As she and Ong both point out, such a focus on gendered responsibilities works to shift local criticisms away from the wider capitalist exploitations enacted through structural adjustment policies that do not provide jobs and welfare at home, policies that could make life much easier for these families in many ways.

What is clear in all these cases is that gendered beliefs and expectations drive these economies. It is also clear that despite limitations placed on their agency, women are active agents in their engagement in this work and in their creative redefinition of their roles and responsibilities. In this, they are increasingly able to push the boundaries of domesticity and traditional gendered hegemonies, even while also participating in the neoliberal economy and so helping to construct it. One way to see this agency in this light is not only to analyze how women are redefining motherhood but to look beyond the domestic realm, narrowly conceived, and ask how they are redefining what a good life means, and how mothers can legitimately work to provide such a life for their families and themselves. These kinds of narratives emerged in my discussions with postsocialist worker-mothers from Gagauz Yeri.

"Driven" Mothers in Gagauz Yeri

In the familiar capitalist gendered hegemony, women are expected to stay at home and men to work in the public realm. Yet ideas about what makes a good mother, good work, and a good life vary across cultures, and among some people the reality of women working for wages outside the home has already been absorbed into the sociocultural understandings. As Mary Zimmerman, Jacqueline Litt, and Christine Bose point out, "Scholarship on US racial ethnic minority families ... identifies a broad conception of motherhood that includes patterns of paid work" (2006, 206; see also Collins 1990). Indeed, ideas about motherhood, migrant work, uplift, and progress are variably conceived according to changing political and historical contexts, differences in women's educational and employment background, and differences in women's identities; but they are also conceived in terms of identities such as class, rural versus urban residence, ethnicity, language, and local ideas about civilization. Such specificities inform migrants' decisions, power, and agency, as well as their experiences of migration and its impact.

The importance of this difference between women is very clear in the case of the formerly socialist states, where local gendered hegemonies regarding worker-mothers stood against capitalist ideals that separated women and men into private and public realms, respectively, and where notions of uplift involved a communal socialist ethic (even if socialist hegemonies were locally resisted in some ways, too). In formerly socialist states, desires for uplift may come into conflict with long-held beliefs among this "last Soviet generation" concerning Soviet-style and Russian modernity and socialism (Yurchak 2006). Women's legitimations of their work abroad through recourse to conventional notions of gender roles and the local panic over their migrant work thus reflect negotiations over past socialist and prospective neoliberal gendered moral economies. Yet in these negotiations, mothers are consistently figured as the key to social order, past, present, and future.

As in other cases of migrant domestic work cited above, in Gagauz Yeri women commuters usually achieve levels of education and hold jobs that would place them in the middle or even upper echelons of societies. In the past in Gagauz Yeri, educated professionals such as teachers and doctors held a distinct status from those who primarily did *kolkhoz* (collective farm) work, but now all have been placed in the same lot. As Tatya explained, in some ways "it is the same for everyone." Most Gagauz women undertaking migrant labor are aged thirty to fifty years and are educated at least through technical school; some have a university education. Some were formerly employed by the state as teachers, administrators, nurses, engineers, doctors, bookkeepers, and even professors, while others worked as traders or in local stores. Even if they managed to keep their jobs, these women are no longer able to live on the wages they make; thus the feeling that people of all different locations in society are now in the same boat.[8] As Tatya also mentioned, whatever their wages and status before the fall of socialism, most women who leave for Turkey make between US$30 and US$50 a month in Moldova (where the per capita gross national product is US$710). The women represented here have these wages, but they also have some other resources: they are just wealthy enough to make the initial trip to Turkey but not quite wealthy enough to be able to make do without working abroad. And though they are experiencing similar economic dynamics, it should be noted that the women in Gagauz Yeri who seek work abroad do so for different reasons. Migrant labor becomes a solution for women whose family's lot is sliding downhill, for those who are scrambling to maintain their status, and for those who hope to take advantage of new opportunities to climb upward. Whatever their reason, migrant labor works for them. In 1999, 80 percent of the Moldovan population lived below the poverty line; only with the help of remittances from work abroad did this figure fall to 36 percent in 2004–5 (World Bank 2004, 2005; Government of the Republic of Moldova 2004).[9]

---

[8] For more on women's situation in post-Soviet Moldova, including the effects of migration, see Pamela Abbott (2007) and Mihail Peleah (2007).

[9] Although these data do not specify particular populations within Moldova, I would argue that these dynamics are reflected in the Gagauz case. The World Bank cites the poverty level for 2005 at 35 percent of the population; this has decreased even more dramatically in recent years (http://povertydata.worldbank.org/poverty/country/MDA, accessed June 8, 2015). The most data about this migration come from the International Organization for Migration and show that 40 percent of the working population are abroad. Some 66 percent are men, most of whom work in the Commonwealth of Independent States (most often doing construction in Russia or Ukraine) (37 percent are ages twenty-one to thirty years, 28 percent are ages thirty-one to forty, 23 percent are ages forty-one to fifty). Of the working population of women, 34 percent labor abroad. Many of them (36 percent) are thirty-one- to forty-year-old mothers with children who work as housekeepers in Turkey or Italy (Spain, Cyprus, and Greece are the other locations). These populations are well educated (42 percent have a secondary school education, 28 percent hold vocational school

Even though they may work multiple jobs, the women of Gagauz Yeri still have primary responsibility for household labor: cooking, cleaning, and child care. They also participate equally with men in farmwork. As women in a socialist state, all were subject to the double or even triple burdens of working outside and inside the home, often including work on a *kolkhoz*. Some in rural areas now have their own plots to tend while continuing to work on the collective farm. These responsibilities are no less of a burden now for women, who have adapted their informal economic strategies to include migrant labor abroad.

Women justify this new kind of work, and their new desires for upward mobility, by appealing to their roles as worker-mothers. Even so, as with other migrant domestics, their discursive practices focus mostly on their maternal duties. These same obligations become the fodder for communities at home to criticize migrant women for their absence from their families. However, what is distinctive in these debates over morality in Moldova and separates them from debates represented in ethnographies of migrant workers elsewhere is the tension over women's new engagements in capitalist activities in the neoliberal global economy as domestics and consumers in Turkey. We also find here migrant working women objecting, even if quietly, to capitalist exploitation, something not as widely seen in narratives of women in historically capitalist societies.

Before fully assessing the shifting gendered moral economies, let us carefully attend to what the gendered notions in this community are—what it is like to be a worker-mother in Gagauz Yeri and Moldova from the perspective of both migrant mothers and their communities at home. Throughout the ethnographic descriptions of this below, I provide the context in which I acquired this data and give a sense of this unusual place through a narrative of the first of six trips of four days each I made to Gagauz Yeri in the fall of 2004, when I met many of the women whom I came to know better during my stay.

---

degrees, and 20 percent are university educated). 42 percent are seasonal workers and 27 percent work abroad for less than one year at a time (most of this number, 56 percent, had worked in Turkey). As reflected in this survey, most go abroad to increase their wealth and to pay current expenses. In terms of getting information about jobs and traveling, they trust their friends and relatives over other sources. Because Russia is close and the networks are well established as a result of Russian administration, it is cheap and easy to enter Russia ($96); Turkey is four times as much ($442), and Italy eight times as much ($2,000), yet wages in these places change accordingly so that wages in Russia are lowest, those in Turkey are higher, and Italy is the highest among the three (IOM 2004; IOM 2005; Lücke, Mahmoud, and Pinger 2007).

Raising Children and Communities

WORKING AND MOTHERING IN MOLDOVA AND TRANSNATIONALLY

September in Gagauz Yeri is harvest season, the time to pick grapes at the *kolkhoz* vineyard and family plots, if you have one. The Moldovan countryside is rolling and green this time of year; chestnuts cover the ground, and corn stalks are stacked in the work-yards of village houses, ready to be shucked for fodder. I had met Tatya's family years before, in the spring of 2002. At that time, Tatya's younger sister, Lidya, was working in Istanbul caring for my grandmother. Lidya was working in Turkey to pay for the expensive medical care for her daughter's epileptic condition. I was staying with my grandmother at the time, and Lidya and I became fast friends, spending her days off together and talking into the wee hours of the morning about her life, Gagauz Yeri, and my research.

When I went that spring to Moldova for a week of exploratory research on this migration at its source, Lidya encouraged me to stay with her family in Congaz (figure 1.1). So, during the time of fasting before Orthodox Easter (not an entirely appropriate time for visitors, but the only time I had), I was hosted by Lidya's youngest sister, Pasha, and her extended family—her husband and mother-in-law, four children, and Lidya's son, who also stayed with them while Lidya was away. It was cold then, and the Moldovan hills were marked by naked black vines and grass charred by the sun and rooted in soppy soil—the Moldovan mud that villagers there are so proud of. Tatya, at thirty-four the eldest of five siblings, was working in Ankara (the capital of Turkey) at the time, so I had not met her.

It was hard to keep track of Lidya's whereabouts in Turkey and Moldova, so the only contact I had had with this family since 2002 was sending them the many pictures I had taken. Even then, I was unsure of the reliability of the mail until I returned in 2004 and found the photographs displayed around the house. This time around, I called Pasha through her sister-in-law, Elena, who lived next door and was the only one in the family with a phone, but since Pasha was working on the day I was to come, Tatya came to greet me and became one of my hosts.

To get to Congaz in 2002, I had taken public transportation, which involved a bumpy ride on a *marshrytka* (minibus) down Lenin Avenue, the paved two-lane highway traversing southern Moldova north to south that goes straight through Gagauz Yeri. Congaz is approximately two hours south of Chişinău, the capital of Moldova. With a population of 10,000, Congaz is

Figure 1.1. Congaz Church, Gagauz Yeri, Moldova, 2004. Photograph by the author.

billed as the largest village in the world. Nonetheless, with so many people working abroad, the streets are often deserted. Some drive horse and carts or ride bicycles, and a few own cars, mopeds, or motorcycles with sidecars. To get around, most people hitchhike; this is free and the most comfortable means of transportation. Otherwise they take the bus (the next most comfortable, but also most expensive) or the *marshrytka* (which is cheaper).

In 2002 I had come alone, but in 2004 I was joined by Diana, a Russian- and English-speaking Gagauz ethnologist who had offered me her assistance.[10] Though Diana lives in Chişinău now, her hometown is Comrat, a city of 70,000, the capital of the autonomous region of Gagauz Yeri and one of three urban centers in the region. She accompanied me on my reentry to Gagauz Yeri to introduce me to people from her family who had been to work in Turkey. Her family became a sort of surrogate family to me in Moldova. After spending one day in Comrat, we traveled together to Congaz,

---

[10] Diana is a scholar at the Academy of Sciences in Chişinău. I met her through connections with other anthropologists who work in Gagauz Yeri.

about a half-hour trip. I had arranged for Tatya to meet us in town, and she directed us to the local *internat* (an orphanage or school), where she had friends who had been to work in Turkey. On this first trip I interviewed a bookkeeper, Tatya's friend Miriam, and a cook who worked in Gagauz Yeri about their labors abroad. As I did so, Diana's discomfort with village life became clear, indicative of stratifications in Gagauz Yeri. So when Tatya invited me to stay with her and offered to introduce me the following day to teachers at Congaz Elementary School who had been to Turkey, I jumped at the opportunity.

Congaz Elementary School is off Lenin Avenue (figure 1.2). When I arrived, afternoon classes had begun, so the corridors were empty. After checking in with the principal, I was led to the teachers' lounge, a small, narrow room with two desks, some bookshelves, and a large window looking out onto the school playground. Three teachers were waiting to speak with me.[11] These teachers had taken leaves of absence from their jobs to go to Turkey in 2001–2.

In some ways, as Tatya put it, their reasoning is simple: they go to make money for their families. "We go to Turkey because of the money. If there were a lot of places to work—you know, state jobs, to support us and to build a life with—we wouldn't go. Perestroika [the political and economic "restructuring" of the Soviet Union under Mikhail Gorbachev in the late 1980s] ruined us. Before that, with very little money, you could buy something. Now, in order to get money you have to go either to Moscow or to Turkey." They spent this money on their children and families. In 2002, Marina left for six months because she needed money for her husband to have an operation. Even though she works two jobs, as a math teacher and an administrator, she earns less than US$100 a month. The second teacher, Alina, also held down these two jobs, while her husband was employed by the church to stock their stoves for heat. She explained that she had gone twice to Turkey over 2001–2, for six months each time, to pay for her eldest

---

[11] I sat at one empty desk with Marina, who volunteered to go first. Yet even when the second teacher sat down with me and Marina went to the other desk to take care of some administrative matters, she continued to comment frequently, and conversations involving all four of us arose. The "interview" therefore amounted to an informal conversation, though a recorded one structured loosely around my interview guide, with all these women at once. This format, which took anywhere from half an hour to two hours, was common to all the recorded interviews I conducted as well as to the many nonrecorded conversations I had with women in Gagauz Yeri and Istanbul about their commutes to Turkey. In these exchanges, usually more than one interviewee was present, most often they were all women, and a comment from one would often prompt others to add their own comments—whether that meant agreeing or arguing.

Figure 1.2. Congaz Elementary School, Gagauz Yeri, Moldova, 2004. Photograph by the author.

child to attend university. She worried that without another trip abroad she would be unable to pay for her second child's education. "Veeeery little pay," Marina summarized, and all chimed in in agreement. This, in addition to the fact that they have to buy their own supplies for classrooms (pens, paper, and chalk) and endure school conditions that sometimes mean that classes are canceled in winter because of lack of heat. Moreover, Marina explained that students often did not do their homework because they were troubled at home. She noted that this was because mothers were away in Turkey. Alina went on, "Hard, hard. It is hard to live here. It is expensive here. Food is expensive, living is expensive, it is all expensive. . . . Whoever wants to give a wedding has to take out a loan. Then she goes to Turkey to pay off the loans." The women were keen to point out that they went for the money and that they needed the money to help their families with emergency hospital bills, but also for more long-term investments such as a university education and for status enhancers, such as a big wedding.

We soon moved on to discuss what life was like for working mothers in Gagauz Yeri. Galina had gone to Turkey twice, for three months and then six months, to get money to buy her musically gifted child a violin and to educate him at the music school in Comrat. She explained that while they worked as teachers, at home there was even more work to do. "We do it all ourselves" she said, implicitly indicating that they had no hired help as the women in the Turkish households they worked for did, and explaining what the double or even triple shift in this context meant.

> *Galina:* And not just work in the house. Here, we also work in the fields on the weekends. We collect the corn, we till the land. . . .
>
> *Leyla:* Both men and women?
>
> *Galina:* Together, everyone does it because it doesn't work with one person. It is hard. There is a lot of work—cows, birds, sheep, all of it. Because there is no money here. We have things to buy, but there is no money. So, at home, you eat that [what you grow on the farm]. We make our own bread for ourselves. It is very hard; there is a lot of work. . . .
>
> *Leyla:* And the men?
>
> *Galina:* Yes, they also help out. They do things—[make] the bread, [take care of] the wood stove. But they also work a lot for money, and it is hard for them too.

During the interview at the *internat* the previous day, Tatya had also talked about how women's work involved not only employment, but also work in the fields alongside men in the family, and housework. Sitting around a makeshift desk off the *internat* kitchen with her friend the bookkeeper, Miriam, and Diana, Tatya explained that she had returned recently from four years of commuting to work in one household in Ankara. The woman she had cared for had died, so she would not be returning to that job. I inquired about what she was doing now that she was back.

> *Leyla:* Are you working now too?
>
> *Tatya:* No [There is none].
>
> *Miriam:* They have land. They work there . . . in the fields.
>
> *Leyla:* That is work, too.
>
> *Tatya:* It is a lot of work, but without money. It doesn't count as pay.
>
> *Miriam:* You do that for what you need at home.

Leyla: What are you working on?

Tatya: We are working in the fields . . . we do housework.

Miriam: Now, just wait until the fields are finished, and anyone can go wherever. . . .

Tatya: And then where? Maybe Moscow, maybe elsewhere, I don't know.

Mothering, keeping house, working outside the home to pay for a hospital visit or a child's education, working in the fields—are all part of being a working mother in post-Soviet Gagauz Yeri. That all of these jobs, especially working outside the home, are taken to be ideologically legitimate means of making a living for a woman and constitutive of the duties of the worker-mother is part of the particularity of the situation of women from a formerly socialist state. This distinguishes these women from other working mothers who do migrant domestic work but who only have recourse to a discourse of motherhood to legitimate their travels abroad. Women in Gagauz Yeri, by contrast, have long had roles as workers.

That night, we huddled around a meat stew, fresh beets, a cabbage salad, and wine in Katya's unfinished kitchen. Both the meat and the wine indicated that I was a special guest. After dinner, we piled onto her husband Victor's motorcycle with sidecar and went over to Pasha's house. Pasha's and Tatya's sister-in-law, Elena, who Pasha proudly announced was a doctor, was there as well, as were Pasha's husband and her children. We ate cookies and drank "new wine," an unfermented sour juice made from newly harvested grapes.

When visitors are present and on other special days, women are expected to drink (wine and local moonshine were the most common alcoholic beverages) and participate in lively socializing with men, even if "good women" are also expected not to overdo it.[12] That men and women would sit around and talk together thus was not unusual. I was generally offered a drink in whatever home I entered, and men, women, and children would all join in if there was enough to go around. Social norms dictate regular drinking in mixed-sex gatherings in Gagauz Yeri. This is a norm that distinguishes these women when they go to Turkey.

Elena, the doctor who is Tatya's sister-in-law, told me that a number of years earlier she too had gone to Turkey to earn money to pay for her

---

[12] Men may even be paid in wine. For another case of this, see Douglas Rogers (2005).

daughter's wedding. Her husband had died, and she had been particularly strapped for income. She suggested I visit her clinic the next day and meet some nurses who also had worked in Turkey.[13] These women, when I spoke with them, all said that they took leaves of absence to go abroad "for the money . . . for the children." Three told me they had gone only once, in 2000. One had gone four times, for three to six months each time, between 2000 and 2002. Another nurse explained that for six months in 1999, they had not been paid at all, so she had gone to Turkey to work for five months in 2000. She reiterated what I had heard from others: even when they were paid, they made at most about $50 a month. And just as at the elementary school, the state employees at the clinic had to use some of their wages to keep up the grounds of the institution themselves. Elena explained that the state was no longer supporting upkeep, particularly since that clinic was due to be closed in favor of the expansion of one in a town about forty minutes away. Tired of the dilapidated conditions, they had recently come together to repaint the rooms and hallways, and the place smelled of fresh paint.

These women had various specific reasons for needing money: one had gone to Turkey to earn money to pay for medical expenses for a sick child, several had gone to pay for a university education for their children, and another had gone to pay off her daughter's wedding expenses. Like the others, all referred their economic need to work in Turkey to their role as mothers, which was their articulation of a gendered moral economy. If they had a job in Moldova that paid enough for these things, they insisted, they would have stayed in Gagauz Yeri.

One of the ways in which women articulate their image of a good worker-mother is through narratives of the hardships of life in Turkey, of saving their money, and of the sacrifices they have made to further their children's opportunities. As noted earlier, narratives of mothers' martyrdom are common in explanations of migrant domestic work (see. e.g., Parrenas 2005). Yet for former socialists, working as a domestic is a particular blow to their status, and thus their defense of their choice is adamant. Many women talked about saving every penny to send home. One nurse from the hospital explained that she only saw her wages for two days before she sent them to her family.

It is usually in this context that these women spoke about how hard the work was. Most admitted that their work in Turkey was not physically but

---

[13] These interviews progressed much like the one with the teachers. We sat in their office at the hospital with four other women; I asked questions and let them tell their stories and talk to each other about their experiences.

psychologically challenging: coming from a former socialist context, and one in which they had perhaps worked as professionals, several said that it was hard to get used to serving someone else, making the time abroad pass quickly, and adjusting to the multitude of exploitations to which they are subject as foreigners both inside and outside their work household. Several women explained that, as undocumented workers, they were at the whim of their employers.

All the women I interviewed talked about how much they missed their children when they were away, about the joys and pains of hearing their voices over long-distance phone calls and how they counted the days until they could return home. Victoria, from the urban center of Comrat, who had started going to Turkey to work as a textile merchant in the mid-1990s but more recently had worked as a domestic (and whose narrative of bad and good employers appears in chapter 4), explained:

> There are women who stay two, three years. I cannot do that at all. One year goes by hard as it is. I miss my mother and daughter too much. I only have one daughter! But you have to go for one year, again, you have to go.

Many also talked about missing their homes in Gagauz Yeri. One woman, Ekaterina, Diana's sister-in-law, also from Comrat and a single mother of a young boy, had left him in the care of her mother while she worked in Turkey caring for an elderly lady. She now worked for a day-care center in Comrat. She exclaimed, "I even missed my walls!" Such stories are similar to other migrant domestics' stories globally.

In their narratives, these women perceived this hard wage-earning labor and the absence from their homes, families, and communities as a motherly sacrifice they made for their children. This emphasis on mothering should be considered in the contexts of both the Soviet socialist and pre-Soviet eras. As many feminist scholars of the region have pointed out, as worker-mothers, women were expected to fulfill their roles as producers for the state and, even more important, as reproducers of the nation (see Verdery 1996). Although socialist economic policies and ideology secured some workers' rights for women, it still upheld the idea that women's *primary* roles should be as mothers and sacrificers for the socialist republic.[14] In fact, a cult of motherhood reaches back to prerevolutionary times in Russia, where even

---

[14] For evidence and discussion of the socialist ideology's incompleteness in regard to women's rights during the Soviet era, see Wendy Goldman (1991), Elizabeth Wood (1997), Anna Temkina

now the trope of the "suffering woman" is "mythical" in its proportions (Ries 1994). Women's suffering is representative of the dilemmas of the "Russian soul" itself, and women are viewed as its repository (du Plessix Gray 1989).[15] The Russian women's "litanies" described by the anthropologist Nancy Ries involve "poetic inventories of suffering, sacrifice, and loss" that complain of the burdens of women and problems with the state and the economy, but also "romanticize and legitimate women's double burden itself" (1994, 259). So, even though a discourse of martyrdom may be common to migrant women's narratives, there is a specific and deep-seated historical context for it in Russia and the republics of the former Soviet Union.

In her study of women traders from the former Soviet Union, Marta Bruno argues that these types of representations of good mothers play out in how women's new economic activity is perceived. Whereas Russian men who trade are often cast as speculators, women are viewed as participating in trade to make money for their families because they are desperate, and thus are not as suspect (1997, 72). That women's labor is represented as "desperate" is part of the valuing of certain economic activities over others in the former Soviet Union and Eastern Europe (Smith and Stenning 2006). Even with a history of women's participation in the workforce, we see how notions of the desperation of mothers can help women morally legitimate otherwise illegitimate work abroad, and the upward mobility gained through it.

Kaldirmak (UPLIFT)

In Gagauz Yeri, migrant women's expectations of the returns on their sacrifices were very high: they were trying to lift up (*kaldirmak*) themselves, their families, and their communities. Indeed, while some went to Turkey to pay off hospital emergencies, most went to improve their conditions and move up in the world. They went so that they could throw a large wedding, or buy a violin, or send a child (who otherwise would have simply stayed in the village) to university, or renovate their homes. Emerging here is a new gendered moral economy that opens spaces for women to take on new roles as responsible mothers who are both nurturers and providers, making the

---

and Anna Rotkirch (1997), Susan Gal and Gail Kligman (2000a), Kathleen Kuehnast and Carol Nechemias (2004), and Hemment (2007, 5–8).

[15] Again, and as noted in chapter 1, the trope of women as depositories of the nation's soul is familiar to the dynamics of gender and nationalism in other nonsocialist or postsocialist contexts as well. From my own research in Turkey, I found this to be true in the case of Turkish women, for instance (for one example, see Kandiyoti 1997).

best of their migrant opportunities to engage in the neoliberalizing economy. This allows them to imagine and construct new horizons for themselves and their families.

This seeking of uplift was evident as Tatya and I walked through her village together. She pointed out the construction and rebuilding of individual houses with better materials and noted that every one of those households had at least one person abroad earning money. Gas heat, new markets, and better housing had come to the village with the help of these wages, Tatya explained. She insisted that the only way to improve the conditions in her village was to go abroad to work. Emphasizing personal responsibility for community and family uplift, she said, "People have to do things for themselves now—and they do—and that is how things get better for them." In another conversation, Anna, a local librarian and staunch communist, complained, "Our villages are falling apart." She herself had worked abroad, and she sympathized: "People are trying to lift themselves up [*kaldirmak*] by going abroad to work." But what else could they do? She went on, "There is no state left!" These assessments indicate that in this formerly socialist and neoliberalizing setting, these commuter laborers see themselves as the most resourceful and responsible people in the community. They see migrant labor as a route to help their children advance and to better their village homes and lives, not escape them.

In their discursive practices, we find that commuter women's desires constitute an emergent gendered moral economy focused on change. These new notions and actions allow women to seek advancement and independence from family obligations. These kinds of narratives uphold women as worker-mothers, but they also rupture conventional gender hegemonies and offer potential "moments of creativity" for women. As one young woman whose father had worked abroad for more than ten years put it, "You can tell the people who have worked abroad: they hold themselves in a different way, they have self-respect now, they were drowning and now they are able to keep their heads above water." Maybe they are even trying to swim, I commented. These transformations in their lives at home are accentuated by their migrant labor experiences abroad. As Ekaterina, who mentioned missing her walls, explained, "When I came back to my home, I looked around and got very depressed. The floors are dirty, the walls crooked, there is no running water, no washing machines." She paused. "But then I thought, well, *I* can change that."

These women also quietly recognize the personal benefits of migrant labor. Though it is true that most of their wages do go to benefit their children and homes in Gagauz Yeri, in conversations with these women over time, I heard other, whispered reasons why they went to Istanbul to work. One woman fled an abusive husband whom she did not feel she could divorce. Sveta and her friends, whose stories we hear in more detail in chapter 4, had Turkish boyfriends and went to restaurants in Istanbul, and felt they had gained some freedom from the dictates of their communities in Gagauz Yeri. Tatya complained that a major difference in her life since she had returned to Moldova was that she had no time to herself, no days off, no vacations, and no time to visit with her girlfriends. "There, you can buy things for yourself and your kids. Here, you don't think about buying things like that." One of the nurses, Maya, who had worked for a good family, talked about what she learned in Turkey: "That it is necessary to talk like this, act like that." What she meant was that she had learned politesse and ways of acting in what she considered a more sophisticated manner. In a certain sense, women found *worldliness* in their work abroad: Alina reminisced about seeing the sea and going on a boat, Maya about wearing pants for the first time, Tatya about shopping in Istanbul, Ekaterina about getting her hair cut at the beauty salon. Tatya explained that she became "caught in the middle," and Maya commented, "One of my legs is still standing in Turkey."

Straddling Moldova and Turkey, even as they criticize Turkish households, they try to transform their own homes to have as many conveniences. Indeed, such things as wallpaper, kitchens open to other rooms, and washing machines are new signs of status in the community. Anna, ever the critic, even claimed that they were not changing enough, or in the right ways. She explained that both Angela and her other daughter, Inna, had gone to Turkey, "but they don't do anything different!" Inna had married a Turk, and Angela intended to keep commuting to Turkey to support her children as they grew up in her Gagauz village home. "They are leaving, sure, but they aren't really doing anything new or different. If it were me, I'd leave entirely. What is there to do here? Why don't they take advantage of their opportunities?"

By means of their geographic mobility and labors abroad, these women are struggling to better their community's and family's lives, as well as their own. Their new economic activities and desires and their continued insistence on being good mothers amount to a new gendered moral economy. This morality is grounded, still, in Gagauz traditional gendered socialist values: they would rather go abroad to work than stay at home and not work at all. But it also allows for and seeks to legitimate new and better ways to make a living, consume, and be a worker-mother. These new ideals align more with neoliberal tenets of self-reliance and entrepreneurship than with socialist ones, a point I return to at the end of this chapter. But their discourse of motherhood in some ways resists, even while inadvertently aligning them with, the conventional views expressed by Gagauz community members who would restrict women's social and physical mobility. These debates represent contestations over shifting gendered moral economies and have particular salience in the postsocialist context.

Contesting Gendered Moral Economies

As women push and poke at local gendered hegemonies and notions of appropriate uplift through their work abroad, local communities are in a panic. Local customs hold that mothers, whether working or not, should be in Gagauz Yeri with their children. When the topic of women's migrant (especially to Turkey) labor comes up in Moldova, eventually one hears unbridled anger and a deep sense of shame and sadness directed at commuter mothers for "abandoning children" and "splitting up families." This not only is true for Gagauz Yeri but also forms part of the discursive landscape of Moldova more generally. The alarmist rhetoric surrounding "trafficking in women" is one of the contexts in which this discussion about commuter women takes place. The fear and panic are fed by Moldovan and international NGOs, which, overpowered by concerns over trafficking, highlight in their campaigns how orphaned children are the main targets of traffickers. Mothers who decide to leave for work thus face considerable moral ambivalence from their communities, for as mobile working mothers they themselves are now also seen as potential victims (IOM 2005). These kinds of accusations leveled against migrant mothers are also to be found in Gagauz communities, where women who go abroad to Turkey are perceived to be running off with men, or at least running around with them while they are there. These women are also accused of wanting too much. Thus, the debates focus on women's perceived sexual and consumerist desires, in addition to revolving around their roles as mothers.

These debates also home in on women's work as *domestics* in *Turkey*, a practice viewed as not providing a legitimate means to progress and modernity. In other cases of migrant women, we saw that mothers were less able than daughters to legitimate their work abroad through desires for uplift and progress, even if it was for their families. Even so, there was no question of whether uplift and progress *could* be achieved in the destinations daughters and mothers sought to work and from which they brought back consumer goods. But the case of migrants from Gagauz Yeri is complicated by the fact that Turkey and domestic work are perceived as "backward," which creates an opening for community members to criticize migrant working mothers for seeking uplift for themselves in the new economy represented by Turkey. They see these transnational worker-mothers not as creating a better life for families and communities but as selfish individuals stirring up social disorder.

As I sat in Pasha's living room one evening with Tatya, Elena, and a neighbor who had been to Turkey to work as a domestic, along with two others (Pasha and her mother-in-law) who had not, the talk turned to how people used the money they earned. Those present said that many women threw large and expensive weddings, built big new homes, or filled their homes with new services (running water and gas heat), appliances (washing machines, heaters, refrigerators, televisions, satellite televisions), and novel products. When I asked the elderly babushka that evening whether in her day people were concerned about building up their homes in such a fashion, she replied, *"Bizimkiler cok azitti"* (Our people are out of control). Several others, even those who had been abroad themselves, concurred. They noted that whereas people used to help each other, now it was everyone for him- or herself. Thus, migrant women transgress accepted norms about legitimate ways to make a living, about appropriate degrees of consumption, and about upward social mobility.

Interestingly, as in other ethnographic studies of migrant workers elsewhere, though men also leave the village for work, the blame for social disorder is routinely laid on women's shoulders. For instance, in the context of a group interview with Miriam and another employee, Lara, the cook at Congaz *internat*, Miriam publicly scolded Lara. Lara had a baby and an alcoholic husband, and had expressed a desire to go back to Turkey. Within Lara's range of hearing, Miriam remarked loudly, "There are women here who are very into themselves, *relaxed*, who leave their husbands and children, even though they know how they'll become drunks and get worse when they go." Such public critiques help police the boundaries of gendered obligations in Gagauz Yeri. I witnessed several similar scenes in which leaving the village for work as a way to try to provide for children was denounced as a responsible option for women because it would make a self-destructive husband worse, and leave him as a burden on others.

However, regarding those commuter women's husbands who did take care of their house and children, many of the women I spoke with exclaimed: "They make the bread now!" Tatya explained that men now did the domestic work that was traditionally associated with women: "They pickle the vegetables come fall, cook for the kids, dress them and send them off to school." Tatya said that though she sent her husband the money, he was the one who put the gas line in, or paid the university fees, and took care of the children. Life in the village was hard, and she appreciated him for doing these things.

Although women like Tatya may quietly respect their husbands, villagers more loudly pronounce husbands left behind to be abandoned and pitiable. That they do "womanly" tasks is an indicator of disorder in the village. Men who assume that their wife in Turkey is running around with Turkish men, then go to Russia for work and find themselves a Russian woman, are also viewed as pitiable. They are seen as making that decision because their wives left, as having no other choice, though perhaps they are regarded as less of a fool than a man who stayed.

Women who leave to work abroad are perceived as not upholding their gendered duties, whether or not the new transnational family actually functions well. As in the case of the mobile Filipina workers observed by Parrenas (2005, 2008), in Gagauz Yeri too, communities and families do not accept migrant women's revisioning of motherhood and working. Most children and Gagauz communities with absent migrant mothers insist that caring and nurturing are the mother's role, not the father's, and that the mother needs to be home to do it.

In Gagauz Yeri, the fact that women *work* is not itself a problem ideologically (as it is in the Philippines in Parrenas's studies, as well as elsewhere), yet interestingly, their mothering roles at home are still emphasized and become a point of contention. Even though men are also choosing to leave, it is the Gagauz women who are at fault and who are regarded as bad wives and mothers. Even when children are left in the care of their grandmother, an option befitting traditional gender roles in the area, this is not perceived as appropriate. Miriam expressed a common sentiment: "This is not right. These women are too old to go running around after children, to sit and do their homework with them. A child needs [his/her] mother." On a midnight tour down the muddy lanes of one Gagauz village, Anna, a librarian, and her husband, a high school biology teacher, pointed out to me all the houses without lights, and some under construction. Almost every other house was dark and empty. The mothers were in Turkey, they explained. (This was in stark contrast to Tatya's insistence that people were trying to better themselves.) Diana, the Gagauz ethnographer, even worried aloud to me that Gagauz female migrant labor could lead to the extinction of the Gagauz people. These narratives reveal the judgment that it is women, and mothers in particular—not men, and not the economy—who are at fault for a man's drinking and philandering, for the abandonment of children, for the breakup of families, and even for the dissolution of their communities.

Thus, a Gagauz mother's decision to go to Turkey instead of Russia was purported to cause even more disorder. In general, perceptions of Turkey in Gagauz Yeri and Moldova are rather negative. Turkish products and the markets that sell them in Moldova are negatively valued. Anna, a university-educated village woman and the communist mentioned earlier, was working as the librarian for the local cultural center. She had worked as a domestic in Istanbul for several years, alternating her time there with her daughter Angela's time there. On one of several visits I made to her village home, she described her experiences in Gagauz Yeri and what it was like to work in Turkey. She felt that the fact that everyone, even women on the lower rungs of the village hierarchy, could go to Turkey to earn money was problematic. She was particularly upset about Turkish male–Gagauz female relations. She complained that everything had become "bottom-up" (*alt-ust olmus*), saying this about the women (presumably other than herself and her daughter) in her village who went to Turkey to work:

> Women who wouldn't be looked at in this village are treated like queens by Turkish men and come to think of themselves as something. Then they don't want to return to their husbands.

Thus, women who go to Turkey are accused of abandoning their motherly duties because they desire such treatment.

These migrant women are compared to those who chose to stay. For instance, Tatya's sister Pasha and her husband had *not* gone abroad to work, and were struggling to run a new business in their village. Pasha works as a cook at the Congaz *internat* in addition to working on the farm. They have four children (sometimes caring for a fifth, when her other sister Sveta goes to Turkey to work and leaves her son with them). "I can't leave," Pasha explained to me, just as many who had not gone abroad to work did. "I have children to take care of." Miriam, Tatya's friend the accountant at the *internat*, explained that she had been to Turkey once, and then had decided not to go again: "I have one child, a daughter, who was ten years old when I left. She had to wash the laundry, take care of the house, and cook. She asked me not to go. So I don't go."

Interestingly, it is not that Miriam does not migrate abroad to work. It is just that she does not go to Turkey. Instead, she goes for short periods to

Moscow with her husband. Migration to Russia is deemed less questionable than migration to Turkey, as Russia is seen as the site of a valued civilization. In these accounts, the fact that migrant women cross the boundary between Moldova and Turkey in their travels and work is talked about in terms of the loyalties and obligations they transgress as mothers and as former socialists.

If it is not out of a desire to be treated well by Turkish men that a woman goes to Istanbul, according to Gagauz community members, then it is because she is willing to do particularly demeaning types of work to gain wealth, new consumer goods, and upward mobility for her household. This critique would seem applicable to all those who go abroad to work from Gagauz Yeri, but in my formal and informal interviews it was particularly focused on those who go to Turkey. This is not only because Turkey is negatively valued but also because of the type of work Gagauz women are willing to do there—domestic service—to make money. Miriam's commentary reflected this critique:

> In Russia, you do physical labor, but you work alongside your husband, friends, and family during the day and have your own apartment with them at night. And the employers treat you better. They just give you the job to do and let you do it—they do not stand over you telling you how to do it.

The bottom line seems to be, with working in Russia as an option or even staying home and struggling through without having any waged work, why would a woman choose to work serving a newly wealthy Muslim Turk who tells you what to do day and night, alone without your family or friends, with only one half-day off a week, and be thankful for the job, unless you are incredibly greedy and selfish, naive, fleeing your responsibilities to your children, or unhappy with your husband and life and searching for a new one? Commuting women in Gagauz Yeri are thus tainted by their migration to Turkey, their labor, and their consumer activity. They are seen as naive and stupid, and are cast as selfish people who are so greedy for money that they would do anything. They are morally sullied by their association with Turkey and Turkish men, and—worst of all—are deemed bad mothers who want too much.

Critiques and assumptions of this sort make up the particular gendered moral economy that Gagauz women working as migrant domestics both participate in and must cope with to legitimate their work abroad. Many commuter women themselves uphold the gendered morality implicit in these assumptions. Many admitted to me that *"oylede var"* (there are those [women] who are like that) but distinguished themselves from such corrupt or naive female commuters.

Women migrants reiterate adamantly that their work in Turkey is a sacrifice they make to provide a better life for their children and their communities. They present themselves as good mothers by distancing themselves from their association with Turkish products and men and by using the same negative categorizations of Turkey detailed above. For instance, most claim they do not buy anything from Turkey to bring back to Gagauz Yeri, seeing Turkish products as not valuable. When I asked Anna, the librarian, if anything in Gagauz Yeri had changed as a result of the back-and-forth labor migration between Moldova and Turkey and the infiltration of remittances, she replied, "No. We have culture [civilization]; we just need money." Another of Tatya's friends, Valentina, who is a primary schoolteacher at Congaz Elementary School and who is married and has a son, went to Turkey to work as a domestic. When interviewed about her decision to migrate for work, she confronted head-on the reputations of women in Gagauz Yeri who go to Turkey: "I go there for the money, not for a husband." In these narratives, Gagauz women commuters directly confronted and resisted negative representations of them while also participating in images of the "good mother"; they co-opted this category, redefining it, but also upholding this particular gendered morality.

Another way that these women articulate their roles as good Gagauz mothers is through criticisms of the domestic realm in Turkey. Mobile women workers from Gagauz Yeri criticize Turkish "new wealthy" family lifestyles and gender roles and heartily defend the moral superiority of their Gagauz village life. In this context, many insisted that they continued to go to Turkey because they had a good situation there: They were paid and treated well, and their jobs were not hard. Tatya said brusquely, "We do this kind of work here [in Gagauz Yeri] anyway, as part of our regular work. But here in the village, the work is even harder." Several offered a critique of gender and labor in capitalist Turkish society, seeing their own system as morally superior but harder on women. For instance, some saw Turkish women as having easy lives. Such critiques of Turkish lifestyle work in conjunction with negative representations of Turks in Gagauz Yeri and Moldova to show commuting women's allegiance to local moralities in Gagauz Yeri.

All the narratives related here, both those criticizing commuter women and those defending them, speak to common cultural logics tied to local and shifting gendered moral economies. All of these women's judgments about Turkey, Russia, changing wealth and consumption patterns, and types of work, and their ideas about women and gender roles, reveal similar combinations of cultural constructs at work in these communities. Commuter women are criticized for not sufficiently, or appropriately, laboring to gain wealth and for ostentatiously consuming new products for themselves. They are associated with "uncivilized" Turkey and suspected of sexual indiscretion. And they are blamed for being bad mothers. Yet the commuters themselves uphold these very ideals by insisting that they do not buy Turkish products or cavort with Turkish men; by respecting the physical labors required by life in Gagauz Yeri; by criticizing Turkish women as lazy; and, most of all, by asserting that their work abroad is a maternal sacrifice they make for their children.

This kind of complicity in gendered limitations is found as well in other cases of migrant women's work (Brennan 2004). Yet these types of contestations over the destination of migrant workers are specific to this formerly socialist context and to one where the relation between employer and employee is between semiperipheries (not between center and periphery, for instance), where the host society is not perceived as having cultural capital, only economic capital. This lack of value of the host country makes legitimating their work abroad even harder.

Female commuter domestic workers from Gagauz Yeri are associated with a negatively valued east, and they are blamed for societal disorder in Moldova. This blaming indexes an anxiety not only over motherhood but also over the new economic activity of migrant women in Turkey. Even as they uphold some of the negative representations of their labor, migrants respond by asserting a new gendered moral economy based on the idea of hardworking worker-mothers trying to bring order to their lives and communities: through discourses of motherhood in particular, women's labor abroad is made morally legitimate.[16] In doing so, they drive wedges into

---

[16] This is similar to the case detailed by Yulian Konstantinov (1996). Writing of the fall of communism in Bulgaria, he explains the similar moral justifications of new transnational "tourist-traders." He explains that their economic action is anxiety-ridden and is presented as "emotionally colored—an object of attraction, indifference, or repulsion" (1996, 769). He details how market capitalism in Bulgaria is seen as chaotic and ambivalent, and there is a nostalgic seeking out of "socialist" order. The tourist-traders he follows in this context are associated with the new "disorder." The same type of disorder is associated with new traders in Russia, who, according to Caroline Humphrey, are perceived as participating in the "great trash road" from the east and Turkey (2002). These traders are seen as people who transgress not only state boundaries but also loyalties, for money through "unproductive" labor (2002). Konstantinov argues that Bulgarian traders respond to such accusations by seeking order through what he terms "poetics," that is, by interpreting their position in reference to the stable orientation point of a "socialist" economic morality. These transnational traders posit themselves as different from both the

local gendered hegemonies. They defend their actions through a socialist morality of worker-mothers rooted in the past. Even among migrant women there is nostalgia for a time when individuals helped each other in the community, when they were not just out to increase their own wealth—when mothers could remain in Gagauz Yeri. These sentiments could be envisioned as a "socialist orientation" (Konstantinov 1996). Yet in the Gagauz case, we find that these transnational laborers' "poetics" (as Herzfeld [2005] and Konstantinov [1996] might call them) also appeal to an emergent moral economy. Migrant women from Gagauz Yeri, then, are not only desperate formerly socialist mothers and workers trying to assuage conditions of poverty but also new entrepreneurial spirits trying to lift themselves up. Ironically, it is a discourse of desperate mothers seeking family survival that helps them do so.

In upholding and redefining what it means to be a good worker-mother, commuter women are constituting new ideals for what is appropriate consumption for the household; what is necessary to provide a future for your children; and what kinds of rights to expect as a woman, a worker, and a citizen. The current gendered moral economies in Moldova are structured by Soviet socialist experiences, even if women's assertion of individual responsibility for the fate of their families and communities indicates a shift to neoliberalism. The worth of this new capitalist oppression can perhaps be limned by analyzing the returns, economic and other, on this migrant work for the commuting women, their families, and their communities.

Returns

From these debates, we can conclude that the consequences of migrant domestic work from Gagauz Yeri and the gendered moral economies they assert are different from other, historically capitalist, cases in some ways but also similar to them. In the societies in which most instances of migrant domestic work have been examined, women have taken up migrant labor

---

"immoral speculators" of the new capitalist economy and the "suckers" waiting for the state to help them (2002, 765). They align themselves with hardworking people and a socialist morality. However, they also assert their moral worth in terms of being brave, imaginative, and adventuresome entrepreneurs. For Konstantinov, this latter representation, along with traders' attempts to normalize trading activities, represents a new "prospective moral economy." Konstantinov's analysis is one of a few addressing the value of transnational labor in the former Soviet Union and Eastern Europe. Yet it stops short of its gendered dimensions, even though the tourist-traders he writes about are all women. The current analyses of migrant domestic workers from Gagauz Yeri moves forward from where he leaves off.

for the uplift of themselves, their families, and their communities, expanding their roles as mothers to that of transnational mothers and including *working* and *providing* as part of their definition of good mothering. Their wages and their new discourses of motherhood gain them new power and agency in their households and outside. Yet ideas about women's domesticity remain strong (Parrenas 2008) and cause considerable conflict in local communities. In such contexts, women are able to legitimate their work only through activating discourses of desperation and survival, not by appealing to opportunity and uplift as men are able to. Even though these migrant women are not the most desperate in their communities or in the world, and even though they also assert that their goals are lofty, to improve their own and their family's lot, discourses of desperation and motherhood dominate in their legitimations of their work abroad. This state of affairs shows the ongoing power of the idea that a woman's primary role is to be a mother. Such discourses of motherhood, moreover, hide the variety of capitalist exploitations migrant women face as global workers.

For women from Gagauz Yeri, things are different. For them, being a good mother includes working in the public realm or on a farm. These duties are seen as compatible. Women seek to continue to fulfill these obligations by migrating abroad to work. With neoliberal capitalism taking root and the nostalgia for a precommunist Russia, one might imagine a new legitimacy (in the former Soviet perspectives on capitalism) for the bourgeois stay-at-home mother and housewife (see Gal and Kligman 2000a).[17] Yet even if arguments in the formerly socialist world that women should stay home align with the purported place of women in the private realm under capitalism, we cannot presume that capitalist hegemonies have taken over. Certainly, this particular hegemony has not taken root in any predictable way in postsocialist Gagauz Yeri. And this is true of other parts of the former Soviet Union as well: despite having to maneuver and make up for the failures of socialism, many women in postsocialist states, whether migrants or not, continue to uphold working and mothering as compatible and important features of their lives (Berdahl 1999; Onica 2008). This gives women from formerly socialist states recourse to a different set of ideas about women

---

[17] An interesting question to pursue in the future would be whether mothering is emphasized more than working. That is, is the stay-at-home mother finding a new moral ground in Moldova now? If so, this would constitute not a traditional ideology in the same way as in Parrenas's case but a complex one that draws on pre-Soviet times to justify the role of a stay-at-home mother, one that is perceived as progressive in a new context in which capitalism may be beginning to be valued over Soviet socialism.

than is available to those in historically capitalist societies. In Gagauz Yeri, migrant work legitimated in this socialist manner allows Gagauz women to continue to hold some power and agency in their households, instead of losing it by not working at all.

And yet, even though working is important to Gagauz women, as it is for other migrant women, the strongest legitimation of their work abroad is still connected to their role as nurturing mothers. They too try to expand this category to a transnational and even neoliberal one, positioning themselves as better mothers than those who stay home. In so doing, they are also forming new ideas of what constitutes a good mother and of appropriate upward mobility. Women migrants from Gagauz Yeri are also, like other migrant women, resourceful agents in search of a better life. Their transnational work in Turkey, domestic labors, transnational mothering, and new consumption practices rub against local norms concerning the morality of certain labors and the value of uplift for women workers as opposed to men. In this context, the desperate-mother narrative, which emphasizes the sacrifices that these women make for their children, works to purify their transgressive practices and defend women's economic activity. These discourses of desperation and motherhood reassert conventional gender hegemonies, but they also underpin slippages in both old and new gendered hegemonies and help gain women some benefits and freedoms.

That women from Gagauz Yeri do *domestic* work as migrant workers still locates these former socialists fully in the private realm, though now as waged workers. It also excuses men from such duties. Yet for women in Moldova's postsocialist context, waged domestic work also represents a *loss* of their public role, a *drop* in their status. It does not reassert but *newly* constructs these women's domesticity. This observation points up particular drawbacks in this postsocialist example of migrant labor. However, perhaps because of the dramatic shifts in Gagauz Yeri from socialism to neoliberal capitalism, the Gagauz migrant women's narratives tend to harbor more critiques of the capitalist exploitations women face as worker-mothers laboring informally abroad than might be found in historically capitalist contexts. The women of Gagauz Yeri who described their experiences to me criticized the effects of shifting structural economic dynamics, such as the loss of state jobs and welfare assistance, which became part of the reason for going abroad to work.

Tatya admitted that it may have become somewhat harder in the village because of labor migration, and that she had become used to the convenience of household appliances. "Here we have to bring the water inside the house ourselves," she said, but then added, "But it is changing here, too—I bought a washing machine for our house!" Such products are new necessities for Gagauz households. Yet, she sighed,

> Even when you save, you sometimes can't make ends meet because then other things fall apart. Before you migrated for work, you used to be able to raise your food, and not have to buy it, but now, since you are in Turkey, there is nobody to take care of the land and the animals. It makes it harder here in some ways.

This cycle also forces her to go abroad again, something many women expect their daughters will do when they become mothers themselves.[18] Moreover, in the early 2000s, it was easy and cheap to go back and forth between Moldova and Turkey, though, as the women pointed out, every year the fines for undocumented migration go up.

These women are growing increasingly weary of maneuvering in this visa regime and of living in fear of being solicited for bribes, deported, imprisoned, or abused by police or others. These mobile worker-mothers are frustrated by the cost of going abroad, by not having health care, by having to work illegally and pay fines for overstayed visas, and by the general insecurity of undocumented migrant work. In discussions with them, it became apparent that what some want most from their state now is not a job that pays and social services at home but freedom of movement, fewer fees for crossing borders, and legal work opportunities abroad, with recourse to legal sanctions if they are exploited.

Ironically, this solution would also help buttress neoliberal capitalism. Migrant women's labors abroad and what they want from the state work to excuse the Moldovan state from providing for their economic needs *within* Moldova. This outcome aligns with the dictates of structural adjustment policies requiring the state to withdraw from offering social services and job creation in Moldova. The women's transnational labors are changing perceptions of needs at home while upholding some more traditional ideas, but they are also creating new and increasing expectations and personal obligations that implicate the women more directly in global neoliberal processes. In

---

[18] Indeed, these women did not seem to think migrant work would change things for their children in the long run. They indicated that they did not see this as a temporary form of work for women in their communities, saying that when their daughters became mothers, they too would leave to work in Turkey. Whether this is a long-term and multigenerational strategy will be an interesting question to follow. However, at this point, there are no data on the next generation.

women's new visions of motherhood in Gagauz Yeri, we hear a new moral value placed on self-reliance as opposed to reliance on the state for individual, family, and community welfare. This is a new kind of worker-mother: a neoliberal one as well as a transnational one. Such arguments justify neoliberal rationales for state retrenchment that affect all global women. In this way, the migrant working women of Gagauz Yeri experience many of the same shortcomings of migrant domestic work found by global women elsewhere.

I am hopeful that the returns on migrant work are not all harmful, that there are some identifiable advantages to this work for women in Gagauz Yeri. Especially when we treat narratives of motherhood and desperation by women migrants as performances and see women themselves as agents, we can see how there may be slippages in gendered hegemonies that help women gain some freedoms. According to Parrenas, such narratives of a mother's martyrdom help children better adjust to their mothers' absence (2005). And in the host society, performances of desperation can help gain women sympathy on the job and off. Yet these are not just instrumental performances. In these narratives, migrant women are not simply hiding an underlying economic motive, nor are they only trying to relieve some psychological pain caused by their guilt over not being home with their children. Rather, they are sincerely jockeying for moral capital in their home communities. There are deep and complex reasonings for their actions: they are trying to live moral lives, and are finding new gendered ways to do so on shifting economic ground. In the context of Gagauz migrant domestics who work in Istanbul, women's narratives move through various frames of reference as women work out the changes they are undergoing and initiating (see Ries 2002). Individuals are flexible in their interpretations of their experiences, but this is not necessarily equivalent to a demonstration of a "false consciousness." In fact, it shows an openness of meaning, an attentiveness to contexts—a very human "flexibility" (Pesmen 2000). The narratives of martyrdom by mothers or of loss by children and communities in Gagauz Yeri are *both* demonstrations of real caring and desperation and, in particular contexts, performances of accommodation or resistance to gendered moral economies.

This chapter has explored the ways in which shifts in the global economy are understood, practiced, and constituted through changing notions of gendered responsibilities. What clearly emerges from the individual narratives is a sense that motherhood, whether as part of a past socialist vision or an emergent neoliberal one, is the key to social order. Commuting mothers are blamed for the loss of social order. Their responses also evoke this discourse, pushing the limits of local norms in Gagauz Yeri to position themselves as better worker-mothers than those who stay. In so doing, they assert new ideas of what makes a good worker-mother and a better socioeconomic order. At times, this logic of motherhood as the key to social order and the new identities and labor practices of commuters may work to contain and oppress women and align them insidiously with neoliberal rationales. However, at other times and places, their concept of desperate and sacrificial motherhood may work in their favor to defend their migratory and economic actions and to guide the way to a better transnational family life. It may provide the reasoning for them not only to contribute their share to the household budget but also to expand their imaginations, gaining them a kind of worldliness and allowing for new desires, and even helping them to construct new lifestyles and move up in the world.

As we have seen so far, some gendered moral economies are specific to the post-Soviet context. Yet these justifications are also refracted through women's personal experiences in terms of their urban or rural residence and lifestyle, education, work history, wealth, and as part of a Russophone and Russophile population in Moldova and Gagauz Yeri. Such particularities hold the key to a deeper understanding of how working abroad is an expression of women's desire to maintain or improve their status.

Chapter 2

Uplift in Gagauz Yeri

If it is difficult for women from Gagauz Yeri to legitimate their work abroad to their communities at home because they are mothers, then making matters worse is that they work in Turkey. Women in Gagauz Yeri conceive of their travels as journeys in the margins of Europe, from a fallen but nonetheless modern and civilized post-Soviet space to an uncivilized but nonetheless capitalist Turkey. For other migrant women on the move from the global east, south, and periphery, uplift and progress, both money and modernity, can legitimately be found in their destinations: the global west, north, and center. Mary Beth Mills (1999) and Aihwa Ong (1987) describe the lives of young, rural, uneducated, and single girls encouraged by their families to seek modernity in urban life. Denise Brennan examines the case of young, uneducated sex workers who seek a ticket to civilization—and out of the Dominican Republic—on the arm of a European husband (2004). For the educated Filipinas who work as migrant domestics, as Rachael Salazar Parrenas details, true uplift is legitimate only when they themselves return to their families and households. Yet Filipina migrants' destinations—Italy and the United States (Parrenas 2001, 2005) and Taiwan (Lan 2006a)—are deemed not only wealthy but also civilized places. This helps Filipinas legitimate their migrant work and absence from their homes. For migrants from Gagauz Yeri, however, Turkey is a place to gain money but not modernity. For them, Russia is still the ultimate locus of civilization. This is one of the peculiarities of the Gagauz women's migrations compared to those of other migrant domestics. It is also a peculiarity of the Gagauz post-Soviet experience as compared to other post-Soviet and postsocialist states. These sentiments harbored toward Russia and Turkey, explored in the first part of this chapter, also help determine the returns on migrant women's labors, or how women's work and wages are seen to improve—or corrupt—the status of their families and communities at home.

These gendered moral economies are also influenced by other overlapping subjugations and social locations in Gagauz Yeri. Close ethnographic attention to women's work backgrounds and subjective experiences reveals that even in a small place like Gagauz Yeri, being a good worker-mother and pursuing uplift can mean different things to different women. Such attentiveness to difference also brings to light a more general dynamic: how certain women seeking opportunity abroad are perceived as more worthy of upward mobility than others. In chapter 1, we saw that while both Tatya and Anna go abroad to work, Tatya insisted that communities were being helped by migrant work, whereas Anna saw the desertion and decline of Gagauz Yeri. The reason for the discrepancy in their views has to do with the differences between these women and their conceptions of upward mobility. As described in this chapter, legitimate uplift is constructed variously through ideas and experiences regarding language skills, civilization, and ethnicity in Moldova, but it is also understood through differences in and valuations of types of education and work experience, wealth, and rurality versus urbanity. All of these particularities complicate the gendered moral economies—the economic location of worker-mothers and ideas about their morality—at play in women's migrant labor. Simply adopting the category "postsocialist women" would erase much of the diversity of this place and these women.

Recognizing diversity in Gagauz Yeri requires us to conceive of the home of migrants and Moldova more broadly as already transnational, with migration simply adding a new dimension to this transnationalism. Diversity is commonly analyzed by scholars working in the host country of migrants. They recognize differences in race, gender, class, and ethnicity between different migrant populations in the destination country and between migrant domestics and their employers (Constable 1997a; Chin 1998; Lan 2006a). Less common are analyses of the diversity of the "home" itself (but see Gamburd 2000; Parrenas 2005; Oishi 2005). In this book, I highlight the diversity of both host and home.

Looking at these diversities and particularities ultimately helps us better understand the transformations in women's lives and the changing ideas about women in Gagauz Yeri and Moldova. Such a perspective more deeply reveals that women are not passive pawns of the global economy but active agents maneuvering for the maintenance of status or specific kinds of upward mobility in their communities. It is then possible to see how complex notions of identity intersect with ideas about gender to drive the transnational neoliberal economy.

It is not only such particularities that structure women's migration opportunities but also their relationships with their communities at home in Moldova and, to be taken up in later chapters, their relations with employers and their experiences working in Turkey. To illuminate first their identities back home in Moldova, this chapter delves into the history of Gagauz Yeri and Moldova, the relationships of the republic and the autonomous region with Russia and Turkey, and the diversity of women's lives in this small, fascinating place.

Turkish Blood, but Russian Souls

As discussed earlier, women in Gagauz Yeri who migrate to Russia for work are viewed in a more positive light than those who go to Turkey. In part, this difference in perception is related to the kind of work women typically do at each destination—construction work in Russia, domestic work in Turkey— but in larger part it has to do with the different valuations of Russia and Turkey. Whereas worldliness and upward mobility can be obtained legitimately through working in Russia, this is not true for working in Turkey, according to many in Gagauz Yeri. Such a marked difference in valuation and in the returns on labor can be better understood by examining the source of the high value placed on Russia and the Russian language in Gagauz Yeri, the debates over language in Moldova more broadly, and Russia's role in Gagauz independence.

Language serves to stratify Moldova, and, as a Russophone autonomous region, Gagauz holds a particular place in the hierarchy. Though the state has at times tried to present "Moldovan" as a citizenship identifier, the term still more or less refers to ethnic Romanian speakers of Romanian (about 65 percent of the population).[1] More than 35 percent of the state of Moldova's population are not Moldovan and speak primarily Russian. The relevant groups include Russians, Ukrainians, Bulgarians, and Gagauz, some of whom also speak their native languages. During Soviet times, university education and public life were predominantly conducted in Russian or Moldovan, and Russian was the language of power and privilege.

The resiliency of Russian in Moldova has posed considerable challenges to the Moldovan nation-state's attempts to institute a common Moldovan language for its population. This has caused great consternation among Moldovan nationalists, who point out that Soviet colonialism separated them from their Romanian roots.[2] The conflict between Russian speakers (and Russian influence) and Moldovans has violently split the country and informs everyday life in Moldova. Many in Gagauz Yeri cite virulent daily battles over Russian and Russian influence, from trying to negotiate bus rides when the driver insists that he does not understand Russian to conflicts over the history and languages their children learn at school.[3]

For people in Gagauz Yeri, speaking Russian is a mark of education, urbanity, age, politics, allegiance, identity, employment, and even station in life in Moldova. There are many reasons why Gagauz Yeri became and remains overwhelmingly Russophone in language and Russophile in orientation. This history, like any, is contested. In the nineteenth century, as the Balkans experienced nationalist movements against the Ottoman Empire and conflicts within various Orthodox Christian churches in Eastern Europe, the Gagauz migrated from Bulgaria (where they settled from central Asia and had adopted Orthodox Christianity) through Romanian territories to Bessarabia, now part of present-day Moldova, where Russia offered them land privileges. Although they retained their Gagauz language, they adopted the Russian language as well, and joined the Russian Orthodox patriarchate (as opposed to the Bulgarian or Romanian Orthodox churches). It was at least from this period that the Gagauz allied themselves with Russians

---

[1] Moldovan is considered a dialect of Romanian. In this book, this language and the people who speak it in Moldova are referred to as Moldovan.
[2] One drama in this debate is Romania's entry into the European Union (EU) in 2007 and its consequent offering of Romanian citizenship to ethnic Romanians in Moldova. This has caused great concern both in the Moldovan government over the loss of its population and in the EU over the flux of new immigrants.
[3] See Elizabeth Anderson's (2005) work on history texts in Moldova for more. For more on nationalism, see Hulya Demirdirek (2001).

against Romanians in the region. In the late nineteenth and early twentieth centuries, Russians and Romanians fought over Bessarabia, including the region in which the Gagauz resided. Many elderly Gagauz recall the harsh conditions under which their communities labored during the interwar period of Romanian rule. From the Gagauz perspective (as opposed to the Moldovan one), it was a relief when the Soviets prevailed in the region after World War II and created the Moldovan Soviet Socialist Republic (Moldovan SSR), whose borders now constitute the current borders of an independent Moldova. As a border republic of the Soviet Union, the Soviets upheld the Moldovan SSR as distinct from Romania, even though much of its population was ethnically Romanian. The Soviets instituted the Cyrillic alphabet and relocated Russian-speaking populations from other parts of the Soviet Union to the Moldovan SSR. The Gagauz region in the south and the mostly Russian-speaking Transniestria in the east were key to the new "multiethnic" (yet Russian-dominant) Soviet socialist republic. In Gagauz Yeri and Transniestria, individuals were educated in Russian and taught to see Moscow as the economic and cultural center. With the fall of socialism and Soviet control in Moldova, and as Moldovans ruminated over reuniting with Romania, Gagauz activists asserted their desire for autonomy and gained Gagauz language rights and status as an autonomous region in 1995.[4] They were supported by both Russia and Turkey in this effort.

Gagauz Yeri is especially Russophile and thus offers a particular post-Soviet and postsocialist experience. In this, it is similar to parts of Ukraine and Belarus, as opposed to other formerly socialist states. Ties to the Soviet communist past and to Moscow have not been severed entirely in Gagauz Yeri.[5] Statues of Lenin are still prominent, and signs and television programs are mostly in Russian (figures 2.1 and 2.2). People in Gagauz Yeri generally still see politics in Moscow, more than in Chișinău, as determining their fate. For instance, on my first visit to Gagauz Yeri in 2002, I sat with Lidya's uncle, aunt, and cousin, watching Russian television. Every time Russian president Vladimir Putin appeared on the screen, Lidya's uncle would shout to me in Gagauz: "Putin—our president!" Links and identification with Russia and the Soviet Union and even communism remain strong in Gagauz Yeri both politically and culturally. Many people in Gagauz Yeri

---

[4] For more on this history, see Atilla Erden, Melvut Ozhan, Piri Er, and Doganay Cevik (1999), Charles King (2000), Harun Güngör and Mustafa Argunsah (2002), and O. K. Karanastas-Radova (2004).

[5] The use of symbols of the communist era were outlawed in Moldova in 2012, but it is unclear whether such laws have been imposed on Gagauz Yeri.

Figure 2.1.   Statue of Lenin in Comrat, capital of Gagauz Yeri, Moldova, 2004. Photograph by the author.

identify themselves quite simply as Russian. Even Diana, an ethnographer of Gagauz cuisine who introduced me to her family in the region, does not speak Gagauz; her ethnographic research was conducted in Russian and her book on Gagauz cuisine was published only in Russian.[6] The Gagauz

---

[6] During a formal event to celebrate the book's publication, it was telling that while all of Diana's colleagues at the Academy of Sciences of Moldova praised her in Russian, the Gagauz words of support offered by a representative from one Gagauz Television station, Yeni Ay, were lost on her (though I suspect that later someone privately translated them to her).

Figure 2.2. Gagauz- and Russian-language signs for Museum of History and Society in Comrat, 2004. Photograph by the author.

autonomy movement saw the development of Gagauz Television, a venue for the establishment of formal Gagauz. However, when I sat down to watch one of the Gagauz stations (Gagauz Radio and Television) one evening with a young Gagauz woman in her early twenties (who otherwise would have been watching Russian-language television, but was humoring me), I was surprised to find that though the show began with "Gagauz Televiziyon!" in Gagauz, the rest of the broadcast was in Russian. There is now a Gagauz-language newspaper, *Ana Sozu* (Mother Tongue), but it is not widely read, and it carries a Gagauz-Russian lexicon in the back of every issue, presumably because otherwise readers would not understand the words.

This situation may change, as Gagauz is now being taught in the public school system and the younger generation can read, write, and speak it somewhat (schoolchildren are also required to take Moldovan, Russian, and English or German, but are taught in Russian). The formal Gagauz they learn is different from the demotic Gagauz their parents or grandparents speak, which mixes more freely with Russian (or, in the case of the interwar generation, even Romanian).[7] Sitting around the dinner table with Tatya and Victor and their daughters, Victor and I tried to converse in Gagauz, which in its formal form is the Turkic language most similar to the Turkish spoken in Turkey (Azeri is a close second). At times, whole sentences of Victor's were lost to me. Sensing my confusion, his second daughter objected in giggles: "Dad! Speak Gagauz! Not Russian!" Perhaps the distinction between Gagauz and Russian is being newly defined for this new generation.

To not speak Gagauz is not unusual for the literate of Gagauz Yeri aged thirty or over, especially for those urbanites educated through the university, where Russian or Moldovan predominates. As for people of a younger generation with whom I spoke in Gagauz Yeri, most know some Gagauz from their parents, particularly if their parents are not formally educated and especially if they were villagers, yet they do not speak it regularly. With new Gagauz language rights, it is hoped that the youngest generation, now in elementary school, will revive the language, yet it has not really taken off. I want to be careful not to undermine the significance of Gagauz language and identity revitalization to certain individuals here, but I think it is fair to say that one of the effects of Gagauz autonomy in this context has been a continued space for the Russian language and Russian political influence in Moldova. Gagauz autonomy and new migrations to Turkey created some space for identification with Turkey, but it is Russia—and the common historical, linguistic, religious, and cultural heritage between it and Gagauz Yeri—that remains most relevant and valued by Gagauz individuals.

Many in Gagauz Yeri still cling to the beliefs and ideals of the Soviet era, but several developments mark Gagauz Yeri's difference from this time, including a new religiosity, new connections to the outside world through online technologies and travel, newly renovated homes built with wages from abroad, and a new transnational exchange between Turkey and Gagauz Yeri. This transnationalism includes a Turkish presence in Gagauz Yeri as much as a Gagauz presence in Turkey. Turkish business, state, and educational institutions now punctuate the landscape of Gagauz Yeri alongside new Gagauz institutions. In the streets of the regional capital of Comrat, one hears mostly Russian, some Gagauz, and sometimes Turkish. Turkish businessmen stroll by watching young women walk around. Women wear urban fashions—in the early 2000s, this involved spiked heels and tight clothes

---

[7] In Gagauz Yeri, spoken Gagauz also varies a great deal depending on location. In the southern town of Vulcănești, for instance, the spoken language is said to sound more like the Turkish spoken in Turkey.

with more zippers and buckles than seemed possible—just as in Chişinău, and some smiled and flirted with the men. In cafes, I overheard discussions about getting female companions to accompany Turkish businessmen to dinner. These kinds of relations were commonly talked about and disapproved of in Gagauz Yeri. Turkish businessmen, representative here of the dark side of the shift to global capitalism, were seen to be "ruining girls" in Gagauz Yeri, as in Moldova in general. As a result of these views, any connection with Turkey, even through wages gained in migrant domestic work, was greeted with a great deal of ambivalence.

Statistics on migration do not take into account stratifications according to language, but language skills in Russian or Gagauz and ideas about Turkey as opposed to Russia do affect migration in various ways. Most migration from Moldova is to Russia. Romania is a close second, Italy is third, and Turkey is fourth (IOM 2004; Lücke, Mahmoud, and Pinger 2007). Individuals' choice of routes is determined and legitimated not only by the need for a job but also by the languages they speak—Gagauz, Russian, or Romanian—and by their notions of connection. Whether one is a Russian or Gagauz speaker or, alternatively, a Moldovan speaker makes all the difference. Moldovans tend to travel to Romania and Italy, as the Moldovan language is a dialect of Romanian and a Romance language that is closely related to Italian (Onica 2008). For individuals in Gagauz Yeri, among other Russian speakers in Moldova, especially men, travel to Russia for construction work was predominant. This preference was facilitated by the fact that, until recently, visas were not required for travel to Russia. Although some women also go to Russia for this kind of labor, many new opportunities in Turkey have opened up for women in particular. This is a general trend, and certainly some Moldovans also seek jobs in Russia and Turkey. Because of the broader influence of the Russian language in Moldova, many ethnic Moldovans also are familiar with it. Moreover, construction work or work painting houses, for instance, requires little language competency. Further, until recently the borders to Russia were still open to Moldovans. Because of the ease of the border crossing, many Moldovans also found work in Russia.

Gender plays a significant role in decisions about where to migrate for work because of the type of work available at the different destinations. Most men who migrate go to Russia or Ukraine or other Commonwealth of Independent States countries to work in construction (where language matters less), whereas most Moldovan women working abroad are in Italy and Gagauz women are in Turkey—in both places to work as domestics (in these jobs, language matters more). Some women do join their husbands to work in Moscow and some men go to Italy, but in general few men go to Turkey because there are fewer jobs there for them.[8]

In Gagauz Yeri, while everyone said that the reason for going abroad was because they were desperate mothers—the gendered moral economies described in chapter 1—other moral reasoning also came into play in both the motivation for women's migrant labor to Russia or to Turkey and in understanding the value of the returns on these migrations. Travel to work in Turkey was conceptualized as a pragmatic step to obtain cash for household support, whereas travel to Russia was broadly understood as going to a valued motherland. Most women I came to know were grateful for the employment they had found in Turkey, yet they saw their connection to Turkey and the Turkic world as an ancient blood relation that was not relevant to their current identity as Russian and Orthodox or even, to some extent, as Gagauz. When asked why they traveled to Turkey for work, many cited their language connection, and gave the analogy of Moldovans' relationship to Italy: "We go to Turkey, just as Moldovans go to Italy."[9] Their migration opportunities are shaped in part by their Turkic language, but this is certainly not a return to an honored motherland for an ethnic diaspora. As one migrant, Stesha, put it:

> Okay, I'm a Turk. It is in my blood. . . . I feel close [because of it]. [But] Gagauz are different [from Turks] . . . [and] because we grew up in the old Russian Soviet [times], we think of ourselves as Russian. We say "we are Russian."

---

[8] Local male informal labor is widely available in Turkey, whereas migrant females are in high demand as live-in domestics. Chapter 3 covers the demand for the latter in more detail.

[9] When I brought up the question of why Gagauz go to Turkey, the common response (right after talking about money for their families) was: "For the Gagauz [women], Turkey is like Italy for the Moldovans. We go there because the language is similar." At least since the nationalist era in Romania in the late 1800s, which marked the end of Ottoman rule there, Moldova, like Romania, has taken care to mark its historical difference from other Slavic peoples of the region. Moldovans present themselves as tied to peoples who speak Romance languages as opposed to Slavic ones. The Romanians are unique as the only Orthodox Christian population who speak a Romance language instead of a Slavic one. Moldovans in Moldova see themselves as part of a group of "Latins," but certainly not as Italians. This kind of connection is posited as similar in the Gagauz-Turkey case and is seen as a reason to commute to Turkey, but not because it is modern. Yet Italy, being Western and Christian as well as capitalist, holds a higher value than Turkey. Cristina Onica argues that Moldovans who go to Italy also are accused of being bad mothers by their communities at home (2008), yet it would be interesting to know whether they hold a stronger legitimation than their counterparts from Gagauz Yeri in Turkey.

Many also took pains to point out the difference between Gagauz and Turkish languages, and the importance of seeing Gagauz Yeri as separate from Turkey. Another migrant worker I spoke with argued that "we may have Turkish blood, but we have Russian souls." This reference to soul highlights the difference between Turks as Muslims versus Gagauz as Orthodox Christians. Indeed, like most other Moldovans I encountered, the individuals whom I got to know in Gagauz Yeri were strongly prejudiced against Muslims. Yet this concept of a Russian soul connotes something beyond a mere religious affiliation. It is something more about culturedness, but also about culture as a civilizational idea.[10] Because of the Soviet legacy, the relationship between language skills and identity in this social field is a complex one that is not always related to ethnicity. Taking a cue from Peggy Levitt and Nina Glick-Schiller, who distinguish between "ways of being" and "ways of belonging" in transnational fields (2004), we find that even while individuals' ways of being have inserted Gagauz women into a field between Gagauz Yeri and Turkey, this does not determine their ways of belonging, which in this case remain firmly embedded in their identities as Russian speakers and Orthodox Christians.

Many migrant domestics from Gagauz Yeri saw Turkey as a step toward some type of low-level worldliness. As one twenty-three-year-old Russian-speaking, university-educated Gagauz woman put it, "I want to see the world, and I guess Turkey is an okay place to start." Some denied Turkey even this small worldliness. As Anna responded when I asked what else besides remittances she may have brought back from Turkey: "We have culture; we go there for the money!" Travel to Russia, by contrast, *was* conceptualized in diasporic terms, as a return to a homeland lost with the dissolution of the Soviet empire. In the context of Moldova, Russia, for these individuals from Gagauz Yeri, might be considered in the same light that Moldovans consider Romania: a closer, relevant center of modern history, religion, civilization, and identification, and a place of linguistic and cultural identification. Most people I interacted with in Gagauz Yeri identified as Russian. A few, such as the ethnographer Diana, said that they were Gagauz before they were Russian. But even she then later admitted that she had a "double consciousness," an acknowledgment that she identifies as both Russian and Gagauz equally. Most associate Gagauz identity with rurality, working on the land, and hard physical labor. Gagauz rurality is idealized

---

[10] See also Dale Pesmen (2000) on the Russian soul.

as traditional, but it is also seen as somewhat backward from the perspective of Gagauz urbanity.

Gagauz positionality demonstrates the transgression of identity boundaries in Moldova: being Turkic speaking, Russian speaking, and pro-Soviet and pro-Russia in Moldova positions the Gagauz as some sort of potential fifth column. Their traveling to Turkey to work as domestics adds new dimensions to the crossing of these boundaries in terms of geography and politics, the type of labor they conduct, and how they use their earnings. Identity boundaries within Gagauz Yeri between women, constructed by differences in their locations as urban or rural, their professions and work experience, education, and wealth, also come into play and overlap with these ideas about Christians (Romanian Orthodox; Russian Orthodox) and Muslims; the Turkish, Russian, Moldovan, and Romanian languages; and Russians, Turks, and Gagauz in various ways. In conveying the women's narratives in the next section, I pay particular attention to these identifications and the material culture of their households, because such details vividly reveal the families' current socioeconomic status in Gagauz Yeri and because the women themselves often use the money they earn to renovate their houses.

Diversity in Gagauz Yeri

Though all the women in Gagauz Yeri with whom I spoke identified with Russia over Turkey, there were several points of difference in their identities that determined their capacity to gain status in their communities through their work abroad. This observation demonstrates how diverse postsocialist women and local ideas about uplift can be. The diversities—or particularities, as I refer to them here—in Gagauz Yeri can be seen in the experiences of three different migrant women and their families. Two are rural, one is urban; two were educated through university, the third through technical school. Their wealth, work experience, and status both under socialism and after socialism varied, even though their sense of belonging and relatedness to Soviet Russia is similar.

What becomes clear in these narratives is that women express that they go abroad to work in order to provide a better future for their children, but doing so means different things to different people—according to their ideas about civilization and to their particular subjectivities in Gagauz Yeri. Thus, they seek out work in Turkey not only to meet general basic needs but because of specific ideas about how to maintain or advance their family's lot. Having to pay for an operation for a family member is one critical reason for working abroad, but women also enter migrant work to buy a violin or afford a university education for a child, to pay for satellite cable, or to throw an elaborate wedding. Though all the women I met had adequate resources to go abroad, some were better off than others and were going abroad to maintain their status, whereas others went abroad to improve it. Whether or not women and families were perceived to be better off as a result of their migrations had everything to do with these preexisting positionalities.

These women's experiences clearly reveal that women's choices to migrate for work are driven morally as well as economically. These kinds of drivers are manifested in women's choices of the kind of migrant work they engage in—construction work in Russia or work in the tourist trade or as a domestic in Turkey—and in what they do with their earnings. Their choices and reasons are based on their moral obligations as worker-mothers, but also on their particular status in terms of rurality or urbanity, past work experiences, education, language, and ideas about civilization. To illustrate this, I return to my time in Gagauz Yeri in 2004 and describe my experiences with three families, beginning with the rural lives of Tatya in Congaz and Anna in Tomay and moving on to discuss the urban lives of Stesha and her family in Comrat.

Rural Lives: Tatya and Anna

After our chat at the café, described in the introduction to this book, Tatya and I walked through the village of Congaz and behind Lenin Avenue some twenty minutes to her house. Other than Lenin Avenue, most roads in Gagauz Yeri are dirt or, on that rainy day, mud. Carefully making her way across a few specks of solid ground, Tatya pointed out that every other house was under construction. Many residents were rebuilding their homes with new or better materials or decorating them in more elaborate ways. The sense was of uncertain transience and constant mobility. Buildings, like the people who inhabit them, move: they are in the process of coming down or going up. If I were seeing them only at this moment in time, instead of over the course of three months, it would be difficult if not impossible to tell the difference between collapse and construction.

On entering Tatya's rural courtyard, she showed off her animals—pigs, geese, and rabbits. Their cow had recently died from disease, yet that they had once had one spoke of their relative wealth in the village. We took off our shoes and put on slippers before entering through the main entrance of the house. Tatya paused to proudly, if shyly, show me how the entrance had been newly decorated. It had wallpaper, a carpet on the floor, and a full wardrobe with mirror. She led me through her daughters' rooms, which she had also recently refurbished: new rugs hung on freshly painted white walls, as is the Moldovan style. Tatya pointed out that one room and the hallway had straight walls and so could be wallpapered. Villagers build these homes themselves, and a straight wall, I discovered, was difficult to achieve without novel building materials; straight walls are highly valued for both the inside and outside of houses. As was typical, the main level of the house had several rooms for stocking wine and pickled vegetables. The living room/main bedroom, where Tatya and her husband, Victor, slept, had a television. A Christian icon hung in a corner of each of the two bedrooms.

The kitchen was closed off to the hallway by a door, and before opening it Tatya apologized: "We haven't got around to [redoing] the kitchen yet." The room was a kitchen in process. There was a new refrigerator (not turned on) and a counter and sink (which someday they hope will have running water). From there we put on outdoor shoes to step down into another workspace. This space was not fully outdoors, as it had a roof, four walls, and a door to the garden in back, but it was sufficiently outdoors (one did not wear slippers, and the work done in this space usually required frequent trips outdoors), so I will call it the outdoor kitchen. This space held a washing machine (not connected to a water supply), a gas stove, and a peat-burning oven. The latter, main oven was fed with peat from the outside of the house and tiled on the inside of the house. Their middle daughter had just baked a full week's worth of bread that day, and the place smelled delicious. Attached to the outdoor kitchen was an indoor bathroom with a bathtub. This bathroom was also expectant; there was no running water. It was decorated, as I found is typical of migrant households in Moldova, with foreign products. The shampoo, conditioner, face wash, body lotions, and shaving materials were all from Turkey and were laid out on display.[11] Tatya explained that they bathed on Saturdays, as it takes all day to heat sufficient water.

The outdoor kitchen led to the backyard, where the family's vineyards were located. Tatya and Victor also grow potatoes, watermelons, beets, tomatoes, cucumbers, and cabbage for their own consumption. A well of water stood by the kitchen door in the yard. Laundry was hung out to dry.

---

[11] Daphne Berdahl (1999) also notes how women in formerly socialist eastern Germany used items from the West for display.

Further off, a narrow plank over mud led to an outhouse. Some people have water piped into their houses in Gagauz Yeri (particularly in Comrat and the cities), but most do not. As for heat, the main oven also served to heat the outdoor kitchen somewhat. Similar but smaller stoves (also tiled on the inside of the house and fed with peat from the outside) heated other rooms. This year, however, Tatya's family was anxious to try out the new gas heating, for which Tatya had gone to Turkey to acquire funds to purchase. The Soviets are acclaimed in Gagauz for taking care of village needs, and Tatya and Victor did have electricity. Unlike houses in the cities, however, they had no running water or gas heat connected to their homes. (Even in the city, hot water was irregularly available, and heat only during certain months.)

Tatya and Victor have lived in this house since they were married, adding on to it where and when needed. Tatya had completed her education through tenth grade and then worked selling wares at a Chişinău outdoor market for a local Congaz merchant. She lived in Chişinău then and reminisces about it fondly, "At that time, there was employment. It was very nice. . . . I would get my salary. What I wore was free. Where I slept was free." When she married Victor (also from Congaz), she moved back to her home village and they set up their own household. "Ever since," she sighed, "it has been hard work." She and her husband have three girls. When I was there, the eldest was attending university in Chişinău, which was paid for by Tatya's work abroad. Their middle daughter was about to finish high school, and there were worries about how to pay for her university education. After their first two girls were born, Tatya and Victor had decided to have a third child, hoping for a boy, who would help out with the household by bringing in a bride,[12] but instead they had a lovely and loved third girl, Iulia, age eleven and attending seventh grade at Congaz Elementary School.

Marrying in their early twenties and having three to four children by thirty was typical among the women I met in Congaz and other villages. Meeting the household and family needs—mostly the needs of their children, nieces, and nephews—is the reason most women give for their annual commutes to Turkey, while their husbands sometimes go for one to two months at a time to Moscow. This is true for Tatya and Victor, who try to alternate their stays abroad so that one parent is at home to care for the children. Over dinner that evening, I asked when they—husband and wife—got to see each other. Victor replied, "We miss each other," and they both smiled at each other, suggesting that this absence had indeed made their hearts grow fonder and

---

[12] Among the Gagauz, this is a common expectation for the youngest son.

that perhaps this distance was not entirely detrimental to their marriage. During the socialist period in Moldova, men in Gagauz Yeri frequently went to Moscow to work in construction and in refurbishing and painting the interiors of houses, and, like Victor, they continued to do so now. Occasionally, women accompanied them. This work is shorter term, but it pays close to what one would get in Turkey. Russian employers give the couple a place to stay and the evenings to themselves. So, in this instance, transnational migration worked quite well, even if the family was divided for a portion of the year. Tatya's family, among the lower- or lower-middle-status villagers, worked abroad to improve their children's educational opportunities and better their households.

In another village, Tomay, about one hour from Congaz, Anna and her eldest daughter Angela shared a single job in Istanbul as domestics, alternating times away from the family, between 2000 and 2003. Angela has two children and works the night shift as an emergency medical technician for the Tomay hospital. Anna is university educated, staunchly communist, and from a relatively wealthy family. Her home has a fully functioning indoor kitchen, with running water and gas heat—the kind of kitchen Tatya aspires to build with the earnings from her trips abroad. Anna works as a librarian for what she calls the "anticultural center" because of the way the town cultural center is falling apart. Her husband holds degrees in animal husbandry and biology; he teaches biology in the high school during the school year and herds sheep in the summer. Anna's middle daughter, Inna, went to Turkey for a university education (an option some have also turned to for educating their children) and married a Turkish man. They now live in the United States. Whereas Tatya had worked as a salesperson for a Congaz merchant without remarking on it, Anna made a point to tell me that nobody in her family, however desperate, had turned to trade, and related this fact directly to her communist upbringing.

Anna's household holds more resources than Tatya's. They have a satellite dish, a car, a phone, a working indoor kitchen, and a computer with Internet access. It was to maintain their status and keep this more modern household running, as well as to provide for her youngest daughter at home and the two grandchildren also living with them, that Anna went abroad to work.

Even between these two village women, Tatya and Anna, there existed a stark difference not only in resources, education, and work background but also in how they related to Soviet ideals that discouraged "working in trade." Because she was in a higher socioeconomic stratum, Anna could live up to such ideals. Although both women sought uplift, that concept meant different things to each migrant working woman. Their differences also underscore the problem with generalizing a "postsocialist woman."

It is not only how much wealth a family has but specifically how a family *gains* wealth—through trade or other work—in these communities that determines status in Gagauz Yeri. In terms of wealth differentials, though small differences among people seem to be generally tolerated and supported, a person who gains a great deal of wealth and is ostentatious is regarded with great suspicion. If people are equally poor, poverty is perceived as bearable, but rising above the crowd tends to promote jealousy. Jealousy is seen as a motivating factor for gossip, and in such small communities gossip can serve as a form of social control.[13] According to Nancy Ries (2002), people who are doing well financially in post-Soviet Russia are considered "smart," meaning "active, energetic, ambitious," as well as "shrewd, always on the lookout for opportunities to make money or gain power; and especially in the current context, it seems to mean negotiating the margins of danger and taking risks, but only those for which you have adequate 'cover'" (300). Ries also explains how trade in the Russian context is seen as immoral speculation. People who make money through trade are suspect, and honest, hardworking people are perceived as getting the short end of the stick. If a family should gain wealth through what is perceived as hard labor, however, its social (and geographic) mobility is deemed legitimate.[14]

In this particularly rural but not necessarily socialist sense, hard work (usually the connotation is physical, often agricultural, labor) is much admired among the individuals in Gagauz Yeri I came to know, and serves as a source of dignity. Trade is thus not only "profiteering"—making money off other people—but it is "easy" money, not requiring physical labor. These moral judgments are transferred over to migrant work as well. Construction work in Moscow thus is more legitimate than trade. As for migrant domestic work, its place is ambivalent. It is not as bad as speculation, but it is perceived as easy (not physically demanding) work. Also, to work as servants for bourgeois families is seen as especially degrading for former socialists, raised to believe in social equality. Yet women cleanse this labor and the wealth gained from it through discourses about the duties and sacrifices of worker-mothers trying to improve their children's lot. Some villagers,

---

[13] For further discussion of the dynamics of inequality in the Russian case, see Pesmen (2000), Ries (2002), and Humphrey (2002). For other formerly socialist countries, see Patico (2005) and Wanner (2005).
[14] This greater understanding of legitimacy with regard to social mobility resonated in insightful comments in helpful personal conversations and email exchanges with scholar Hulya Demirdirek.

such as both Tatya and Anna, have gone to Turkey to work as domestics because they felt obligated to do so as worker-mothers. Nevertheless, their cases suggest the diversity of women villagers from Gagauz Yeri who go to Turkey, the differences in their perception of needs, and differences in what they regard as legitimate means to fulfill them. These amount to differences in their articulation and practices of a gendered moral economy. What is clear throughout these discursive practices is that these women's migrant labors are about particular forms of uplift. The fall of the Soviet Union and the opening of borders created new opportunities for families and individuals to fulfill desires for upward mobility. Looking ethnographically at the differences among women and families in these villages (and a few cities) helps illuminate how women operationalize power and agency in seizing these opportunities and deriving gains from them.

Urban Lives: Stesha and Her Family

Women from urban areas of Gagauz Yeri, such as Comrat, also go to Turkey for work. Whereas villagers seemed to labor primarily as domestics in the 2000s, several urbanites I met had initially gone to Turkey in the 1990s as tourist-traders or to work in sales, and only later had returned to work as domestics.[15] In Comrat, Diana led me to her Aunt Rosa's house. It was this family, in both Comrat and Istanbul, with whom I stayed most often and got to know best during my research. On my next trip to Gagauz Yeri and on every one after that, I stayed with Rosa's sister, Katya. I used this household as a base for trips to the surrounding Gagauz villages. Rosa and Katya had both been to Turkey to work as domestics, following Rosa's daughter, Stesha.

Rosa's household is in a dual apartment complex of about ten two- to three-bedroom apartments two blocks up from Lenin Avenue and the center of Comrat. Katya lives in the apartment complex next door but uses it only to sleep; she eats, bathes, and spends her entire day at Rosa's. As a result, she neither heats her own place (except at night, when she would call for me and say, "Okay, let's go back to the refrigerator") nor pays for water. Rosa and Katya are two of six siblings, three sisters and three brothers.

Rosa had worked at a pharmacy for many years until she contracted breast cancer in the late 1990s and needed treatment, which, in the absence of state health care, had become very expensive. At the time, her daughter

---

[15] Tourist-traders are not exclusive to urbanites, but urbanites may have been the first group to engage in tourist-trading.

Stesha was completing work on her bachelor's degree at Comrat University and teaching English to elementary schoolchildren. I spoke with Stesha in her home in Istanbul, where she lives with her Turkish husband, a textile merchant with whom she now works.

Stesha: I was getting $15 to $20.

Leyla: A month?

Stesha: Yes. And we'd have to wait three to four months for that salary. At that time, they were not giving it to anyone.

Leyla: Is that right?

Stesha: Teachers, doctors, would wait a long time for their salaries. Me? I was always taking out loans. You take out a loan. You get your salary. You have to wait three or four months, but you receive [only] one month's pay. At that point, you've acquired so much debt [that] you get your salary and you give it away.

Leyla: You give it right away to pay your debt.

Stesha: And immediately you take out more loans. It's like that. It was very hard. And because of that, of course, after I came here [to Istanbul], $100 was like honey to me.

When she left Comrat, Stesha had been married for one year to a local man and had a baby girl, Ljuda. It was not a happy marriage, and she and her husband separated. To help pay for her mother's chemotherapy, Stesha had left Ljuda in the care of her mother and aunt and sought opportunities abroad.

Stesha: I went first on August 17, 1998. Exactly one year before the earthquake [in Turkey].... I had a friend here. She had come one year before and persuaded me to come. Back then, business was good.... I got a job as a salesperson.

Leyla: You worked in a store. Because you knew Russian?

Stesha: Yes, because I knew Russian. My friend was working in a different place than me. In 1995, Turkey's [economic] condition was good. In 1998, by the time I came, business was already beginning to decline. It was hard to find a job. And I wanted good money. For instance, they were offering $60 a week. I got a job for $100 a week. I found a good job.

Among Stesha's urban, university-educated set in Gagauz Yeri, many had already been to Turkey to work as salespeople in the mid-1990s. At that time, tourist-traders—*chelnoki* in Russian—doing *alis-veris* ("trade" or "buying" in Turkish) participated in what came to be known as *bavul ticareti* ("suitcase trade" in Turkish, described in more detail in chapter 3). As Yulian Konstantinov (1996) wrote regarding Bulgarian tourist-traders, typically during this time a government-approved bus full of traders, mostly women, would be rounded up and conveyed to Istanbul for a week or so, during which time they "touristed" shopping malls set up for their benefit near the neighborhood of Laleli in Istanbul (see also Yükseker 2000, 2004). Russian-speaking women, who were perceived to be talented at sales to such groups, were in high demand in Laleli then.[16] Alongside this suitcase trade in Laleli and elsewhere in Turkey was the prevalence of work as an entertainer or sex worker, the source of the infamous image of the "natasha."

Stesha went to Turkey at the tail end of the booming nineties trade. That she was willing to work in sales distinguishes her from others in Gagauz Yeri, like Anna, who see such trade as sullying. From Stesha's perspective as an urban, well-educated woman willing to participate in business, and one from a generation younger than Anna, working in Turkey as a salesperson for tourists—which used her language skills (Russian and English) and business savvy—seemed appropriate and formed a sort of worldliness marked by the opening of the states of the former Soviet Union. Still other women sought out educational and cultural exchanges and opportunities in Turkey. However, going to Moscow to work in construction was not an attractive option to Stesha, no matter how much she and her family needed the money; for her, such work was too menial. For Anna and her husband, though, and for Tatya, there was less shame in working in construction in Moscow or doing domestic work in Turkey than in engaging in any type of business trade anywhere.

When the tourist trade declined in the late 1990s, Moldovan women like Stesha, in their thirties or older, who were married with children, began to seek out work as domestics and caretakers; Stesha, her mother, and her aunt all followed suit. Katya's friend Victoria, with whom I spoke in the city of Comrat, had gone in the mid- to late 1990s to work in sales and to trade, bringing back goods to sell in local Comrat markets. Then, in 1999, as she

---

[16] Although both academics and laypeople generally regard domestic work, petty trading and sales, and prostitution as separate labors, many women participated in a little of everything, or switched jobs according to opportunities (see Uygun 2004).

put it, "we started working for the families." Rosa had gone for about eight months in 1999, and Katya before her, but only for about a month. Katya had not liked Turkey, and decided instead to follow a friend to the United States, where she found employment for close to two years. She had recently returned from working as a domestic for a wealthy Russian-speaking family from formerly Soviet Azerbaijan who worked and lived outside Washington, D.C. She was the only person I met in Moldova who had been to the United States; few even make it to Western Europe. Stesha's family members were not proud of the domestic work they felt they had to do, but, like Tatya and Anna, they justified it as relatively easy work for good pay, and worth doing for the sake of bettering their children's lives. With their earnings from abroad, Katya and Stesha supported the household of Rosa, her mother (the elderly babushka of the household), and Stesha's daughter, Ljuda. Katya also helped her own daughter and her daughter's family, who live in Tiraspol, the capital of the unrecognized, Russian-dominated breakaway Transniestrian Republic, which used to be part of the Moldovan SSR.

Both Rosa's and Katya's homes would look familiar to anyone who has been inside an urban home in Moldova. These households held some similarities with village homes such as Anna's, but they also held key differences from other homes in Gagauz Yeri I had visited. I immediately noticed one major difference in urban homes: Rosa and Katya had shelves filled with books, and newspapers strewn across the floor. The television was set to a world news program, and commentaries abounded. Katya is an avid crossword puzzler, which, she explained, was a good way to exercise the brain. As we sat one night covered in the brown-and-white blankets I saw so often at the outdoor markets, peeling apples and watching television, she explained to me, partly in English, partly in Russian, and partly using sign language, that she would wake up in the middle of the night with the answer to a clue. It was hard to find her without a puzzle close at hand.

Rosa's and Katya's walls were straight, and wallpapered, but the women gave them little thought; the walls had been built not by them but by the state. There was carpeting on the floors, and the kitchen and bathroom had piped water, which even ran hot at certain times of the day in the winter. Katya had a dining room. Framed pictures hung on the walls. They had gas heat with radiators, even if it was turned off at times. Also, Russian was spoken here more than Gagauz. In fact, Katya did not speak much Gagauz, and my interactions with her were translated through Stesha's daughter and through Rosa, who spoke Gagauz and Turkish. They were able to do so because both had spent a good deal of time in Turkey; the young girl was also taking Gagauz and Turkish classes in school.

Speaking Russian is an indicator in Gagauz Yeri of higher education; it is considered the language of civilization, progress, and urbanity. In this family's imagination, as I learned from spending time with them, villagers outside Comrat were a bastion of authentic Gagauz life, especially as manifested by the home-grown vegetables and fruit, their work in the fields, their cooking with peat-burning ovens, and their Gagauz language skills. Stesha's family was unaware of recent changes in the villages—the gas stoves, piped-in heat, and new educational opportunities—or that many villagers do not speak Gagauz. Like the ethnographers of Gagauz Yeri with whom I had spoken, they too identify "the Gagauz" as above all a rural people tied to the land. Villagers and urbanites can have different levels of education and work experience, resources, and migration opportunities. At the same time, urbanites tend to stereotype rural life and to not acknowledge rural transformations. As the foremost Gagauz poet and ethnologist Luba Chimpoesh put it to me, despite their traveling abroad, "you have to remember, the Gagauz will always be villagers." Interestingly, this rural versus urban distinction was also reflected in the perspective that the urbanites were more "Russian." As Stesha said, "I am Russian because I speak Russian and went to Russian schools. I knew little Gagauz. In the cities, we did not speak Gagauz."

Despite urban dwellers' claims of difference, in Gagauz Yeri, ideas about Russian both as a language and as a civilization associated with modernity and progress were common to both urbanites and villagers, and exceedingly important to migrant women. They also held sway in their decisions to go to Turkey or to Russia, and the perception of whether or not they were better off as a result. These notions overlap with subjectivities regarding wealth, work, and education, and intersect with notions of gender, to create the gendered moral economies in this case of migrant domestics.

Conclusion

Until relatively recently, social stratification in Gagauz Yeri was relatively stable. There were educated professionals (doctors, teachers, engineers), and then there were workers on the *kolkhozi*, or collective farms. Women's and men's roles, while pliable in practice, were socially well defined. Urban and rural differences were more obvious as well. The collapse of the Soviet Union and the neoliberal institution of structural adjustment policies that have reduced the government's role in social welfare have transformed many of these traditional distinctions in Gagauz life. The earnings of women migrating to Turkey to work have contributed to these transformations. The gendered moral economies expressed in Gagauz Yeri are shifting along with these changes, underscoring how things are changing for women in complex ways.

The women's accounts presented in this chapter deepen our understanding of these processes. New distinctions have emerged in Gagauz Yeri, along the lines of the kind of work migrant women workers will undertake, whether in trade, construction, or domestic service, and where they undertake it, Istanbul or Moscow. Yet even older distinctions involving wealth, education, work experience, rurality versus urbanity, Russianness, and civilization still serve the Gagauz women as a frame of reference. Notions regarding the morality of new kinds of women's work and migration, which are defined by women's specific social locations, also help shape their agency: women make particular choices based on these gendered moral economies.

The moral views expressed about their work makes migrant domestics from Moldova unique in the literature on women traveling the peripheries of Europe. The women in Gagauz Yeri share positive ideas and values connected to socialism and to Russia, which is seen as a progressive country, and stereotype Turkey as "backward." For them, Turkey may be a good place to make money, but it is not a place to proceed toward modernity. They thus see their journeys as at once going "forward" into a capitalist global economy but "backward" to Turkey. These views and conceptions come to the fore when mobile workers and those who remain in Moldova justify their labor, and describe how they experience and interpret migration. These ideas also influence women's views on domestic work and the Gagauz insistence on their difference from Turks—especially Turkish women—that I will describe in chapter 3. This context makes it more difficult for them than for other migrant domestic workers to morally legitimate their work abroad to their communities, to admit to some of the valuable experiences their "host society" offers, and be recognized for the uplift they bring to their families.

Gagauz women's narratives concerning the need to journey to Turkey for work vary from other migrant women's accounts represented in ethnographic research to date in that they are refracted through the gendered hegemony of Soviet socialism, reflecting in turn the historical background of many who live in Gagauz Yeri. But a socialist past is not the beginning and the end of their difference from other migrant women. Rather, Gagauz women hold particular positions according to their intersecting subjectivities with respect to their rurality or urbanity, age, education, ideas about and experiences of wealth and work, language, views of civilization, and ethnicity. Thus, the similarities and differences in reasons for deciding to work abroad for global women do not necessarily align along regional or national lines (because they are "Gagauz" or "Moldovan," "Filipina" or "Mexican," "capitalist" or "postsocialist"). Rather, to compare migrant domestic work, we must analyze women's overlapping subjugations in class, age, ethnic, religious, language, educational, professional, and rural versus urban identities. Illustrating these configurations of subjectivities through women's narratives of the conditions in Gagauz Yeri and motivations for migration helps us better understand the ways in which the post-Soviet collapse and neoliberal adjustment were and are variously experienced and imagined by women. Moreover, it complicates the anthropological notions in "gender and postsocialism" literature that would generalize their experiences as postsocialist at the expense of understanding other forms of identifications in these women's lives.

As Sherry Ortner argues, it is important to recognize specific cultural identifications as a form of agency through meaning making and potentially a source of "thick resistance" to dominant discourses that would see people's lives as solely determined by and understood in economic (here, survivalist) terms (1999b; see also Herzfeld 2004). The point is that while some meaning for these women is structured by their relationship to the Soviet Union and its political and economic collapse, their former position as Soviet socialist subjects, and the imposition of neoliberal capitalism on a formerly socialist structure, much of their agency lies beyond a simple reaction to these shifting political economies or dominant discourses. Instead, it is found in their differences as women in a particular place trying to uplift their families and communities according to their ideas—ever shifting—of what uplift means. Women migrants, in all their diversity, are coming from communities in Moldova that are already transnational. In traveling to work in Turkey, they enter a novel transnational context, and while working in Turkey they find new kinds of gendered moral economies.

Chapter 3

Desiring a New Domestic

Just as shifting gendered moral economies in Gagauz Yeri inform women's reasons to seek domestic work in Turkey and their returns on that work, so too do changes in gendered moral economies in Turkey construct the demand for domestics from Moldova.

The desire for "Moldovans," as Gagauz women generally are called in Turkey (as most in Turkey do not distinguish Gagauz from other ethnic and language groups in Moldova), is structured by transformations in what constitutes the "modern" Turkish household. For middle- and upper-class families, hiring Gagauz women characterizes what is deemed a contemporary lifestyle in a way that hiring local domestics or women from the other formerly socialist states and Eastern Europe does not. As I came to know, employers explain this preference not as a matter of economics—that migrant labor is cheaper—but as an expression of cultural ideas based on their views of modernity: the professionalization of domestic work, and notions of gender intersecting with ideas about citizenship, class, race, ethnicity, nationality, and religion or religiosity. Migrants from Moldova are taken to be white,

European, cultured, educated, attractive, hardworking, and trustworthy, but also desperate, oversexed, and ambitious. This image works with the broader economic and ideological conditions of migrant domestic work in Turkey to construct the desire—the gendered moral economy of demand—for women from formerly socialist states as domestics. Such notions also help employers negotiate the vulnerabilities and inconsistencies that arise in hiring a live-in domestic worker who, whether local or foreign, undertakes this work illegally (see also Nare 2011). Indeed, this migration is not sanctioned and regulated from the top down, by the Turkish state, but rather is driven by specific gendered moral economies as they play out between individuals. Examining these ideas thus is vital to understanding the discursive practices in the transnational social field of labor as it takes shape in Turkey.

Along with the views of the women themselves, their communities at home in Gagauz Yeri, and staff at the IOM, the employers' and employment agents' gendered moral economies construct the social field of women's transnational labor migration. My concern in this chapter is to illuminate the Turkish context and employers' points of view, especially those of a Westernized, wealthy, and secular elite in Istanbul. This will help us, in the following chapter, to better understand the moral and economic fields women from Gagauz Yeri enter as migrant domestics in Turkey. I begin by briefly comparing the demand for migrant domestics in Turkey with that in other cases of mobile labor. I then detail the emergence and image of a diaspora of women from formerly socialist states in Istanbul. This image has worked itself into the demand for "Moldovans" as a way to achieve new lifestyles among Turkish middle and upper classes. However, such new desires, represented in the shifting gendered moral economies, are fraught with tensions, which create dilemmas for employers who hire mobile workers from Gagauz Yeri—the final topic of the chapter.

The Demand for Domestic Workers in Turkey

Middle- and upper-class families in Turkey hire domestic workers for many of the same reasons that families in other parts of the world do, but there are some unique features to this pattern of migrant employment. Traditionally, domestic work in Turkey, especially caring for children and the elderly, was the charge of the women of the household, who would have received assistance through extended family networks. But, especially in urban settings like Istanbul, the nuclear family has increasingly become the norm, and some Turkish women have begun to work outside the home. Nevertheless, women in Turkey, like women the world over, are saddled with gendered structures of inequality and traditional ideas about women that dictate that their primary responsibilities are as household caretakers. Since Turkish men have not assumed more responsibility for housework, working women in Turkey, as in other places, are burdened with the "second shift." Yet even if women in Turkey do not work, changing visions of a new Turkish middle- and upper-class woman and a new type of modern lifestyle continue to demand household work and care that can really only be achieved by hiring a domestic. Thus, waged domestic work is one way to meet the challenges and status concerns.

In Turkey, in the past, a local working class, often migrants from villages, met these household needs. Households often hired such women to help with monthly cleaning and caretaking. However, this workforce is now less available for this type of flexible, intimate, under-the-table work, and less likely to do it for low pay. Moreover, private child-care or elder-care homes are not widely available and are too expensive for many families. Although the state provides some more reasonably priced institutionalized care, the facilities are often plagued by poor conditions. Also, there are strong cultural preferences for performing such care inside one's own home. This is especially so for the elderly, who often prefer to end their days in their own home. Thus, how to provide this care work has become a very real problem for middle- and upper-class families in Turkey.

Migrant domestics have come to be a solution to this dilemma, but such work in Turkey remains unregulated. In some states, as detailed by Nana Oishi for Japan, migrant domestic work is also illegal, and gendered hegemonies encourage women to stay home and provide care for their families (2005). In other cases, however, and especially where women are increasingly working outside the home and local women's labor is unavailable for domestic work, states support the immigration of domestic workers (Chin 1998; Lan 2006a; Parrenas 2008). The Global Cooperation Council countries of the Middle East, having legalized migrant domestic labor, are a case in point (Oishi 2005; Mahdavi 2011). In these states, even though gendered ideologies dictate that women remain at home, increases in oil-generated wealth have led to desires for new lifestyles, ones that involve hiring foreign domestic workers as a new form of conspicuous consumption. Households also hire foreigners because there is no local labor to fulfill this demand. In Turkey, a representative of the Interior Ministry informed me, since there is a surplus of "unskilled" labor, laws to allow migrant domestics to work in the country are not even under consideration. Arguments to legalize this labor also conflict with local gendered hegemonies that still assert the priority of a Turkish woman's role as caretaker and housekeeper, even if she also works in the public realm. The upshot is that, in Turkey, the labor market for foreign domestic workers remains underground.

Migrant domestics meet the practical needs of many families in Turkey. In some cases, migrant labor is the only kind available for this type of work and is cheaper than local labor. Among some people in Turkey, this reduced cost may be a primary reason for hiring a migrant worker. An article in the weekly magazine *Tempo* and the employment agents I spoke with clearly presented migrant labor as a "great deal" economically (Ergul 2002).[1] Employment agents asserted that local workers would not do certain chores—especially caretaking for an invalid elder—for a wage that foreigners would accept. As one agent crudely told me, "Turks won't wipe someone's ass for that much." Another particularly articulate agent advocating a new way to hire household help explained: "Some people still come and say they want a young village girl and want to pay them $300 a month. That just doesn't exist anymore. They [Turks] have gotten smarter too. You won't find a Turk for under $500 a month." It is thus not just that an employer may not want a "village girl" but that even if the employer did, local workers do not exist for this market anymore. Indeed, the working class has lost its local, rural-to-urban migrant character in Istanbul. Many internal migrants have their own families in Istanbul and do not need a place to stay. They are thus disinclined to take live-in positions. Foreign migrant domestics are more readily available for live-in arrangements than local workers, for they are looking for a place to stay. This dynamic has partitioned the labor market for domestic work into local laborers, who work in households during the

---

[1] In 2005 (as opposed to 2002, when the article was written) the average monthly wage for a Moldovan or other foreign domestic began at $400, but some were paid as high as $600 or more, and some were also given "road money" (*yol parasi*) for their days off, amounting to $10 to $15. By comparison, Turkish live-in domestic workers were asking at least $500 a month. Employers and agencies do well in this transaction, at the expense of the domestic workers. Agencies take anywhere from 25 percent to 40 percent of the first month's pay from the employee and the rest (60 to 75 percent) from the employer. Some guaranteed employers that they would replace the worker if the worker left within six months to one year. Some agents actually encouraged employers to take the fee out of the employee's pay, too, leaving domestics without pay for their first month. Some had "trial periods" of one week or one month. A newcomer might take a hard job for a low salary, but women who had commuted for five to six years by 2005 had begun to smarten up. Many now have family, friends, or boyfriends in Istanbul with whom they can stay on their days off. They thus have begun to ask for a full day off per week. Most agencies in 2005 encouraged employers to give a full day off, but most employers wanted live-ins to take only one day, morning until night.

day and are charged with doing the heavy cleaning, and migrants, who work as live-in caretakers (Akalin 2007).

Women from Moldova who come to work as domestics enter this field of work with a particular value placed on them: as cheap and desperate. However, it is not only such practical considerations that determine the demand for these migrant workers as caregivers. Members of the secular, Westernized, and wealthy class in Istanbul I interviewed are seeking out new kinds of professionalized domestic care work for their homes.[2] For them, migrant domestic work is not only an issue of fulfilling household and caretaking labor but of employing someone in what is deemed a civilized and neoliberal manner and hiring someone who has the capacity to work in such a household. Moldovans are valued as educated and skilled, hardworking and trustworthy, seen as civilized and modern "White Russians" with the ability to correctly execute the job of being a caretaker for the contemporary Turkish household.

As many feminists have pointed out concerning care work in other contexts, migrant domestic work is accompanied by a transfer of emotional resources. Money is exchanged not only for physical labor but for providing intangible affective services such as love and caring (Hochschild 2002; Misra 2003). Michael Hardt and Antonio Negri argue that in the new demand-driven, postmodern global economy, consumers increasingly expect these kinds of affective services, or "immaterial labors" (2001). In this case, the upper classes in Turkey seek out Moldovans to fulfill new conceptions of the affective labor appropriate to a "civilized" household. According to Ayşe Akalin, migrant domestics are perceived to hold the gendered capacity for this type of flexible care work—the type of work that one might do out of love, as a family member would—and thus able to carry out the duties of an "ideal housewife," while Turkish women employers can proceed to fulfill their public role (2007). This indicates that the demand for Moldovan caregivers is more about changing household lifestyles in Turkey than it is an economic calculation. It shows that the demand side of this social field of transnational labor is also a shifting ground of gendered moral economies.

It is a common understanding that domestic work is always gendered. In most cases it is expected to be done by women, and thus is "women's work." Yet gender is not the only consideration. Women from the global south in first-world nations are often in demand not only because they are cheaper

---

[2] Some Turkish sociologists have dubbed this elite population "White Turks" (Yavuz 2000). For a critique of this categorization, see Christopher Houston (2002).

than local labor but also because of assumptions about qualities associated with their citizenship, class, race, nationality, ethnicity, and sexuality (Bakan and Stasiulis 1997a, 1997b; Moors 2003; Zimmerman, Litt, and Bose 2006; Anderson 2007).[3] As Bridget Anderson puts it, "Race, nationality, and immigration status interact to give migrants a particular place within labor markets for home care" (2007, 248; see also Oishi 2005). In Italy, employers stereotype women of certain nationalities as good domestic workers—honest, trustworthy, clean, and flexible (Nare 2011). And in Taiwan, Pei-Chia Lan found that employers and agencies hire migrants, considered racially and ethnically inferior, because they are believed to be better suited to domestic work than local workers (2006a and 2006b). In such contexts, the domestic work and so-called dirty work they do are hidden, while the woman of the house can be envisioned as "doing it all" (e.g., Palmer 1989). Indeed, in the case of migrants in Malaysia, described by Christine Chin, when migrant women take care of this dirty work, the woman of the house can distance herself from it, and achieve modernity (1998).

Even within the category of migrant, employers often make distinctions. For instance, Lan shows that whereas Filipinas in Taiwan are admired for their English-language skills and education, Indonesians are preferred because they fit the profile of the "docile," "obedient," and "stupid" maid whom employers can modernize (2006b). Moreover, third-world women are also valued as more "traditional" (if "backward") in their femininity and as inherently more nurturing than first-world women who have chosen to work outside the home (Ehrenreich and Hochschild 2002; Anderson 2002). These overlapping subjugations also work to create an oversexualized image of such racialized women (Constable 1997b; Chang and Groves 2000; Brennan 2004). This sexualization is compounded by the situation of domestic work itself, which places the worker in the caring role traditionally fulfilled by mother, wife, or daughter-in-law, women who hold sexual reproductive roles in the patrilocal household as well.[4] Thus, migrant domestic workers are desired because of particular ideas about gender, but also because of class, citizenship, ethnicity, race, nationality, and sexuality. This complex of overlapping subjugations is as relevant to the demand side as it is to the supply side of this form of labor.

---

[3] This is also true for those who form minorities in the global north, such as African Americans in the United States (see, e.g., Rollins 1985; Zarembka 2002). Historically unequal relations of power, such as colonialism, also often mark these relations (Hansen 1992; Buijs 1993; Momsen 1999).
[4] As Barbara Ehrenreich and Arlie Russell Hochschild (2002) and Denise Brennan (2004) note, both representations condition the demand for sex workers as well.

In the case of migrant domestics traveling to Turkey for work, such processes are also at work, but there are some interesting twists to them, which makes this case particularly disruptive to conventional academic understandings of who does migrant domestic work, where the work is done, why migrant domestics are in demand, and what kinds of needs they fulfill. Women from Turkey mostly appear in the social science literature as migrants themselves, and even as domestic workers in Europe (e.g., Erel 2009). The employment of women migrant workers from Gagauz Yeri in Turkey forces us to see women from Turkey and employers of domestic workers worldwide as diverse.

In its regional pattern, this case resembles the cases of south-south migration in East Asia mentioned earlier, in the Philippines and Taiwan (Constable 1997a; Chin 1998; Lan 2006a, 2006b). It is especially similar to the example of Vietnamese workers in Taiwan, cited but not elaborated on by Lan (2006a). She briefly notes that in this migration pattern, Vietnamese women are considered racially superior to their employers but held back by their socialist state. According to Lan, because ultimately these Vietnamese women are perceived as backward by their employers, they end up in a similar situation as in other examples she cites in which migrants have lesser status than their employers (Lan 2006a). As in some of these examples from East Asia, in the case of migrants from Moldova to Turkey, the women employers are not from countries in the top tier of wealth. However, even though migrant domestics from Moldova come from a postsocialist periphery, in Turkey their race, ethnicity, citizenship, and class—even their religion and lack of religiosity—mark them as closer to the civilized West in many ways. Hiring them thus can reflect an employer's modernity. Although some of the "dirty work" they do is still hidden, migrant caretakers from Moldova are also deployed as visible markers of the employer's neoliberal ways. Ethnicity preferences in the demand for migrant domestics can indicate a desire for a new lifestyle, but as we saw in the instances of migrant labor in East Asia (and elsewhere), the preference is often for a third-world woman who is considered more traditional than her employer (Lan 2006a). The case of Moldovan migrant domestics in Turkey, by contrast, is more akin to how employment of an English nanny marks an American household as elite.

In Turkey, migrant domestics from various parts of the former Soviet Union and Eastern Europe, but especially Moldova, because of their location in what is considered in Turkey to be the West, their education, presentability and attractiveness, "whiteness," secular lifestyles, work experience, and ethic of hard work are seen as modern, not as traditional. It is their difference from tradition and their similarity to their employers that makes them valuable. Often noted of the women from the former Soviet Union and Eastern Europe are their light eyes and hair color, which are highly valued features of (often foreign) beauty in Turkey. These women's "put-togetherness" is another admired feature. They do not dress, for instance, as the local working-class woman who normally fulfill these roles are sometimes held to, in a loose, perhaps even traditional, dress. They wear jeans and slacks (not long skirts, as would be expected of local domestics) and blouses; they have their hair styled and do their nails, just as the woman of the house does. They are not all good cooks, but they know how to do household accounting. In their time off, some read books and seek out people to talk with about the books they are reading. They speak freely with the men of the household and in the neighborhood. They are Orthodox Christian, but not particularly religious. In Turkey, such secularism is a key feature of modernity. These characteristics distinguish them, in terms of expectations of their labor, from the local working-class women, marked as villagers, who fulfilled the role of domestic worker in the past and continue now to do the heavy housework on a regular but not live-in basis (Akalin 2007). In sum, consuming Moldovans' services provides an upper-class home in Turkey with an image of itself as a "civilized" household that hires professional domestic labor, not just a village girl.

However, the very characteristics that contribute to Moldovans being seen as desirable as domestic workers also cast them as morally ambiguous. Women from the former Soviet Union and Eastern Europe transgress traditional Turkish codes of class and gender, which assume a domestic worker to be of a lower class, uneducated, and religiously conservative. Transgressing these assumptions makes women from Gagauz Yeri seem ambitious and driven women in their employers' imagination—morally loose or overly sexual (something accentuated by the fact that in Turkey, Orthodox Christians are reputedly more sexual than other women) and potential competitors with the women of the house for the children's and husband's love, and for their status as a "modern" woman. In the end, these migrant domestics are subjected to much the same sexualized imagery as migrant domestics in other contexts, who are marked as racially inferior, traditional women. As a result of these complex relations between women employers and their migrant domestic workers, and because this system works through problematic representations of women of a certain class, race, ethnicity, nationality, citizenship, religion, and religiosity, migrants are much more vulnerable to the exploitations of the illegal labor market than are their employers.

New gendered moral and cultural ideas are perpetuating this transnational labor migration and neoliberalism in this case, but shifts in the notions of civilization in Turkey, as in Moldova, are fraught. These shifts have created, but also complicate, the desire for Moldovan domestics, leading to contradictions in employers' expectations for domestic work and of domestic workers. In investigating these shifting gendered moral economies, we may discover the value of Moldovans to employers in Turkey and how it came about that they are in such demand. To understand this value, I begin with a description of Turkish contact with and imaginings of women from formerly socialist states in the 1990s with the phenomenon of tourist-traders and "natashas" in the Istanbul neighborhood of Laleli. I then move to discuss the particularity of the demand for Moldovans in the context of changing Turkish households. I conclude with an analysis of the gendered contradictions and conflicts of this particular case compared to others.

Laleli and the Natasha

Laleli is located on the European collar (*Avrupa yakasi*) of the Bosphorus Strait, which connects the Black Sea in the north to the Sea of Marmara in the south, and eventually on to the Dardanelles, the Aegean, and the Mediterranean (figure 3.1). In Istanbul, one is said to live on the Anatolian collar (*Anadolu yakasi*) or the European collar (*Avrupa yakasi*) of the Bosphorus (*Bogaz*, meaning "strait" or "throat"). The European collar of Istanbul is further divided by the Golden Horn, a body of water that runs into the Bosphorus. South of the Golden Horn is the Imperial peninsula, where the Byzantines centered their empire, and the Ottomans, in the late fifteenth century, took over. Topkapı Palace is located here. The Saint Sofia (Aya Sofya) rises above the skyline, as do the Blue Mosque and the Mosque of Suleyman, built by the famous Ottoman architect Sinan for Suleyman the Magnificent, the famous sixteenth-century Sultan. So well-built is this mosque, Sinan claimed, that even at the Apocalypse its dome would not crumble. Instead, he boasted, the entire structure would slide in one piece into the Golden Horn (figure 3.2). Because of its complex history, this area is the main site of tourism in Istanbul.

Most tourists approach the Mosque of Suleyman from the Golden Horn and the north. Yet behind it, just to the south, lies the neighborhood of Laleli, Turkish for something decorated in tulips. Laleli is so close to the mosque as to practically be in its shadow, yet oddly, from Laleli, one cannot see this famous mosque. Its hiddenness is an apt metaphor for Laleli's proximate

Figure 3.1. Bosphorus Strait and bridge connecting the Asian and European parts of Istanbul, 2004. Photograph by the author.

marginality from official tourist sites and its role as a place of passage for working-class people who labor in the tourism industry or on its periphery. The neighborhood is thus a borderland of sorts, nestled between different areas and populated by different types of people, some transient: backpackers who come to see the remnants and reimaginings of imperial Byzantium or the Ottomans and stay in the cheap hotels; religious conservatives from the nearby neighborhood of Fatih; working-class people who reside in the larger area of Aksaray and Unkapanı; and students from nearby Istanbul University. Since the early 1990s, adding to its marginality, Laleli has become known for the presence of women from the former Soviet Union—the so-called natashas—and as a borderland for trade and gender (Yükseker 2004).

As the anthropologist Banu Nilgün Uygun explains, "natasha" is "a generic name popularized by the Turkish media whose referent conveniently slips back and forth between a young and beautiful woman and a prostitute from the former Soviet Union" (2004, 29). Uygun goes on to note that popular media in Turkey represent these women

Figure 3.2. The Mosque of Suleyman, seen from the Golden Horn in Istanbul, 2009. Photograph by Terry Ruthrauff. Reproduced by permission.

at best, as tragic heroines created by the collapse of a system—as beautiful, educated and civilized women who, out of economic despair, are forced into the laps of uneducated, uncivilized, vulgar Turkish men. At worst they are portrayed as cunning, manipulative entrepreneurs who break homes, take away "our" money and spread STDs. (29)

In the 1990s, this image was even popularized in a song, "Natasha Disco," by Erkan Ocakli. These women are partitioned even further, according to Ildikó Bellér-Hann (1995), a social scientist who spent time on the Black Sea coast observing the flood of women from the former Soviet Union and Eastern Europe in the early 1990s. She writes that it is hard to pin down a general representation of Muslim women from the former Soviet Union, but Christian women are generally divided into "White Russians" (*beyaz Ruslar*), summoning an image of beautiful, fair-skinned people, and others, such as Georgians, who are considered "dark and vulgar" (1995, 222). The women from the formerly socialist regions west or north of Turkey are considered "clean, safe, better organized, and somewhat richer" than those from the regions east of Turkey, such as Georgia, a state regarded as "dirty, dangerous, warlike and extremely poor" (222). Whether considered white or not, migrant women from the former Soviet bloc countries are accused of causing family feuds, divorce, theft, crime, and disease. This natasha image is something with which all women from the former Soviet Union and Eastern Europe in Turkey must contend. And it is a double-edged image, for though it makes migrant women fair game for sexual harassment, the more positive face of the image, of a modern and civilized if desperate woman, helps create the demand for female merchants, store clerks, sex workers, and domestic workers from the formerly socialist states.

Laleli and the natasha are linked in the public consciousness in Turkey because, after the fall of the Soviet Union, Laleli became and continues to be a locus for small-scale unregistered and unregulated trade between women from the former Soviet Union and Eastern Europe and local men, mostly involving the sale of leather goods and clothing. This is when women coming from former socialist states in Eastern Europe and Russia, and also Kurdish men driven from the cross-border trade in southeastern Turkey by the Turkish state's counterterrorism efforts in the 1980s and the 1991 Iraq War, developed what came to be known in Turkey as the "suitcase trade" (*bavul ticareti*) (Yükseker 2000, 2004).[5] Because the women buyers entered the country on tourist visas to buy in Turkey and resell in their formerly socialist cities and towns, and because they were allowed to carry only two suitcases across the border without being taxed, they were also commonly known as "tourist-traders "or "shuttle-traders"/"shuttlers" (in Russian, *chelnoki*). According to the sociologist Deniz Yükseker, Turkish merchants liked working with women traders from the formerly socialist states because they found the women to be trustworthy and respected them for being hardworking (2000). The traders also were perceived to be beautiful women in desperate straits, whom the men felt sorry for and sought to help. Yükseker posits that the intimate, sometimes sexual, relationships between traders and merchants that developed helped to secure some level of trust in this unregulated trade and brought in up to US$9 billion in currency to Turkey before the trade declined, later in the 1990s (2000). Even so,

---

[5] The Turkish state has waged a war against Kurdish separatists, particularly the PKK (Kurdish Workers' Party). This war, which was at its height during the 1980s, took place on Turkey's border with Iraq and Iran, where many Kurds live. Kurds constitute up to 20 percent of the Turkish population. Because of the violence between the PKK and the government and the concomitant economic devastation in the region, many Kurds moved to Istanbul and other major cities seeking work. A vibrant trade between Turkey and Iran and Iraq also existed in this region, but came to a halt with the first Iraq War. The continuation of the 2003 Iraq War no doubt contributed to the continuing migration of those Kurds left in the region to Istanbul and the permanency of their settlement there.

wholesale stores for leather and clothing continue to predominate in Laleli, as do signs in Russian. Store merchants and customers alike commonly speak Russian. Some Russian-speaking women are employed at these stores, but for the most part they shop rather than work in Laleli.

Yükseker, on one hand, argues that "femininity" helped the tourist trade and was operationalized by women for economic ends (2004).[6] Bellér-Hann, on the other hand, analyzed the influx of women from the former Soviet Union through Turkey's border with Georgia to the cities and towns of the Black Sea coast of Turkey and considers that the tourist trade (which was initially seen as legitimate, even if not legalized by the government) became a sort of camouflage for sex work (1995). As on the Black Sea coast, the phenomenon of sex work by women from formerly socialist countries emerged in Laleli at around the same time as the tourist trade, and has increased since. As one woman from Gagauz Yeri told me, "Laleli changes at night." There are many cheap hotels in Laleli, and activities ranging from those defined as "consumption" to those strictly defined as sex work take place.[7] Uygun points out that Turkish men of rural and marginal backgrounds seek out these companions to experience romance and sex in a way that traditional conservative values bar them from doing in their own marriages or in relationships with Turkish women (2004). She argues that the availability of women from the former Soviet Union for these jobs and their real or perceived differences in education, work experience, and personal and business relationships have led to a new demand among Turkish men for different, more "modern" trade and even sexual practices with women.[8] Needless to say, this availability of migrant women and the image of the natasha have affected the demand for migrant domestic workers from Moldova.

White Turks and White Russians

The desire for women workers from the postsocialist republics has coincided with the demand for new types of domestic work in Turkey and new

---

[6] Yükseker seems to use "femininity" to refer to sexuality, but separates its use in these trading relationships from prostitution.
[7] "Consumption" is a word in use at the IOM-Moldova connoting the hiring of a young woman by an entertainment establishment to get men to buy drinks; such women may or may not provide sexual services.
[8] For another interesting analysis of the ways in which this transnational trade has shifted, see Mine Eder and Özlem Öz (2010).

household lifestyles. During my stays in Turkey in the early and mid-2000s, it was particularly Moldovans who fulfilled these new desires. To understand why, we must plumb Turkish notions about gender, primarily, but also about class, race, ethnicity, nationality, religion, religiosity, and citizenship with respect to local Turkish laborers and migrant workers coming from different regions of the former Soviet Union and Eastern Europe. Moreover, it takes an understanding of the historical shifts in middle- and upper-class expectations for laborers and lifestyles in contemporary Turkish households.

Since the late 1990s, women from many formerly socialist nation-states, including Moldova, Bulgaria, Turkmenistan, Uzbekistan, Armenia, Azerbaijan, Romania, and Ukraine, have taken up domestic work in Turkey. These women are often preferred to local workers, and among them, Moldovans have come to hold a particularly high value—so much so that in 2002, when I first started looking into the phenomenon, the term "Moldovan" (*Moldovyalı*) had become synonymous with the best of migrant domestics. Because of language skills and ethnic commonalities, it was women from Gagauz Yeri who made up the majority of this mobile worker population. But most people in Turkey are ignorant of the existence of the Gagauz, let alone their connection to—or disconnection from—Turks in Turkey. For most employers and others in Turkey, the Gagauz are thus indistinguishable from other Orthodox Christian women who come from Moldova.

A 2002 issue of the popular weekly *Tempo* headlined a story about the new Moldovan workers:

> They are hardworking, cultured, educated, and a great deal [economically]: Don't you have a Moldovan maid yet?
>
> - If you say no, you have been left behind the times, because Istanbul's luxury homes are teeming with Moldovans.
> - They may not have permission to work here, but nobody is saying anything about it.
> - If you want to catch up with the times, what you need to do is simple: Go to the Moldovan Bazaar in the heart of Istanbul. (Ergul 2002, author's translation)

Despite calling on prospective employers to go to the "Moldovan Bazaar" (that is, Laleli), the article interviews employment agents in the heart of Istanbul's wealthy neighborhoods, who place migrant domestics in Turkish homes. The article details agents' views contrasting the virtues of Moldovan domestics with the "laziness" and "lack of discipline" of local workers, stating that the latter delay undertaking certain tasks or avoid them altogether. It is professed that domestics from Turkey care too much about their own comfort (*rahat*) to be disciplined workers. The *Tempo* article theorizes that women from Turkey are not good workers because they suffer from Ottoman pride (*Osmanli gururu*): they express distaste for the jobs they are given to do and are concerned with not being slighted by their employers. As one agent told me, they "take TL 500 million [about $500 a month] and then look for ways to slack off. A delicate admonition from the head of household can prompt them to be greatly offended." "But foreigners," the article continues, "have gotten over themselves; they come here with two university degrees, but don't have any complexes. 'Give me US$250–300 and I'll do it,' they say." As a result, the article continues, agencies that act as go-betweens for those seeking help and those looking for work have found that the middle and upper classes in Turkey are beginning to favor hiring migrant domestics. Among the many foreigners available, Moldovans are further distinguished. As one agent quoted in the article put it, "They are very hardworking; they will get up at the crack of dawn and start washing windows."

This article summarizes what I found to be the view of the agents at the more than twenty agencies I surveyed and among the employers with whom I spoke by phone or in person. I collected agency advertisements in newspapers, and, since my uncle was looking for a new domestic worker to care for my grandmother, I inquired on her behalf, speaking with them by phone and in person. Stesha (the urbanite Russophile, Rosa's daughter, introduced in the last chapter) and other women from Gagauz Yeri, knowing my research topic, all suggested I look into the agencies, saying that the agencies determined to a great extent the jobs women get and their lives in Istanbul. This gave me an opportunity to do so.[9] Supplementing this research, I spoke informally with fifteen employers over the course of my research and taped six interviews with individuals who employed migrant domestics. Four of the six formal interviews I conducted were with employers drawn from the upper echelons of Istanbul society, to which the *Tempo* article refers. It should

---

[9] Admittedly, this part of my research was less than ideal transparent anthropological practice. I did not tell the agents that I was studying this phenomenon, but instead approached them as a prospective employer's granddaughter, and I was not observing how actual employers themselves interacted with the agencies. (I should note that nobody from my investigations was hired.) However, taking on this full insider's position, I was able to ascertain the variety of ways these agents positioned themselves as service providers in this undocumented and informal labor market and the range of attitudes and values held toward employers and employees generally.

not be assumed, however, that these are the only people in Istanbul hiring Moldovans. People of middling means also hire them, and many cite similar reasons for doing so. Just as the reasons that the women from Gagauz Yeri have for working in Turkey differed according to their particular location in the local class hierarchy, so too did the reasons for hiring them. I met people of middle-class status in Istanbul who hired migrant domestics to show that they were moving up in the world, while others hired them as a way to retain a hold on their declining class status. Most of the individuals I highlight here, however, were from a very wealthy class and were trying to distinguish their novel form of globalized modernity from the traditions of past generations by means of distinctive demands for professionalized domestic work.

Some of the employers I spoke with were hiring live-in laborers to provide child care, while others were looking for migrant couples to live in and take care of their second home (usually called a "villa," outside the city), and still others were seeking in-home caregivers for their elderly, invalid, or sick family members. A job's location in Istanbul can reflect what kind of job it is. At that time, elder care and care for the sick were generally to be found around Sisli, Nistantasi, or Osmanbey on the European collar. These neighborhoods were the middle- and upper-class family neighborhoods in the 1950s to 1970s, and many elderly remain there, alone. Their children, the middle and upper classes of today, have moved to more newly prosperous neighborhoods either on the Bosphorus—in Etiler, for instance—or on "the other side" (*öbür taraf*), the Anatolian collar (in Suadiye and Fenerbahçe, for instance). People living in these latter neighborhoods tend to have child-care needs. In Istanbul, even moderate middle-class households hire a cleaning woman. Traditionally, this domestic is the wife of the doorman, who is called in to do heavy cleaning (*büyük temizlemek*), meaning dusting thoroughly, vacuuming and scrubbing floors and rugs, washing the windows, and sometimes doing the laundry and ironing as well over the course of one day every ten or fifteen days (Özyeğin 2001).[10] Such a woman is called a day worker (*gündelikçi*) and received the equivalent of US$15 to $40 a day in 2005. As Akalin notes, an overnighter (*yatili*) is usually hired separately (2007). She is a live-in domestic who may cook (though sometimes cooks

---

[10] Traditionally, apartments in Istanbul have doormen or concierges, who live with their families in a basement apartment. This is true for urban Turkey more generally. For an excellent study of the relationship between working-class women from these families who work as domestics and the women they work for, who live in the apartments in Ankara, see Gul Özyeğin (2001).

are hired separately) and do some neatening up as part of daily housework (*evişi*), but most of all she is expected to act as nanny (*çocuk bakıcı* or *dadı*) or caretaker for an elderly, sick, or invalid household member (*yaşlı bakıcı* or *hasta/yatalak bakıcı*). Many of these jobs are now located in large apartments in Istanbul *sités* occupied by a Westernized elite.

The home in which I interviewed Ayşe, a young, thirty-something mother of twins, was in an area of about fifteen four-story apartment blocks.[11] As I waited to go to her home on the Anatolian side in July 2004, I sat in a cafe nearby in the height of comfort. I lounged in a plush chair in a modern tea garden (*çay bahçesi*) overlooking a large yacht club on the Sea of Marmara. A group of young women chatted nearby. Wearing designer jeans and tank tops, they drank cappuccinos (not Turkish coffee) and talked about university life in the United States. At another table, some mothers and their children drank tea from mugs (not, in traditional Turkish fashion, from small tea glasses) and scolded their children in Turkish and English. Elsewhere, a young couple drank Coca-Colas and flirted obviously. A man rode by on a luxury Mongoose-brand bicycle, wearing spandex biker shorts, leather biking gloves, and no shirt. He was fit and evenly tanned. A woman in khakis and a pressed, bright white cotton T-shirt carried a Hilfiger bag to a sailboat docked at the yacht club. Behind the tea house was a large Migros (a relatively expensive grocery store chain) and next to it a sports plus gymnastic salon, called "Powerful," where a middle-aged woman rode a stationary bicycle in a room with windows looking out over the sea. The paper that week had reported that fewer than 1 percent of the Turkish population attend gyms.

This scene could as easily have come from the American shores of Long Island, or perhaps the southern shores of the European Mediterranean, but in this neighborhood it illustrates the lifestyles of an urban elite and secular sector of the Turkish population, who live in luxury gated communities called *sités*. The *sité* in Istanbul is described by Turkish sociologists as a clean and orderly place where the old or new wealthy classes seek escape from the disorder and insecurity of Istanbul life, overrun by pollution and noise, crime, and earthquakes, and by "uncivilized" and "irresponsible" people from villages in Turkey (by some estimates more than 60 percent of

---

[11] That the buildings are only four stories also makes this a safer environment than others, should an earthquake hit. Many Turkish high-rises that were built in the 1980s are known for their shoddy construction, a fact confirmed by the experiences of the August 1999 earthquake. Many people died when these apartment buildings collapsed.

the population of Istanbul are migrants from these villages, many of whom are Kurds from southeastern Turkey) (Öncü 1997; Öncü and Weyland 1997; Keyder 1999). Within their gates, the *sités* offer twenty-four-hour security, shopping plazas, satellite television, movie theaters, tennis courts, and pools.

In talking with a number of employers in different *sités*, I found a group of individuals representing an *Istanbulu* (from Istanbul) upper class. These families consisted of men and women educated in universities in Europe and the United States or in elite colleges in Turkey; many had worked abroad or work for multinational corporations in Turkey. The newlywed couple who owned this particular apartment was well educated in private exam-entry foreign language high schools in Istanbul. Ayşe, whom I had met through a family member, had previously worked at an advertising agency, while her husband worked for a multinational corporation. Two other heads of households I interviewed were a generation older than Ayşe and her husband. I also had met them through family contacts, and both were well educated and spoke at least two languages fluently. These older couples have children studying in Ivy League schools or working in the United States. One of these latter individuals, an international businessman named Ahmet, drove a large luxury car, an extravagance that in Istanbul means "I have my own parking space wherever I go." These two households had sought out migrant couples to live in a separate apartment on the grounds of their respective villas, second homes away from the city: the wife to cook and clean, the husband to take care of the grounds and the dogs and to provide security. One way in which the families in these *sités* or villas distinguish themselves from other classes in Turkey and separate themselves further from disorderly villagers—and from the crime, filth, and cultural "backwardness" that these villagers represent—is by employing migrant domestic workers. This is a new lifestyle practice, one they engage in to mark their difference from past gendered moral economies of labor in the household, those of their parents' or grandparents' generation. It is one among numerous changes seen over time in household practices in Turkey as those with the means to do so seek to establish themselves as modern, even cosmopolitan.

Transforming the Domestic

To understand this situation and the particular type of modernity and progress these employers intend to embody, and why hiring Moldovans helps them to do so, we must first understand the changes in the relationships between employer and domestic. Also important to grasp is the role of gender in the shifts in what constitutes progress and modernity since Republican era in Turkey. The modernity and progress of the Turkish nation-state were strongly promoted through the image of the modern Turkish woman and family (Kandiyoti 1991; Öncü 1997; Özbay 1999). In the transition from Ottoman Empire to the Turkish nation-state, feminists fought for, and gained, the right to vote and to hold elected office, for equal inheritance, and for the abolition of polygamy. Moreover, veils were outlawed in public, and women began to be employed outside the home and to engage in public lives, including as politicians. Yet patriarchy still had a foothold in both public and private realms.[12] And whether women held public roles or not, their household duties tasks remained the same. Gender ideology locating women in the home remained strong. Domestic workers helped assuage this situation. Common practices included "adopting" a young orphan or village girl to work, whom the employer would then support, and hiring the doorman's wife as a weekly cleaner (Özbay 1999; Özyeğin 2001, 2002).

As the sociologist Ferhunde Özbay argues, the labor of this "other" girl or woman was key to the modernity of the new woman and household in Turkey, and the Turkish state. These domestic workers were often referred to as "women" (*kadın*), as in "I'm going to hire a woman" (*kadın tutacagim*)—a crude term of reference that would never be used for the woman of the house. Yet without these paid domestic workers, the modern Turkish woman and even Turkish modernity could not have been established. It was these laborers who allowed the rising Turkish middle and upper classes to embody the modern urban family ideal. Whether working or not, the women of the household upheld this ideal by hiding the dirty work of domestic labor as well as the domestic laborer herself, much as in the case of migrant domestics in Malaysia detailed by Chin (1998). In so doing, the modern family, and the new state, safely distanced themselves from the "disorder," "pollution,"

---

[12] In the 1960s, feminists stepped up efforts to fight the patriarchal practices that continued to exist in the private and public realms. By the 1980s, violence against women was a rallying point for feminists of all ethnicities and religions in Turkey. Since the 1990s, there has also been an increasingly vocal Islamic feminism movement and, in the 2000s, a budding gay, lesbian, bisexual, transgender, and queer movement. Additional legal freedoms were gained by women in the 2000s, yet violence against women persists and continues to rally feminists. Hopefully, wider public outrage over such violence (such as the recent responses to the murder of a young woman in February 2015) will help their battle gain more traction. For more on women, gender, and feminism in Turkey, there is a very rich literature to draw on. Some examples include Deniz Kandiyoti (1991), Ayşe Kadıoğlu (1994), Yeşim Arat (1994), Şirin Tekeli (1995), Parla (2001), Altınay (2004), Adak and Altınay (2010), Caglar Diner and Şule Toktas (2010), and Simten Coşar and Metin Yeğenoğlu (2011).

and "backwardness" represented by Turkish villagers who did this labor (Akalin 2007).

These villagers were seen as clients by their employer-patrons. The employers were poised to act as a civilizing force for the working-class villagers. At the same time, Turkish working-class domestics were often treated as fictive kin and referred to in such terms, as daughter, older sister, aunt. And, particularly if they were young girls from villages, the job was assumed to be a way for villagers to move up in the world, a way for them to learn urban, modern ways. Like the Taiwanese employers of Indonesians documented by Lan (2002, 2006a, 2006b), employers were positioned to teach them these ways. The villagers were under their employer's protection in this environment, and it was not unusual for them to be given dowries and married off when the time came—a practice usually reserved for parents. They were considered part of the family, but not quite. The symbolic transgressions these domestics made in this case between clean and dirty, modernity and tradition, urban and rural, civilized and uncivilized, order and disorder, and progress and backwardness are characteristic dilemmas of "civilizational discourse" during the Turkish Republican era and are still apparent in local middle- and upper-class practices.

Until the late 1990s, relations between domestic worker and employer were expected to be like those of client and patron, as described by Özbay (1999). The contemporary relationship between women of the house and their local domestic workers in Turkey still is marked by the expectations that the former is a "generous older sister" and the latter is "her loyal lady" (Kalaycıoğlu and Rittersberger-Tılıç 2000). In her sociological study of contemporary domestic workers and their employers in middle- and upper-class Ankara, Gul Özyeğin (2001, 2002) reveals that these "faithful" Turkish domestics manipulate their "charitable" employers through cultural codes of dependency and responsibility, prompting the "patrons" to succumb to "class guilt" and provide favors and gifts for their employees beyond what they pay them. Many of the ideas discussed by Özbay for historical Istanbulus thus still hold sway in Turkish domestic worker-employer relations today, even if considered an old-fashioned way of doing things—what many would term *à la Turca*, a phrase that retains the French Orientalist language and perspective to refer to a "backward" but "typical" Turkish way.

The employers I spoke with rebelled against or at least sought to dissociate themselves from these practices. Asserting themselves as more "modern" than their forebears, ironically, they continued to participate in the very categories that the older civilization discourse employed in many ways, even if they had altered the paradigm somewhat. Unlike those following the "old" ways, they did not refer to taking responsibility for "civilizing" a villager. In fact, the village domestic worker was perceived as a visible blot on the modernity and order of the household, which the employer sought to scrub out entirely. The foreign domestic worker from the former Soviet Union and Eastern Europe, especially Moldovans, became a solution to their dilemma. As Akalin argues, this segmented the market for domestic labor in Turkey into local workers for heavy cleaning and migrants for caretaking (2007).

Employers I spoke with remarked first and foremost how their process of hiring a live-in domestic worker was markedly different from the old practices. These individuals were not interested in just hiring a woman or a girl, or in bringing in a country cousin, whom they would help financially and teach how to work in a modern household before the employee could start her own household. Instead, these employers used employment services (*danismanliklar*) or answered advertisements in newspapers. They collected a number of appropriate candidates (*aday*), whom they then interviewed formally (*görüşmek*), sometimes several times. As they represented it, they evaluated the candidates according to experience and education. For baby caretakers (*bebek bakıcı*) in particular, the young mother I interviewed who lived in the apartment complex near where I lounged earlier, Ayse, explained to me that specialized knowledge of babies is sought, as well as trustworthiness (*güvenilir birisi*). I spoke with her in her large two-bedroom apartment, where the caretaker stayed with the twins in their room. She went on to say that when you hire a caretaker, she should do nothing else but caretake. In the case of baby caretaking, the domestic is expected to do everything associated with the babies—washing, feeding, playing with them—but nothing else, including cooking and cleaning, other than to pick up after the baby. This separation of duties is key to the professionalization of domestic work. To clarify such duties in their villa, Ahmet, one of the Turkish male employers, who had hired a husband-and-wife couple, wrote out a detailed contract of expectations for the employer and employees to sign.

As in the 2002 *Tempo* article, these employers told me they preferred foreign domestics because such workers had specialized knowledge and a professional work ethic (*iş ahlaklari*). Several employers attributed the better work ethic of foreign domestics compared with that of local Turkish workers to their better education. Others suggested it could be their individual personalities. Ayse described domestics from the former Soviet bloc countries and Eastern Europe as different from locals in their ways (*davranışları*) and in what they wore (*giyimleri*), and all the employers I spoke with liked the fact that often, if they have worked in Turkey before, the workers come with references. Ahmet and Ayse both found the women from formerly socialist states they hired to be responsible (*sorumlu insanlar*). They described them as doing what needed to be done (*gerek yapiyorlar*), as trustworthy (*sorumlular*), and as not stealing. In a Mediterranean society in which the suspicion of the envious evil eye is prevalent even in the most Westernized households, as Ahmet put it, their "eyes are not on other people's things." Moreover, he went on to indicate that even if they were shown some kindness and intimacy by their employers (because, after all, they all lived in the same house), they still retained a professional distance and were respectful to their employers. He contrasted this to "our own people," who stole or were even violent, who would stretch the rules and try to manipulate things to their own advantage.

Ahmet spoke about and sought to treat domestics differently from how he had seen his parents treat them in the houses he grew up in. The advertisements and the agencies I surveyed appealed to this type of sentiment. Like the employers, the ads referred to migrant domestics not as "woman" (*kadın*) (as a local domestic would be called), but as "lady" (*hanım* or *bayan*)—a term of equality used for both the woman of the house and the female worker—or even as "assistant" (*eleman*). Ayşe said she encouraged her domestic worker to eat dinner at the same table with the family. Moreover, these employers sought to change some traditional practices in the patron-client relation: they often paid the domestic worker what they considered a generous wage and did not want to be expected to provide anything else, such as gifts, additional money, or favors. That the relationship between employer and the migrant domestic worker was more professional and less hierarchical and clientalist marked the household as contemporary and modern, composed of enlightened individuals who offered rights to their professional employees.

Interestingly, unlike the local domestic worker doing heavy cleaning, who is hidden from view, thereby allowing the woman of the house to present herself as doing it all, the Moldovan is allowed some visibility in the new household arrangements. Like local domestics, Moldovans are often expected to sit in the back of the room, if they are in the same room with their employers, and are encouraged not to take the more prominent seats in the household; the cleaning is done when most people are not in the house. Yet, unlike local domestic workers, Moldovans are sometimes encouraged to be judiciously seen at key moments in the performance of modernity. If the worker is a caretaker, her presence also marks the family as one that struggles to raise their children or care for their elderly or sick family members in the best, most progressive way, a way that requires professional and literate knowledge of child care or medicine. Employers seek migrant domestic workers to reflect their own modern ways; these migrant domestics are seen to hold the gendered aptitude to fulfill this kind of work in a contemporary Turkish home.

Valuing Moldovans

Child care and elder care have become two specializations for which domestics from the former Soviet states and Eastern Europe are particularly valued, and Moldovans hold a particular place among them, according to agencies and employers. This further partitions the labor market by citizenship, race, ethnicity, nationality, religion, and religiosity. Domestic workers are divided into Turk or foreigner (*yabancı*). Foreign domestics, who most assume are from the former Soviet Union and Eastern Europe (though they are not always), are divided further according to their specialty skills, such as language skills, cleanliness, cooking ability, medical or other specialized knowledge for elder care or child care, hardworking nature, cultural capital, religion, and citizenship.

Certain other cases of migrant domestic work involve formerly enslaved or colonized people working for their former colonizers (see, e.g., Rollins 1985; Hansen 1992; Chin 1998; Momsen 1999; and Zarembka 2002; on how ethnicity plays a role in demand, see Anderson 2002). Similarly, migrant laborers from the formerly socialist space in Istanbul are perceived in the light of their historical connections with or disconnections from the Ottomans or Turkey. These connections are racialized in certain ways. In general, individuals from formerly socialist states are regarded with sympathy or pity in Turkey in some ways: they are seen as suffering not from the fall of communism but from communism itself. Yet their weakened state is seen to be an ironic, if deserved, twist of fate, since Turkey, as the most eastern front of NATO, was surrounded by socialist states and lived in great fear of socialism's influence for fifty years. A common exclamation I heard about their situation was, "Imagine! Now they work for us!" Because of Turkey's deeper presocialist historical connection to the region, however, the images of peoples from the formerly socialist states varied according to whether they were from the east or west of Turkey, whether they were formerly under Ottoman rule or not, whether they were Turkic or not, and whether they were

Muslim or Christian. Religion is rarely noted as a determining feature for hiring domestics, according to Annelies Moors (2003), but plays an important role here, along with religiosity versus secularism.

In representations of women foreign domestics, their skills are often aligned with whether they are Muslim (Turkmen, Uzbek, Bulgarian Turk, Azeri) or Christian (Moldovan, Romanian, Ukrainian, Georgian, Armenian). In this post-Ottoman context, ethnicity and religion often are assumed to be aligned. Muslims are racialized as a whole as "Turks," and thus are perceived to hold many of the same characteristics of working-class or rural Turks. The latter, the Christian Orthodox, as Bellér-Hann also noted, are divided by ethnicity or race into those from the east and the Caucasus (Armenia and Georgia) and those from the west, sometimes called "White Russians" (*beyaz Ruslar*) (Ukrainians, Moldovans, and Romanians). The term "White Russian" refers to a historical region that included parts of the western Russian Federation and other parts of the East European countries of Belarus, Moldova, Ukraine, Poland, and Slovakia. It is popularly thought to refer to Belarus in particular, since "Belarus" translates as "White Russian," but this contention is refuted by Belarusians themselves. "White Russian" is also associated with the counterrevolutionary White Army, which opposed the Bolshevik Red Army during the early years of the communist revolution in Russia. Many of these bourgeois White Russians fled Russia for Istanbul during that time. The term "White Russian" in Turkey seems to stem from a conflation of both these usages, further adding to the understanding of people from Eastern Europe and western Russia as also cultured. Another image that comes into play in representations of these women stems from Ottoman times. The Ottomans drew on this population for the most valued women of the harem. The most famous was Hurrem Sultan or Roxalanne, for whom Suleyman the Magnificent, a sixteenth-century sultan, wrote famous love poetry. Hurrem Sultan gained great power when her sons took the throne. Thus, the image of the beautiful, ambitious woman from this region reaches back even to Ottoman times.

In the current context, "White Russians" in general and Moldovans in particular are considered presentable, hardworking, and very clean. According to the *Tempo* article and my interviews, Moldovans are perceived to be good at caring for children under the age of one year. After this age, as the *Tempo* article notes, their accented Turkish becomes a point of concern. Some families are also concerned with teaching their children foreign languages. Thus, for children older than one year, Filipinas have become popular as nannies, valued for their knowledge of English, which they are expected to teach the children. One agency also advertises English-speaking Ethiopians, while another boasts French-speaking nannies. For the elderly and invalid, who often have "bathroom business" (*tuvalet işleri*), which means that they will need assistance from the domestic caregiver in toileting and bathing, White Russians and particularly Moldovans are again perceived to be particularly competent and patient. As one agent put it, for child care and elder care, Moldovans are better: "Turkmen and Uzbeks don't like to work for the elderly; they are slower and get tired quickly." However, Turkmen, this agent assured me (as others also did) are great cooks, especially of dough-based foods such as *böreks* and raviolis. Armenians are also represented in Turkey as exceptional cooks, and the migrant domestics from this region are admired for this skill. Employers contrasted women from Turkey's east (most of whom are Muslim, but not all; Armenians and Georgians are Christian, for instance) to those from the west of Turkey, who, as many employers put it, "don't know our vegetables."[13] Interestingly, since my stay in Turkey in 2005, Moldovans have had stiff competition from Bulgarian Turks, who, as Muslims (and Muslims to the west of Turkey, in the Balkans), are often preferred by employers because they are "more like us" (*bizim gibi*) in some ways. At the same time, Bulgarians are presented as better than domestic labor because they are considered more Western. Taking into account the ubiquitous religious versus secular divide in Turkey, along with the rising class of wealthy among Islamists, the *Tempo* article also argues that hiring a local worker might be preferable for more "conservative" families (as opposed to secular Turks), those concerned with having a similar culture and values (Ergul 2002). On the other hand, it is the lack of religiosity, whether Muslim or Christian, that makes migrant domestics from the former Soviet Union and Eastern Europe attractive to secular families.

These valuations index a different regard among employers in Turkey for citizens of different nations within the formerly socialist sphere. Although migration for domestic work is not sanctioned by the state, even the visa regime in Turkey is conditioned by such cultural ideas about those who are "like us" and those who are not. Visa issues in turn often affect the demand for migrant domestic workers from specific states. Bulgarians and Moldovans differ in this respect as well. Bulgarian Turks, because they are Muslim and considered "kin" (*soydaş*) by the state, do not need visas and

---

[13] However, cooking is not necessarily most important to employers. As Lan (2006a) and Akalin (2007) note, many employers continue to do the cooking themselves as a sign of difference from the domestic worker and intimacy with the family.

have access to citizenship in Turkey, whereas Gagauz must obtain tourist visas to enter Turkey and have fewer opportunities to gain citizenship (Parla and Kaşlı 2009). Bulgarian Turks first came to Turkey when Bulgaria's severe policies against its Turkish minorities prompted more than 300,000 to flee to Turkey when communism fell in 1989. Many settled in Turkey, but most returned after the new Bulgarian government offered them their rights. Kemal Kirişci notes that policies for refugee Turkic "kin," such as the Bulgarian Turks and Muslim populations abroad in the Balkans (e.g., Bosnians) and the Caucasus (e.g., Chechens), were somewhat similar (2000). What is interesting is that Gagauz are not categorized as kin because they are Orthodox Christians and are associated with White Russians. This has made it harder on individuals from Gagauz Yeri to travel to and from Turkey. Moldovans entering Turkey receive a one-month tourist visa, which they can extend for up to three months. Most do so and then stay as long as they can, preferring simply to pay the high "overstayer" fines when they leave. Sometimes employers will pay part or all of these fines, but most migrants pay it themselves. Bulgarians have an advantage over Moldovans in terms of being able to enter and leave Turkey without visas and fines, yet even they are required to exit and reenter Turkey every three months.

For an employer, these dictates can mean the difference between a consistent employee and a high turnover rate; between an employee who stays for a year without a break but then leaves for a month or longer and one who has to take a short jaunt across the border every three months. These are major considerations in hiring a foreign domestic, as they can determine retention of the employee (Anderson 2007). The 2002 *Tempo* article claimed that migrant domestics are unreliable; that "they could leave at any time" (*her zaman olmayabiliyorlar*). Yet agencies and employers weigh these visa issues in different ways. Some said that because of the high overstayer fines, Moldovans stay as long as they can, and thus are preferable to Bulgarians, who have to leave every three months (even if just for a weekend) and reenter. Others argued that Bulgarians do not have to pay fines when they go back and forth and thus are worth the short absence so they can make the weekend jaunt across the border.

Of course, none of these issues would be a problem if employers hired foreign domestics legally. Because Turkey has a large population of local "unskilled" labor, to gain a work visa, employers must fill out paperwork with the government declaring that they need a domestic worker as a "skilled" laborer from abroad because they cannot find one locally. They might argue that migrants hold a specialized knowledge in medicine or education that is needed by their family and that such skills cannot be found in Turkey. But this is a difficult argument to make, and I met only one person, a foreign employee of the IOM-Turkey and someone who clearly had suitable contacts, who had done so. People of the middle and upper classes in Turkey try to stay away from the Turkish government and police. These institutions generally are not trusted, and the bureaucracy is known to still be byzantine. Even so, employers I spoke with expressed a desire to hire foreigners legally if they could in a reasonable manner. In the meantime, the undocumented nature of this migrant labor, and the lack of recourse to legal channels for their migration and work, make gendered notions of value about these women—overlapping with ideas of class, citizenship, ethnicity, race, nationality, religion and religiosity—even more important in determining hiring decisions and trust between employer and employee. Turkic Muslim peoples from Central Asia and Bulgarian Turks are valued for their cooking and for having similar "values"; like local domestics, however, they also are perceived as a bit lazy and not particularly clean or cultured. By contrast, White Russians, Moldovans the best among them, are valued as European, professional, educated, modern, clean, cultured, and very hardworking—domestics who can serve as visible markers of a modern home. These ideas have even made their way into the visa regime in Turkey, which in turn informs employers' decisions further.

These representations and practices of the employers and agencies and their demand for foreign domestics are complex indicators of shifting gendered moral economies—that is, changes in the economy and in ideas about what constitutes a "civilized" household and the gendered labor in it—in Turkey today. In these discourses, we find a desire to live a lifestyle where one can treat domestic workers as skilled professionals. This is a desire only fulfilled, employers here argue, when they hire foreign workers. The shifts in the discourse of civilization in Turkey indicate a concern with a different degree of progress than in the Republican era and a continued effort to become modern. Influential in this is the neoliberal capitalist processes that have made private child and elder care too expensive and not preferable to providing such care at home. Alongside the shifting economic conditions and changes in the family structure in Turkey are new moralities guided by gendered ideas about a modern lifestyle, about becoming a new kind of employer of domestic workers and enacting a new way to employ them. Influencing this discourse are ideas about free-market principles, the conspicuous consumption of new identities, and a concern with individual rights—influenced, no doubt, by the EU accession process. The employers I interviewed described the process of finding help in terms a businessperson might use, as a "market" (*piyasa*) for domestic workers, where the foreign domestic workers have the advantage in terms of skills.

When asked about the undocumented nature of these migrant domestics, employers all felt that there should be open borders and that this foreign labor should be legalized. Believing in free-market principles, they want to be able to hire the best person for the job, no matter what the individual's citizenship is. They insisted that their preference has to do with skills held by these women as modern workers, and that they are not discriminating against laborers in Turkey. If they could find a local worker who did the work like this, they would hire them. In fact, they hope that with open borders, the new workers coming from abroad could teach a thing or two about professionalism to "our workers" (*bizimkiler*).

Whereas an older generation in Turkey felt responsible for civilizing local domestics (who were part of the family, but not quite) according to the then modern urban ideals, a younger generation has given up on that project, envisioning the neoliberal and free labor market itself as a civilizing force for the fittest. In this case, Moldovans, seen as white, cultured, educated women, are marked as having the capacity to be the fittest, whereas local laborers are not (Akalin 2007). These younger families seek a way out of the traditional patron-client relationship and appeal to the market principle of hiring the best worker for the job. Employing Moldovans allows these families to embody these new ideals and statuses. Moldovan and other female laborers from the former Soviet republics and Eastern Europe thus have begun to create new demands in Turkey and to occasion new ideas about domestic work itself, about who should fulfill these roles, and about modern womanhood and contemporary lifestyles.

Gendered Contradictions and Conflicts

Taking on these new forms of modernity in Turkey, however much desired, is a fraught process marked by ambivalence, as is evident in the shifting gendered moral economies of demand for migrant domestics. These migrant domestics are taken as modern by Istanbulus, but in being perceived as such they are also characterized as ambitious and driven. This endowment prompts contradictory expectations of the work of employees, as well as sometimes strict surveillance, poor work conditions, and even termination of employment. As a result, employers often find themselves in conflict with their employees over their gendered labor, womanhood, and sexuality. This situation is not unlike that experienced by racialized migrant domestics in other contexts (see Constable 1997b; Chang and Groves 2000; Hondagneu-Sotelo 2002), yet with an interesting twist, since it is their perceived whiteness and Westernness, not their perceived darkness and inferiority, that cast Moldovans as overly sexualized.

Even as employers in Turkey seeking a new modernity try to position themselves differently from their parents' generation, the tasks of domestic work—cleaning, cooking, and caring—continue to be traditionally associated with the woman of the house, the wife and mother. Even if separated out in representations of the modern and specialized Moldovan, domestic workers are still often expected to be an intimate and compassionate companion to their employers. This is particularly true if they are charged with taking care of children or an elderly person. Indeed, they are valued because (unlike locals) they can fulfill the role of the housewife. Despite their being hired as specialized professionals, conflations of the roles these women play in the house and mixed expectations of the tasks they will perform are commonplace, just as in other instances of domestic work. With Gagauz, as with local domestics before them, these relations of care work are still mostly marked by the use of familial terms. Most domestics I knew called their elderly charges "mother" or "father," or were "older sister" to a young child (see also Akalin 2007). As the other "other woman" in the house, these domestics crossed conventional gendered categories of mother, daughter, sister, wife, caretaker, homemaker, and worker (Özbay 1999).[14] Thus, even though they need domestic help, the Turkish women of the household feel threatened by the domestic worker as a competitor for the affection of their children, husband, or parent, as a cook and caretaker, and even as a lover, but more generally for the role of woman of the house.

These conflations are complicated in the case at hand, for Gagauz women pose an even greater threat than local domestics might in Turkey. Moldovans are not easily identifiable as a working class in Turkey; they are considered educated, modern secular women who are mothers and workers, and thus do not fit the image of the domestic worker as a woman who is uneducated, more religious than her employers, and perhaps from a village in Turkey. These migrant domestic workers, then, not only transgress notions of family, worker, and woman but further disturb category boundaries between clean

---

[14] For more on this in the case of doormen's wives and their employers in Ankara, see Özyeğin (2001, 2002).

and dirty, orderly and disorderly, public and private, civilized and backward, urban and rural, and religious and secular that previously existed in Turkey, when either kin women of the household did this labor or a local working-class villager was hired.

From my observations of households and interviews with employers, I found three sets of conflicts were common. First, while calling for a "professional" caretaker, and even creating and signing contracts with them, employers in practice often contradicted their professed interest in conducting employer-employee relations in a professional way. Though the employers claimed they separated household labors—a domestic might be hired only to do baby caretaking, for instance—in reality, household jobs frequently overlapped. As Akalin argues, women are valued for their flexible labor, for their willingness to do work as a housewife would, out of concern (Akalin 2007). These women are also valued for their ability to do work out of their own sense of duty or morality, in a moral economy of domestic work much like that illuminated by Nare in the case of migrant domestics in Italy (2011). This overlap in duties and the need for flexibility is inherent to the situation of domestic work more generally (see Constable 1997a, 2002; Ehrenreich and Hochschild 2002), and especially when children get older and, for instance, feeding the child segues into feeding the family. Even when the charge is still an infant, chores such as ironing baby clothing blend into the labor of doing cleaning and ironing in general.

In two of the households I investigated, for instance, there were a number of different domestics, and the division of labor was such that the caretaking tasks went to the domestic from Moldova and the cooking and cleaning tasks went to one or two local domestics. The employers were proud to express, however, that the workers got along and often helped each other out. Ironically, even though the caretaker's professionalism stems from specialized labor, if a domestic worker refused to help out with other tasks, it would be seen as unprofessional. Despite the argument that it is their special skills and professionalism for which foreigner workers are hired, it is in fact the Moldovans' willingness to do anything and everything—to *not* distinguish between tasks, and to be flexible—that marks them as good workers as opposed to local workers.

If this was so at the most Westernized of households, in homes of more moderate means or in households somewhat less concerned with Westernized modernity, where the migrant domestic was the sole domestic laborer, such conflations of duties as in the old, *à la Turka* way were routine and expected. In fact, it is important to point out that while most of the employers I describe were from a relatively stable, Westernized wealthy elite, some families hiring Moldovans are seeking to move up into this class (the new wealthy), while those from an older elite may hire Moldovans to maintain their status. In these diverse households, gendered moral economies are constructed similar to those I cite here, but they also vary with the particularities of generation, education, wealth, ethnicity, religion, and religiosity of specific employers. This becomes evident in the second type of conflict between employers and employees, over the ambitions, real or perceived, of the foreign domestic worker.

Moldovans in Turkey are often represented as desperate and as women who are ambitiously maneuvering for a better situation, whether that takes the form of a higher-paying and an easier job or marriage to a local Turk. Though they are admired for being hardworking, the suspicion of their "drivenness" is palpable in these representations and practices. This is a quality that, like ambition (*hırs*), is seen in Turkey as inappropriate for any woman, let alone a domestic worker. Yet the accusation of ambition is also class-based and has to do with the domestics' sometimes rural origins.

For instance, I came to know an elderly Turkish male employer who had cancer and whose children had hired a woman from Gagauz Yeri to take care of him, as he lived alone. A successful lawyer all his adult life, he had lost his wealth and status in his later years. His domestic worker was in the process of telling me about how she was working in Turkey to raise money to build a bigger and better house in Gagauz Yeri when he interrupted her: "You want too much! You are just a villager!" She retorted, "If you can want more for yourself and your family, why shouldn't I?" It seems to me that the chip on this particular man's shoulder about his caretaker's ambitions had to do with his fruitless attempts at maintaining his own power in his family and community, and with his unenviable situation as an elderly man no longer able to support himself economically or physically. It was typical of individuals of this declining class and generation to sigh and express (either outright or in subtle ways) resentment of where they have "ended up"—sorely dependent on (*muhtaç*) foreign women domestic workers hired by their adult children, who have neither the time nor the space to care for their elders in their own homes.[15] These types of conflicts were rarer in households—and among employers of a younger generation—that were more secure in both their wealth and status.

---

[15] On the difficulties of caring for an adult who is used to being independent, see Lynn Rivas (2002).

These conflicts take on a special hue for younger Turkish women of the house, who may perceive the domestic worker's ambitions as aimed at being the woman of the house herself, married to the employer's husband. The third point of contention I came across regularly, and one related to this driven quality, had to do with domestics' womanhood and sexuality. Their well-kept looks, education, and "cultured" ways serve to reflect the Westernization and modernness of homes. Yet these characteristics, as with the image of the natasha, are yoked to a suspicion of women from the former Soviet Union and Eastern Europe as morally loose and potential sexual predators. This dual perspective positions them for conflict and even exploitation. What they wore and how they looked, whom they spoke to inside and outside the home (particularly if it was men), and whether and how they were deferential became sources of contention in the household. These kinds of tensions made working as a domestic difficult for the women I came to know and contributed to why they would leave a job.

Part of the problem in this situation lies in the assumptions about the nature of domestic work as woman's work, in the conditions of waged domestic work, particularly migrant waged domestic work, and in the symbolism associated with domestic work. For decades, socialists and feminists have called attention to the inequities involved in being an unpaid wife, mother, and homemaker and the often hidden—or at best unacknowledged—reproductive labors associated with the housework, care work, and even sex work involved in these roles (Ehrenreich and Hochschild 2002). Initially, feminists argued that paid domestic work and care work held some potential to change this situation. Yet, even if the work is waged, two factors continue to be a challenge. First, even if waged, domestic work is still considered woman's work and bundles the roles of women as kin, cleaners, and caretakers. Second, in most cases, even if it is waged and thus acknowledged as labor, this work, and the women who do it, are often still hidden from view. Barbara Ehrenreich and Arlie Hochschild point out that this invisibility helps preserve the illusion that the woman of the house is doing it all (2002). They attribute this to the Western value of individualism, yet it seems clear that such illusions are found outside the West. In the West and beyond, conspiring with political economic conditions is the domestic worker's symbolic association with "dirty work." In holding a liminal position, the domestic worker protects other household members from real and symbolic association with dirty work. According to Lan, this allows families to maintain or construct new boundaries and hierarchies in the household (2006a).

Care work and domestic work, as we have seen in the case of migrant workers employed in Turkey's domestic space, can be visible work too, showing households to be modern and civilized. However, even when valued for their presumed culture, as Moldovans are, waged domestic workers must also deal effectively with the work that the woman employer does not, such as cleaning and caregiving tasks that place them in association with filth, as in bathing children or helping elderly take care of their "bathroom business." Their labor keeps the woman of the house pure (although still less pure than men). If the woman of the house enters this realm at all, it is as manager. Aggravating this situation is the fact that the woman of the house, her children, her husband, and often an elderly parent are entirely dependent on the care worker for their most basic needs. Especially when the dependent is an elderly invalid who needs help with daily bodily functions and bathing, this can be a quite personal and intimate kind of care (see Lan 2002). If an outsider undertakes such care for a parent, then other family members of the household do not have to do it, thus protecting the traditional hierarchies in which elderly are the most respected (and not the most dependent) in the household. If a domestic caregiver leaves suddenly, there is little option but for an adult child to take on this role, even if temporarily. Thus the domestic worker protects the boundaries between parent and child in the case of elder care in a society in which hierarchy by age is respected among all classes. Yet doing so also can cause resentment on the part of the employers, who then feel the family is beholden to the domestic. This gives the domestic a power that discomfits the employer.

These kinds of conflicts over the gendered nature of domestic work take on particular meanings in specific cases, where differences in class, race, or ethnicity between the woman of the house and the domestic are heightened (Palmer 1989). This is even more so in the case of migrant domestic workers, usually third-world women laboring for first-world women, for issues of nationality and citizenship also come into play. Among the variety of domestic work cases that have been researched worldwide, the relationships between women employers in Turkey and domestics from Gagauz Yeri working in Turkey is peculiar. Gendered notions of citizenship, race, ethnicity, class, and religion all work to visibly mark Moldovans as modern and civilized, not as traditional women. This is different from most cases of migrant domestics, who are seen as racialized, traditional, and backward others, and consequently are deemed appropriate for domestic work. Yet even with these differences in representations, both sets of migrant domestic workers, those considered modern and progressive and those deemed traditional and backward, suffer from being sexualized, and both then are seen as threats to the woman of the house.

Feminists have long argued for acknowledging "invisible" caring and "labors of love," or domestic work that entails taking care of the physical and emotional needs of the family (Constable 1997a, 1997b; Chang and Groves 2000).[16] Hardt and Negri have pointed to the significance of "immaterial labor," which they define as "the affective labor of human contact and interaction" (2001, 292), as characteristic of the postmodernizing global economy. They note: "This labor is immaterial, even if it is corporeal and affective, in the sense that its products are intangible, a feeling of ease, well being, satisfaction, excitement, or passion" (292). Though Hardt and Negri see immaterial labor as a new phenomenon, theirs is simply a new conceptualization of what many feminists have been saying all along. Both these analyses help us to place immaterial or invisible affective labors, such as the care work involved in a domestic setting, in the context of an increasingly service-oriented neoliberal global economy. This global economy is consumer-driven: The demand for affective labors, which are gendered and also intersect with notions of citizenship, race, ethnicity, nation, religion and religiosity, and sexuality, drives the supply for them. With *waged* domestic work, such labors are in a sense made tangible, for they are turned into a monetary value by means of a contract. According to employers I spoke with from the upper classes in Turkey, the battle to make such intangible labors tangible and openly fair drives them to hire women from Moldova over local laborers. This is not a crude economic calculation. In their vision, it is a modern civilizational choice, a morality. Shifting gendered moral economies in Turkey demonstrate how the demand for migrant domestics from Moldova is premised on their presumed modernity. Nonetheless, the situation is rife with conflicts over what constitutes a modern household, a civilized lifestyle, and appropriate household labor in Turkey today.

The perspectives of employers in Turkey complete the picture of the migrant labor circuit between Gagauz Yeri and Turkey at the supply point and the demand point. Just as women migrants from Gagauz Yeri are moving up or down their own class scale back in Moldova and using gendered moral economies to do so, Turkish employers' notions of what constitutes civilization in Turkey, connected to the changes in wealth and class and gendered

---

[16] For a good summary of the feminist scholarship on carework, see Ehrenreich and Hochschild (2002); on affective labor, see Hochschild (2002).

household practices among employers described here, are also shifting in this social field of transnational labor. As the mobile labor circuit enters Turkey, the image of the cultured, educated woman who contributes to the demand and desire for Moldovan domestics works to their advantage in getting jobs, and even in living in Istanbul. Yet the obverse face of the image is more fraught, for it makes migrant women vulnerable to certain exploitations there.

Chapter 4

Working in Istanbul

The shifting gendered moral economies in Turkey create the demand for migrant domestics from Moldova, and construct the contours for Gagauz women's lives in Istanbul. Migrant worker-mothers bring their own perspectives and skills to this experience, navigating the ins and outs of this migration and labor with considerable deft. Natalia's story, given here, illustrates the contradictory effects of their agency. Ultimately, her narrative tells us about the benefits that women gain from this migrant labor, the exploitations they face, and the limits imposed on their upward mobility.

Natalia's Story

I was tooling around the market in downtown Comrat in late October when I met Natalia. She was working with her sister at a stall selling clothing brought from Turkey. The breezy fall had turned into a cold winter in Moldova, and she was selling turtleneck sweaters. She spoke to me in Russian and I replied in Turkish, as I often did in Gagauz Yeri, since most people at the market could understand it. After quick introductions, Natalia said, "I'm going to Turkey in ten days," and launched into her story. She and her sister, whom she nodded to in the next stall over, had both been to Turkey. Her sister had a child, and they needed money, so they alternated their stints abroad, often for the same employer. "How was it?" I asked. "How was it?" she scoffed. "How is working twenty-four hours a day? Serving someone at midnight— 'Natalia, bring tea!'" she mimicked. "And then you have to get up early, at 7 a.m." "Hard," I replied. "Yeah, it's hard," she said.

Natalia had found work in Istanbul through a firm there run by a woman from Armenia. She likes this woman, she said, because she tells it like it is. The agent does not say that the job is a good one, and then you show up at work and discover that you have an enormous villa to clean. For about $50 a week, this agent also provides housing and food in an apartment with other prospective migrant domestics until Natalia is placed in a job. As is typical of such placement firms, the agent takes a 30 percent cut of Natalia's first month's earnings, and then at least another 30 percent of the salary from the employer. For Natalia, the $90 was worth it because, as she told me, if you do not like the job, you can call the agent and tell her to find you another one. You do not have to stay stuck in a bad place. Natalia threw her shoulders back and her head up, and said, "And I speak up." If Natalia does not like a job or it is inappropriate for her somehow, she says something about it: "I am not like some village woman, who will thank God for any job they give me no matter what, and stay quiet," she added.

Natalia understands the ins and outs of undocumented migrant labor in Turkey. She said that she tries to stay away from Laleli as much as possible. She explained that even so, she has to go there sometimes to send things home on the minibuses that transport gifts and remittances to Moldova. She described the extortion that is a routine part of being an undocumented migrant worker in Turkey. "The police give us a hard time," she explained, "and I'm just too old to deal with it. They are younger than I am! I don't owe them an explanation!" She does not want to have to justify her presence in Laleli: that she is just there to shop and send money home; that her family called her and said they needed something and she has to send it; that *this* is why she is in Laleli; that her presence has nothing to do with anything else. I looked at her questioningly for the latter remark, and she continued:

Our women have a reputation in Turkey. How should I put it? Your men fancy our women.[1] And 10 percent of the women deserve the reputation: There is nothing they wouldn't do for ten or twenty dollars. And we have destroyed Turkish families, split up husbands and wives. But the other 90 percent pay for it by being harassed by the police.

During her last commute, Natalia said, her agent had found her a good job in the Bosphorus neighborhood of Sariyer on the outskirts of Istanbul, and she worked there for seven months, for a married couple with a sixteen-year-old daughter. The husband worked in the United States and often was not around. The wife also worked. Sometimes, Natalia said, the wife worked so hard she felt bad for her. "The wife trusted me," Natalia explained. "When I went to work for her, she showed me my room downstairs and told me I could arrange the furniture any way I wanted, and if there was a problem she would tell me." Natalia had a television of her own in her room, and the family had a satellite dish, so she watched Russian television.

Natalia liked that she had some control over when she did which work in this household. Yet there was a schedule. She got up at 7 a.m., made breakfast, and got the teenager off to school. Then she prepared breakfast for the mother. After the mother left for work, Natalia had the place to herself and could do her work on her own time. The teenager got home around 4 p.m., and Natalia would have something ready for her to eat. Then the girl would watch television, talk on the phone, or email, and Natalia could go back downstairs to her room and watch television. Natalia would come back up to make dinner around 6 p.m. At 8 p.m. the mother came home, and they ate together. Natalia cleaned up, and was usually back in her room for the night at 9 p.m. I asked her if she ever had to work after that, for example if there were guests to serve, but she said that in the time she was there, guests came only about three times (this was not the place she referred to in her original statement, where she was on call twenty-four hours a day).

As is customary, Natalia had obtained a one-month tourist visa to enter Turkey, and then had overstayed her visa term by six months. To get a free ride home, she and her sister had turned themselves in to the Foreigner's Office (*Yabancı Şube*) of police headquarters in Istanbul. They decided to risk police abuse to get the free ride. After spending a week at the station's

---

[1] She said "your" here meaning me, as a Turkish person. Unlike most others whom I interviewed, Natalia did not know that I was an American of Turkish descent.

"guest house" (*misafirhane*, which is actually a jailhouse where, when caught, undocumented migrants are housed temporarily)[2] with other undocumented migrants, they were sent by boat to the Ukrainian port of Odessa (see map I.2). From there, minibuses run frequently to all parts of Moldova. Now, after a year back in Gagauz Yeri, she was returning to Istanbul to work. She had acquired a transit visa to go through Bulgaria and would be traveling by bus, a fifteen-hour trip. But because she had been deported, legally she could not reenter Turkey for five years. Natalia had found a way around this, too: she had the name on her passport changed back to her maiden name and so was traveling as a "different" person.

This chat with Natalia touches on the major themes of this book in several ways. Natalia couched her experience in cultural terms, in the frame of the gendered moral economies of the supply of migrant labor, by presenting herself both as an educated Russophone urbanite working abroad as a domestic and as a woman whose duty it is to work to support her family. Her narrative also indicates her attempts to position herself within the new expectations and subjugations that women encounter in Turkey as "driven" women from the former Soviet Union and Eastern Europe, as undocumented migrant workers, and as domestics whose role in the household moves fluidly between that of kin and that of worker. The image of the Moldovan—marked by notions of citizenship, class, race, ethnicity, and religion—creates the gendered moral economy of the demand for women from formerly socialist states in Istanbul as sex workers, tourist traders, and domestics. Yet the dark side of this image, the figure of an ambitious, "driven" woman and sexual predator, subjects these same women to exploitation and disciplinary measures in their places of work and on their days off.

Natalia and others manipulate their high cultural capital in Istanbul to gain employment, but that same cultural capital is used against them, becoming grist for the exploitation of these illegal migrant domestic workers. The women from Gagauz Yeri whom I came to know take pride in being known as "cultured" and hardworking: as many put it, "We don't fear work." But they know they are vulnerable to maltreatment and exploitation as a result of this perception and their status as undocumented migrants. They detailed how they often are not treated as professionals and their work tasks

---

[2] The place is now known as a "return center" (Porla 2011). Regardless, police hold these migrants until there are enough of them to get a group-rate ticket on the boat. This sometimes takes a few weeks. Usually, I heard of them holding people for a week or ten days.

do not have clear limits. They told me how they are taken advantage of as hard workers, underpaid, and have to face various kinds of harassment. A minibus driver from the Gagauz town of Beşalma whom I interviewed illustrated with his notebook the perceived difference between workers from Gagauz Yeri and those from Turkey. If someone hires a Turk, he explained, they will do only the one thing they are hired to do (he gestured to half a page in his notebook). But if you hire someone from Gagauz Yeri, they will do everything, they will do it all (his hand swept over the whole page), and then they will open it up, do the inside, turn it over, and do the back. Yet these very characteristics can backfire to make the working lives of migrant women from Gagauz Yeri very difficult, when employers take advantage of their work ethic or have contradictory expectations. Referring to Turkish employers, Dussa, a teacher from Beşalma, put it this way: "There is no such thing as a good job or a bad job, but there *are* good people and bad people." Natalia, having been to Turkey several times, had found a manageable situation. But unfortunately, many migrant women are able to find "good work" only after experiencing several exploitative situations. In the narratives I relate in this chapter, women detail how those very aspects of cultural capital they are hired for—a strong work ethic, education, culturedness, attractiveness, and modernity—become a point of contention in Turkish households.

Though the high cultural capital of Moldovans in Turkey poses particular challenges, migrant domestics demonstrate a great deal of agency in working through them. Their cultural capital becomes a way for these migrant workers to mollify their chagrin over their downward mobility from white-collar workers to domestics. According to Pei-Chia Lan, Filipinas, who are held in high esteem as workers in Taiwan, do this by pointing to their similarities and even superiority to their employers (2006a, 2010). As in that case, here too, such discursive practices enact and remake class, racial, and gendered differences. However, these practices do not necessarily lessen their exploitation. If contentions heighten into conflict with employers, as undocumented migrant workers they have no recourse to the law. To gain some semblance of trust and security in this system, then, women maneuver inside and outside their workplaces in Istanbul by deploying the gendered notions and stereotypes that subjugate them. Sometimes they are exploited because of these stereotypes: when their employers or police activate them to justify the policing and surveillance of migrant women. At other times, migrant women deftly use these perceptions and stereotypes to their own advantage, to get jobs or money, gain favor and gifts, or secure their own safety. An interesting comparison case is described by Denise Brennan (2004). In her ethnography, sex workers in the Dominican Republic are highly valued by foreign tourists. Because these women see foreign men as potential routes to Europe and advancement, Brennan concludes, "relations across borders reinforce racial and gender stereotypes, hierarchies, and inequalities, but they can also be a vehicle for advancement for women" (99). Women migrants demonstrate a great deal of strategic agency through the manipulation of representations. Those from Gagauz Yeri often said that they "fell into" a job with a good or bad employer. Yet it is clear from their narratives that they are actively evaluating "good" and "bad" Turkish employers in this informal labor market and deploy gendered stereotypes about themselves strategically to find good work.

Although women from Gagauz Yeri obviously "go for the money," because of the undocumented nature of this migration and work, more important than making the highest wage is finding a good and trustworthy employer who treats domestic workers humanely and shows a caring attitude, one often demonstrated in the informal offering of gifts and favors. Such affective rewards function to cleanse the "dirty work" that these women do and build more secure relations in this informal economy. Because of their past experience with the underground economy during Soviet times, such a situation is not unfamiliar to them. To succeed here and now, as there and then, takes a sensibility that, as the famous Russian saying goes, sees the value of 100 friends over 100 rubles.

This dynamic may demonstrate the formerly socialist context of this case of migrant domestic work in some ways, but it can also be found in other case studies. Lena Nare found that domestics in Italy from the former socialist states of Poland and Ukraine seek out moral relations with their employer similar to those I describe for the Gagauz below. But according to her comparative analysis, these practices are common also to Sri Lankan domestics in Italy (2011). She notes that all these migrants prefer using kin terms to make their work relations more familial. For them, migrant work is about dependency and reciprocity as much as it is about wages. She points out that some feminists have argued that such practices can worsen or continue inequality between employers and employees (2011, 180; see also Romero [1992] 2002; Bakan and Stasiulis 1997a). Yet Nare argues that such claims assume "economic maximization" as the ultimate goal, which was not the goal of migrants she studied. For both women migrants from former socialist states and others, such moral economies, whether of socialist origin or not, do not work to hide exploitations but instead can help lessen them.

Taking an even broader view, it is clear that in all these cases, ideas about gender are key features of these moral economies. Just as with the former East German villagers that Daphne Berdahl describes in her ethnography, here, too, gender plays a strong role in women from the former Soviet Union working through new relationships with capitalist others and in conceptualizing their difference from them (1999). Yet we should remember that this could be true of women from other kinds of states and economic backgrounds as well. More generally, employers and employees use gender to make sense of their new relationships across various boundaries. For Gagauz migrant domestic workers, cultural notions of gender help them interpret men's and women's behavior in Turkey, structure these new relationships, and legitimate the work they do. Thus, the functioning of this transnational labor market is determined not solely by economics but also by gendered ideas about good work and decent people.

This chapter presents a complex and nuanced narrative description of Gagauz women's migrant domestic labor in Turkey from their own perspective. Their insights force us to rethink conventional and academic understandings of work, power, and agency in all migrant women's work. Academics; policymakers in Moldova, Turkey, and the United States and at intergovernmental organizations such as the International Organization for Migration (IOM); Turkish police officers; Turkish employers; employment agencies; and even women migrants themselves tend to loosely group migrant women according to the labors they do and the agency they hold. Those who do "sex work"—or those who are willing to use their sexuality for various ends—are distinguished from domestic workers and "suitcase-traders." And they often position these labors along a forced labor–voluntary labor continuum: sex work is perceived as forced labor, whereas domestic work and trade are not. In these representations, sex work is treated as a special case of migrant labor, and women from the former Soviet Union and Eastern Europe, as white, cultured women from the periphery of Europe (not the third world), are treated as a special case of migrant women forced into sex work (a view that dismisses the possibility that they do a variety of work) because of their class, citizenship, race, ethnicity, and religion. However, it is clear from the Gagauz and other cases detailed here that we must see all migrant women as in some way agents who use various kinds of labor (e.g., domestic work, trade, sex work); gendered cultural codes about their reputed attractiveness and assertiveness; and others' pity for them to secure advancement, security, and at times even survival. Moreover, taken as a whole these gendered labors have economic, morally motivated, and affective dimensions. These dimensions, and the overlapping nature of all women's work, affect Gagauz migrant women's agency and exploitations in searching for a good job and in coping with gendered challenges on and off the job.

Finding Good Work

Because the market for mobile migrant labor in Turkey is unregulated, it is not surprising that women's experiences in finding work and their expectations of and experiences with work conditions and compensation varied a great deal and changed over time, especially between their initial trips and later ones, when they had more knowledge of the marketplace. Stumbling onto bad jobs, described as "landing in a bad place" (*kötü yere düşmek*), meant having to deal with spoiled children, with grumpy and mean elderly people, and especially with Turkish female employers' jealousy or men's sexual harassment. Good employers, by contrast, treated them with respect and were appreciative and generous. Although being treated as a professional and being paid well mattered to the migrant women workers from Gagauz Yeri, what mattered more was the respect and care that employers showed them. In a good job, employers treated a domestic as kin in the household and were generous not just with salary but also with food, favors, and gifts. Such affective and material exchanges helped build security and trust.

The women workers' previous socialist experience came into play in their interpretation of these relationships in two main ways. First, the women I met exhibited particular sensitivity to the gender and class inequities involved in the relationship between employer and employee in the market-based Turkish society and in the gendered labor of serving a family.[3] Second, genuine caring demonstrated by employers for domestic workers and reciprocated by the worker helped cleanse an otherwise uncomfortable and instrumental labor-for-money exchange between the domestic and her charge or employer. These women's experience with the informal moral economy of favors during the socialist era had prepared them especially well to participate in undocumented labor under a new economic regime and had provided a basis for their expectations and understanding of this work and its appropriate compensation. In the Soviet era, women in particular were

---

[3] For an interesting case of how Russian teachers reject new expectations that they "serve" a newly wealthy Russian elite, see Jennifer Patico (2005).

adept at negotiating *blat*, a type of informal exchange or bribery for goods or services in the context of lack (see Bruno 1997). It thus is not unusual to them for labor relations to have both affective and economic dimensions. And though such exchanges may result in material gain, we should be careful not to interpret domestic workers' caring for their charges or seeking care from their employers as superficial and instrumental. As in *blat* relations in the former Soviet Union, described in depth by Alena Ledeneva (1998), Dale Pesmen (2000), and others (Bruno 1997; Ries 2002), these women may seem as though they are manipulating kinship and friendship ties for economic gain, but they are also simultaneously acting out of sincere feelings of kinship and friendship.

Though there is something peculiarly "formerly socialist" about these expectations of the rights and obligations extending between an employer and employee, migrant domestics in other contexts (e.g., postcolonial ones) are no doubt also attuned to the ironies, inequities, and conversions involved in the shift from patron-client relations to market-based employer-employee relations, and seek more affectively meaningful relationships with their employers. Certainly, discomfort during such transitions in economic regime is not limited to those from formerly socialist states. Uncomfortable changes from older lifestyles to newer ones are occurring among Turkish employers as well, as a wealthy younger generation seeks to distance itself from the traditional ways of an older generation, including eschewing the traditional treatment of domestic staff. As a result, there is some confusion surrounding expectations of domestic work. Moreover, sensitivities about the conflations of women's roles in the household (kin or worker? family or outsider?) are inherent in the situation of the gendered, affective labor of domestic work itself, especially undocumented labor. In this way, the resulting contentions and conflicts detailed here and the gendered moral economies in play align with what has been observed in other cases of migrant domestic work. These commonalities notwithstanding, there are notable particularities in the case of migrant domestic work performed in Turkey by women from Gagauz.

Domestic Work for Former Socialists

Because of the conflation of roles and the kinds of labor involved, the conditions of undocumented migrant domestic work hold many challenges for women workers, such as not being in control of one's own time or space (Constable 1997a, 2002; Ehrenreich and Hochschild 2002). Women from formerly socialist states interpret and negotiate these conditions in particular ways and are especially challenged by the condition of "serving." The women I spoke with explained that in migrant domestic work, there is no clocking in and out each day, and most women get only part of one day, from 9 a.m. to 5 p.m., off per week (for a well-detailed example, see Constable 1997a). As Stesha, who had worked at two different places in Istanbul, put it:

> It is difficult, very stressful. I mean, one week you have to stay in one house, you don't go out at all, and you serve that family, you cannot act as you like, you cannot eat what you want, you are not at ease, and in the end, it is not your house.

Miriam (Tatya's friend, the bookkeeper at the *internat*, introduced in chapter 1) too explained how in this type of live-in domestic work, even if you have your own room, "You cannot say, 'My work is over now,' then go to your room and shut the door. They can get you up whenever they want and say 'Do this' and 'Do that.'" Miriam indicated that in all of these jobs, "there is no time," meaning that the domestic worker is not on a clock and can be called on at any time to work.

In another conversation, Stesha (Rosa's daughter, introduced in chapter 2) told me that her Moldovan friend Oksana, whom she had met in Turkey and who works in the *site* where Stesha lives with her husband, has an employer who works all day and then comes home and unloads her stress on Oksana. I had spent several Sundays with Stesha and Oksana at Stesha's apartment in Istanbul. On this day, we were sitting around Stesha's dining table, having tea. I interviewed Stesha formally, and Oksana frequently commented as well. Oksana works for a family caretaking a five-year-old girl, and often visits Stesha when she has time off during the week and all day on Sundays. Although Oksana considered her job a good one (she had returned to it several times over the past three years), Stesha, who had also worked as a domestic in several different places, explained some of the difficulties this way:

> They say things like "you can eat what you want, you should feel you are in your own home," but if you go ahead and act like that, they take account of it. If you just open the fridge and eat anything you want like you would at home, later they will ask, "Where is that food?"

Even in "good places," a domestic's time and space are not her own, and she can never really relax. If they are caretaking an invalid who is entirely dependent on them, the domestic's mobility becomes a particular point of contention. For instance, if Sveta (Tatya's sister) went to the store and was out for more than half an hour, her charge would question her why it took so long, what she had done. Such situations are not uncommon for domestics working for the elderly (Rivas 2002). And, as in Nicole Constable's account of the conditions of Filipinas working in Hong Kong (1997a, 2002), in Istanbul domestics found that when and for how long they took showers and how long they were in the bathroom was noted. Also under scrutiny was to whom a domestic spoke on the phone (even if it was her own cell phone) and for how long, and what, when, where, and how she ate—as well as when and what she watched on television, how long she slept, whether she smoked or drank, and even where and when she sat. Discipline could be meted out for transgressions of the employer's expectations regarding these practices.

Even if a caretaking situation was manageable for the domestic worker, it was very hard for them to be away from their homes. The feeling of "not being at home" in the place they lived in in Istanbul was heightened by the fact that they are foreigners who have to deal with things like language misunderstandings and strange foods, which posed daily challenges. Most of all, many spoke of missing their families, friends, and homes in Gagauz Yeri. In elder care or invalid care, often the domestic's chore was to sit with her charge for most of the day and keep the person company. In cases like these, Tatya explained, time passed very slowly; you longed for Sunday, when you would have some time off, and then that day would go by very quickly. Anna and Angela, the mother and daughter from Tomay who for years tag-teamed their trips to work for one family in Istanbul, said they worked in child care so that they would be busy and time would pass more quickly. Yet even Angela admitted to me that she had a daily ritual of waking up and crossing off the day on her calendar: "I'd cross it off at the *beginning* of the day," she emphasized. She just could not wait for it to end.

Another difficulty for these women was the very fact that they had to serve another person. To express this, many I spoke with contrasted this kind of work with the work they could do in Moscow or on their farms in Gagauz Yeri. Olga, for instance, said she would not return to Turkey. She preferred to go to Moscow. She and Tatya explained to me their perspective on how these jobs compared:

Olga: It is hard there [in Moscow]. Construction work is hard. But you work with your friends, and you leave it at night.

Tatya: But it is hard there because it is physical labor, but your mind is at ease. In Turkey, the [Turkish] ladies say, "Look at how you've done this; that is wrong," and this does something to your morale. It is not physically difficult, but it is extremely hard. But in Moscow that doesn't exist. He gives it [work] to you: "You are going to do this room; you do it like this." Okay. They bring you the materials, you work, they leave, they come and check in, say: "Do it like this and this," and that is it. But in a physical sense, it is hard. You have a day off, Sundays, and they give you a place to stay. We would go out with friends on that day, with our own people.

Tatya and Stesha had both worked as traders, for different reasons and in different capacities. Like Natalia, whose story began this chapter, neither Tatya nor Stesha viewed trading particularly negatively, or at least they were able to find the moral ground to participate in it. Anna, by contrast, was proud that she and her family had never participated in sales. These positionalities were also reflected in their respective views of domestic work. Here, we find one of the specificities in the narratives of Gagauz domestic workers as opposed to other domestics: the problem of serving took on particular salience for those who still identified as former communists. For Anna's daughter Angela, as for Natalia, having to do all that work and then act as a servant when guests came was one of the hardest parts of being in domestic service. Coming from a family of committed communists, Angela attested that this sentiment stemmed from her socialist roots. Overlapping with these values was that physical, rural work is particularly valued in Gagauz Yeri. Thus, criticisms of domestic work as indoor and not "hard" work were couched in narratives of physical work (whether rural or construction work) as being harder, more legitimate, and dignified work. This is as much a rural as a socialist morality. With domestic work, women held divergent moralities according to their positionalities, work histories, and current employment, as became evident when they defended working abroad to their community. However, even if one takes into account the differences between women from Gagauz Yeri, these new domestic labors were commonly legitimated and purified through narratives of being a good worker-mother, and also, as we see here, by working for "good people," who offered nonmonetary compensation in the form of understanding and appreciation. These were important considerations in finding work in the unregulated labor market for domestic help in Turkey.

Seeking Good Employers

Problems common to all forms of domestic work include a fluid definition of work time, overlapping duties, being away from home, being in service, and, because of the undocumented nature of the work, the assessment of trust between employer and employee. For Gagauz women working in Turkey, the trust assessment was accomplished in large part through a gendered moral economy of favors. For the women I came to know, what distinguished good places of employment from bad ones were the numerous daily indicators of whether or not the employer would take responsibility (*sahib olmak*) for the domestic worker and expressions of appreciation, such as offers of favors, material items, and kind words. Interestingly, from the Gagauz perspective, while an employer who placed specific limits around the job as "baby caretaker" or "elderly caretaker," as would be expected in a professionalized employment arrangement, was deemed good, many of the other characteristics that the workers appreciated about employers would easily come under the patron-client system, such as offers of favors and gifts and taking responsibility for them. *Blat* of this sort seemed to absolve the economic exchange of the taint of money for labor and create a more meaningful place and secure role for the domestic in the household. This was a means of agency for the migrant domestics I came to know. Although some feminists argue that familializing work relations hides the exploitations that migrant domestics face as workers in the global economy, my observations support Nare's (2011) conclusion that it may also work as a palliative, helping to assuage employees' feelings about exploitative conditions by augmenting the positive aspects of the relationship. Initially, however, many domestic workers from Gagauz Yeri had negative experiences working in Istanbul and only later moved on to more positive experiences.

Many domestics I spoke with said that for a good employer in Turkey, they would do all the overlapping chores without complaint—care for children or elders, clean, cook, iron, wash the windows. But bad employers asked for too much and were not appreciative. Bad employers were those who did not give domestic workers enough time off, did not let the worker out of the house (Miriam was locked inside during the day), and did not allow the worker decent space or sufficient time for herself. Some employers would take money out of the worker's pay to make up for the fees agents charged them. Moreover, some individuals were given a bed in the same room with the child or elderly person they were caretaking. They were not given a drawer or closet for themselves, let alone any privacy.

A Turkish agent who ran her own business on the Asian side, Zeyneb, whom I found to be particularly concerned with her employees' experiences and advocated for them (she had left an agency that abused these women's vulnerabilities), recounted some of the horror stories she had heard of the poor treatment of workers she had placed. She explained, "Sure, there are women who run away, but look at how our people treat them." She described one family who "put the woman to sleep on the balcony, like an animal. Can you imagine? Are these people not human? Don't they deserve to be treated like humans?"

One woman I knew who worked for an elderly invalid was assigned some hooks in a back room where she could hang some of her things, but most of her belongings—clothes, toiletries, and gifts she had bought for her family back home—she put under her bed in the room she shared with her charge. These things were often searched by the employer, who would also check the bags the employee took with her on her way out the door on her day off to make sure the employee had not stolen anything. Others told me that they were expected to take care of pets, and complained that the pets were treated better than they were. Many said that bad employers kept them up until late at night, and then made them get up early in the morning. These negative practices might also be true of good employers, but with bad ones they were taken to an extreme.

Tatya's friend, Olga, a thirty-something villager with whom I spoke at the café in Congaz, described a particularly bad employer in the city of Bursa, outside Istanbul. Olga worked for one month for a family for $300 a month without a day off. She had her own room and bathroom but was hardly there at all: "I got up at 6 a.m. and went to bed at 2 or 3 a.m., working through the night," she said. The problem was that all the women of the house, the wife and two daughters, were around all day and night and demanded that she serve them in various ways, ignoring the fact that she had other work (the cleaning and cooking she was hired to do).

> If they left, you are left alone, you can do your work, but these people were there all day; you have to serve them, you cannot do your own work. So I would get up early to do the work. I'd turn on the dishwasher and the younger sister would get mad: "I can't sleep with that noise." I couldn't

keep up with the work, that is why I left. . . . The mother would say to do one thing, but when you did it, the other would get mad and ask why you are doing that now.

The women even demanded she give them massages. "I felt like I was losing my mind!" Olga exclaimed. Moreover, while she was initially employed to work for one family, she ended up working for their parents, who lived upstairs, as well. Tatya explained that some employers do not tell you what work you will be doing. You only find out when you get there:

They know that you have no other choice [at that point]. They say, "You cannot leave now, you don't know anyone, you don't understand anything, where are you going to go at night?," and you are forced to stay there.

Tatya knew that in this respect, migrants differed from local domestics: undocumented migrants were more vulnerable to employer whims and bad conditions, whereas local domestics had citizenship rights and probably had family nearby to appeal to, and many went home at night.[4]

In the initial years of this migrant labor, women were very vulnerable and regularly exploited for their undocumented gendered labors; it was with these experiences in mind that they sought out better jobs later. In the late 1990s and early 2000s many women from Gagauz Yeri used a local agent (*firma*) to go to Turkey for the first time. One particular firm was incredibly irresponsible in its travel arrangements (overcharging for grossly awful conditions of travel) and employment placements and has since been shut down for trafficking in women.[5] Apparently, this firm consisted of a local woman working with a Turkish man; both were jailed for trafficking. It seems that many different people used their services to migrate to and work in Turkey,

---

[4] Local domestics, as citizens, are offered some form of social security from the state, whereas migrants are not (though they were in their home states to some extent, especially if they had worked there previously). Although new activism is focusing on legalizing domestic work in Turkey, at present local domestic workers generally are not legally employed either and thus also do not receive any social security as workers, but they do receive it as citizens (for more on local domestics, see Özyeğin 2001). For a thoughtful, much-needed exploration of the politics of local versus foreign domestic workers and the possibility for an alliance between the two kinds of laborers, see Danış and Parla (2009) and Parla (2011). These works are part of a burgeoning literature on migration to Turkey, and Turkey's migration regime. For more, see the edited volume by Ahmet İçduygu and Kemal Kirişci (2009) and Kirişci (2000, 2005).

[5] I tried to confirm this firm's closure independently, but my attempts were unsuccessful; the information I received about this particular firm was all by word of mouth.

including some for domestic work. But then a set of parents could not reach one young woman whom this firm had sent abroad. An investigation revealed that she had been trapped in an apartment and trafficked for forced sex work. The local agent, I was told, was found with more than forty passports in her possession, and had had a great deal of plastic surgery done (presumably with the profits). Whether real or not, such stories underscore the dangers inherent—for women especially—in this undocumented travel and work, and illustrate their fears. They also discriminate, for these women, the gullible from the savvy.

In this unregulated employment market, the agencies varied a great deal. Some in Turkey, such as Zeyneb's firm, were run by women agents who respected their clients and took care to place them in good households. Others I surveyed were egregious in their practices, knowing that a newcomer is particularly vulnerable and cheap. One advertisement stipulated "*newly arrived* Moldovans, Turkmen, Bulgars housework, child care, overnight" (emphasis added). Even though none of the women I met had experienced unpaid, coerced labor, many who had employed the transnational firm that was later shut down for trafficking found themselves in abusive working conditions. As a result, some now refuse to return to Turkey. However, many others fled poor situations to seek better employment and have continued to commute. It was on the second or third trip that women began to show considerable strategic insight for finding good work. They had learned the ropes.

As we were sitting around in Rosa's (Stesha's mom's) living room in Comrat one night, Katya, Rosa's sister, came in with a friend of hers, Victoria, who described her learning curve when it came to migrant work in Turkey. Like Katya and Rosa, Victoria was an urbanite from Comrat in her late forties. She had had a bad initial experience, a position caretaking for two small children that she had found through the questionable transnational firm, then found a better one by herself. At her first place of employment, a Turkish person came in to cook, and she was expected to care for the children for $250 a month. She had only two days off every month and was given poor accommodations, being forced to sleep on a makeshift couch in the laundry room. Victoria also complained about her female employer:

> The husband worked [as] a lawyer; he was a good man. But I didn't like that woman at all. The woman was very cheap. She didn't feed me. She gave me very little food. I became sick. . . . I was patient because our family here was in bad shape. Because of that, I was forced to [stay]. My

daughter says to me, why did you put up with it? I'm actually not that patient a person, but I had to stay. I didn't like that woman. They gave me $250. For that much work, that little pay. . . . After that, I didn't go for two years.

Two years later, Victoria's daughter-in-law was leaving a job in Turkey and asked Victoria to take her place. Many of the migrant domestics I came to know found jobs in this way. The arrangement was described as "ready work" (*hazir iş*), meaning that a candidate worker knew someone who had worked in a position and was returning to Moldova for a period of time, and so was looking for a temporary replacement who could hold her place until she wanted to return. Tatya told me that these "ready" jobs were the best jobs because a domestic worker had already checked out the particular employer and established that she was good. Others, like Natalia, found an agent they liked, many times another woman from the former Soviet Union or Eastern Europe like themselves (as in Natalia's case) whom they trusted. Victoria's daughter and son-in-law had just moved to Chişinău, where they were renting a place, and she wanted to help them out financially. "I have to help them. I only have one daughter!" she said.

This time, Victoria really liked her job and employer: "There cannot be a greater man than the owner of this household!" He was single and lived alone in a big apartment, and in an apartment complex where much of his family also lived. She worked there for one year, just for him, "very happily": "I did housework. Everything—cooking, cleaning—for $300. Sometimes I'd get more—'road money' when I came back to my country." Like other good employers (Tatya had also had this situation), this one paid for Victoria's trip back home, visa, and fines. These costs could add up.

In Turkey, the visa regime for entering has remained much the same, but has become a bit more expensive for Moldovan citizens. Overstayers are charged fines according to the amount of time they have overstayed their visas. It costs about US$400 for those who overstay six months, after which the fines double. After one year in Turkey, Victoria went back to Moldova and discovered while there that she could not return to Turkey for a year. The laws had changed in 2002, and an overstayer could not reenter Turkey for the amount of time by which she had overstayed her visa. In this case, it was one year. So her sister took the job. Victoria explained:

She [Victoria's sister] stayed there for two years. A day off every week. And the meals were super. The meals were really super. I mean, on my birthday, a present, on New Year's, a present—he was an incredibly super man. . . . But he is very rich. I had my own room, my own bathroom, everything.

In this case, Victoria did not have to deal with a Turkish female employer or with children, which was a good situation, according to many. Yet what also distinguished this employer was his spontaneous generosity and caring manner. These kinds of expressions cleansed the menial labor these women had to do and transformed the exchange from a purely labor-for-money transaction into one between a generous patron and his client.

Showing compassion for and trust in their employee was another important consideration in finding a good employer. This was particularly important since, should anything go awry, these domestics have recourse neither to legal nor to familial channels. One of the nurses I interviewed in Gagauz Yeri, Maya, who was a caretaker for an elderly diabetic in Istanbul, slept in the same room as her charge. She preferred it this way, she said, so that she could watch the elderly person in case she needed something. As a nurse, Maya said, she was used to such practices. She described how good her employer was with this example:

> I had worked there [only] one week. . . . The second day I was on that job, they called me from my village. My husband had fallen here. He says, "I need you, you go away, and I'm used to that now, but I still need you." "No," I said, "I have no money, I can't leave." They gave me my entire one month's pay that day. I lived with a family like that. I hadn't even worked yet and they gave me a whole month's pay. Good, a very good family.

This act earned the employers her loyalty and respect, and she returned to work for them several times over the years.

The domestics I came to know are often in such emergency situations. Whether needed at home because of a death or accident, or because someone (a child, perhaps) was caught at the border or in Laleli, they sometimes had to leave suddenly. This is another example of migrant domestic workers' vulnerability as undocumented workers in a precarious position. They coped with these situations by appealing to moral economies as well. The response of employers to such a situation would determine the domestics' opinion of them. Sometimes domestics in a bad place would lie to leave the job without having to just quit, and they would find another job instead of returning. But the fact that this was a plausible excuse, even if employers often did not believe them, shows how common such situations were.

Maya, the nurse caretaking an elderly woman, attested that she came to love the family dearly. Many women complained about elder care, remarking that the elderly person was grumpy and would severely criticize them and insult them. But, Maya told me, the elderly woman who employed her insisted that Maya refer to her as an "older sister" and encouraged her to have her friends over on her days off, saying, "The door is open to your friends to come here. If your friends are coming, tell me, we'll buy cake, *börek*, ice cream." Many of the other nurses in the room nodded, saying they had been guests in this house on their days off. Good employers also provided and took responsibility for their employee, from underwriting large expenses such as dental care to small ones such as providing toothpaste, shampoo, and other bathroom products for them. In this unregulated market, it was these smaller things and the daily indications of appreciation—or, alternatively, put-downs—that allowed a domestic worker to distinguish a good situation from a bad one and endure it as a perhaps better, more soulful, and more secure employment than another.

Dining practices and generosity with food were also used to illustrate better employers, ones who treated the domestic as part of the family and thus could be trusted (see also Constable 1997a, 2002). One of the teachers in Congaz, Alina, contrasted a bad place where she had to eat separately to a later, better job, where "from the first day I came, they greeted me at their table." They would encourage her to feel at home in their house: "If you want to eat, go ahead, don't wait for us to get up [in the morning]." This family also demonstrated their ability to treat the caretaker as a "specialist." This good employer actually did separate out the domestic's work as solely that of baby caretaker, something Alina greatly appreciated:

> They [the employers] did the shopping and the cooking. My job was to take care of the baby. "If you have extra time, do ironing, or clean, but if you don't then there is no problem." There was no "Why didn't you do this." "Your job is the child," they'd say.

In a situation like this, where her fines were paid as well, Alina would stay as long as she could tolerate being away from her family in Gagauz Yeri. Yet she was quick to point out that her employers had *learned* how to better treat a domestic. During her first six months of employment there, they did not offer her extra gifts or show appreciation for her with words of thanks. When she returned six months later, according to her, they had changed: "They'd learned to appreciate me."

Many migrants emphasized their gendered vulnerabilities to their employers and to others they met in Turkey, expressing their positionalities as mothers working for the good of their children, as hardworking women, and as foreigners vulnerable to harassment by men and police in the street. With bad employers, this practice could backfire. In other cases, however, it gained them sympathy, protection, and monetary rewards. These narratives were performative litanies that worked to lessen the threat that the Gagauz woman posed to the Turkish woman of the house. But again, this does not mean they were concocted for purely instrumental purposes; they were experiences very real to migrant women. This affective dimension of the compensation that domestics receive as a result of these pleas—compensation that shows the value of working for good people over the amount of work or money—helps this transnational labor market function.

The nature of domestic work itself holds certain problems for all domestic workers, but in this context certain particularities are evident. Here we have seen some of the former socialist specificities of this gendered moral economy in terms of what constitutes good work. First, workers from a socialist background are especially attuned to the gendered and class inequalities involved in domestic work. Second, and particularly salient to their roles as migrant domestic workers in an unregulated market, their past experiences with using *blat* to get by as mother-workers in the informal economy of the former Soviet Union stood them in good stead. But an overriding particularity is their understanding of modern womanhood as having the capacity to "do it all"—as mothers, workers, and wives—and this understanding in turn structures their views of their difference from and even superiority to Turkish women, who are depicted by many of them as inept as handling any one part of it. This perception naturally poses problems for their relationships with female employers. Once they have successfully found a job, they must negotiate the job's various gendered challenges. As they do so, gender turns out to be a key cultural concept and practice through which they make sense of these others they are living with and working for.

Gendered Challenges on the Job

The reputations of Gagauz and other migrant women from Moldova in Turkey make them desirable as domestics. Yet this very appeal, along with the nature of domestic work itself, also makes them *too* desirable to be domestic workers. Whereas in other contexts, such as among Filipinas migrating to

Taiwan for work, whose experiences Nana Oishi (2005) and Lan (2006a) document, this would lessen their demand; in Turkey, it only increases it. Desirability nonetheless prompts particular conflicts. Many Gagauz I spoke with felt that Moldovans are seen as threats to the modern womanhood of the Turkish woman of the house. In some instances the Turkish female employer is not as well educated as the domestic worker she hires or has not had work experience, and thus the educated working Moldovan woman poses a challenge to her employer's power and status in the household in terms of both class and gender. As in the situation of domestic work more generally, Gagauz domestics' lives are characterized by recurring power struggles with their female employers and sometimes with their charges.[6] As many put it, because of this, one of the hardest parts about being a domestic is that it is hard on one's "morale." Some Gagauz domestics interpreted the woman of the house's behavior as jealousy. Whether or not such jealousy is real, this interpretation indicates migrant women's own ideas about class and gender, the roles they feel that women should hold as workers, mothers, and wives, and their presumed differences from (and even superiority to) the Turkish women who employ them. Like migrant domestics in East Asia observed by Lan, Moldovans too "evaluate female employers, while framing their own ideals of womanhood" (2006a, 144; see also Unal 2006). Such ideals, however, even if they also include working as part of the definition of being a "good woman," can privilege women's roles as nurturers of both children and husbands. Gagauz women's understandings of domestic service and its gendered labor in the Turkish household therefore were worked out in criticisms directed toward the education of Turkish women, their mothering style, and their ways of being a wife and even a lover.

Dussa, the teacher and former nurse from Beşalma, told me that she had not considered domestic work or child care demeaning until she saw how it was perceived as such in Turkey and experienced firsthand being "put in her place." Dussa was acutely aware of how foreign women compared with local Turkish domestic workers, who were uneducated and sometimes illiterate. And though the Turkish employers preferred foreign domestics because of their education and culturedness, Dussa pointed out that precisely these characteristics prompted conflict between herself and her first set of employers in a number of ways. The infamous firm, the one later charged with sex trafficking, had placed Dussa with a family that needed child care in a city on the Black Sea coast. Like many of the teachers I interviewed in Congaz

---

[6] For another instance of such power plays, see Pierrette Hondagneu-Sotelo (2002).

who also did child care in Turkey, Dussa complained that Turkish children were spoiled. As one Congaz teacher, Marina, said, "I have children of my own and I've taught kids here, but the children there do not listen or obey." Miriam explained:

> In Turkey, we look after kids fifteen, seventeen years old. But here children much younger than that are already taking care of themselves. Our children are used to working. Turkish children are not used to difficulty or work.

Marina had had a difficult situation like this one as well, and described the challenge of trying to discipline a young child who regularly screamed at his parents and at her. And as Dussa also said, Marina said that when she tried to talk to the employers about it, they shrugged it off, saying there was nothing wrong with their child's behavior.

The issue, it evolved, was not just dealing with rowdy and spoiled children but the faulty mothering style of Turkish women (there was little comment about fathering), according to the Gagauz women I interviewed. Conflicts between the domestic workers and the women of the house often took the form of arguments about disciplining or raising the children. The domestic workers from Gagauz Yeri felt the woman of the house too often undermined their authority over the child, or at the very least did not support it. As a result, many women from Gagauz Yeri do not accept employment as caretakers of children older than one year at all. For Dussa, the last straw was when the young child became very ill and Dussa, who had been trained as a nurse, recognized the illness as a highly communicable disease and told the mother; the mother grew angry with Dussa, saying, "Who are you to tell me this? What do you know?" Yet when they finally took the child to the doctor, they found that Dussa was correct. Even though Turkish employers are said to prefer Moldovans because they are specialized and educated professionals, domestic workers complained that conflicts between employers and domestics over each other's knowledge and mothering role were routine. They interpreted such conflicts as the result of Turkish women's poor mothering style and lack of knowledge.

In this job, Dussa's relationship with the "woman of the house" was also agitated by another side effect of the conflated gendered labor of migrant domestic work in Turkey: men's sexual advances or inappropriately intimate behavior toward the domestic worker and what was interpreted by domestics as Turkish women's jealousy of their attractiveness and insistence on their chasteness. Zeyneb, the progressive domestic worker employment agent described earlier, recalled one employee she had placed who had suffered sexual harassment every morning. The man of the house set his alarm one hour before anyone else woke up so he could go "touch" (*dokun*) the domestic worker. In Dussa's case, the man of the house had once come out of the bathroom from a shower naked and walked down the hallway, past Dussa, to his bedroom. After this, the Turkish woman employer became suspicious of Dussa's relationship with the husband and took this out on Dussa, not her husband.

Although Turkish men are feared as harassers, most conflicts over the domestics' sexuality I was told about took place between the Turkish woman employer and the domestic. Dussa explained that her increasingly suspicious employer began to carefully look her up and down and took great interest in every detail, commenting on what Dussa wore, how she spoke to her employer's husband, how she did her hair, and whether she painted her nails. Many women from Gagauz Yeri I spoke with thought that their attractiveness to Turkish men prompted jealousy on the part of the woman of the house. In this context, and to dispel suspicions, when they got such looks from Turkish women, several told me that they would preemptively seize the opportunity to stake out a position: "I'm here for the money, not a man!" At times this worked, but at other times, they explained, the woman of the house would continue to act out, often in passive-aggressive ways, commenting on how nice the domestic worker looked in a sarcastic manner or one that made fun of her. Such comments accused the domestic of trying to be seductive despite her assumed low status.

Employers frequently policed not only what women wore but also where they went when they left the house, and at what time. The domestics I spoke with complained of being reprimanded for speaking to a man on the street or talking comfortably with the doorman. Whether or not the domestic worker had intimate relationships with men were also a concern. Zeyneb, the employment agent, told me that some prospective employers asked her whether a potential hire had a husband or lover, explaining that they did not want someone who was married or had a boyfriend. "What? Do they want a robot?" she exclaimed. "These are women, after all. I mean, if you and I have lovers, why shouldn't they?"[7]

---

[7] Zeyneb added, "I tell you, even if you give it 100 years, our Turkish mentality will not change. I feel like an alien [*uzalyı*] here." She herself has a five-year-old daughter and employs a Turkmen woman to take care of her, but if she is home at night, she explained to me, and the caretaker wants to go out to a disco and she has someone to take her to the disco, she says, "Go ahead." This domestic worker has a boyfriend. "And why shouldn't she?," said Zeyneb. "Sometimes I even leave

Employers desired a domestic who, in their minds, was presentable, secular, and modern, but these very qualities were constantly under surveillance. Snide remarks also involved the employer saying, as Dussa's employer did, "You are educated. Why don't you use it?" For Dussa, this was a transparent put-down. First, it meant that domestic work did not take education or skill. Second, it indicated suspicion of the domestic as "driven" and using domestic work as a launching pad for something better, perhaps as a wife to an upper-middle-class Turkish man—like the employer's own husband.

This kind of situation could lead to disaster for the domestic, according to some of the women from Gagauz Yeri I spoke with. One story by a cook at the *internat*, whom I interviewed alongside Tatya and Miriam, had heard that a Turkish employer became jealous of a migrant domestic, making working there impossible for her. Therefore, as is often the case, she came up with an excuse to leave the job, saying she was needed at home (even though she would actually be moving to another job). The employer said, "Sure you can leave. But first do the windows." When Tatya and Miriam heard this, their eyes widened and their eyebrows lifted. I inquired further. When, as was expected of a "hardworking" domestic (whether Turkish or foreign), the worker stepped up to an open windowsill to clean the exterior surface of a window five stories up, the treacherous employer pushed her out, later claiming that the domestic had slipped. Whether this is a true story (I was unable to confirm it) or an urban myth, at the very least it indicates the real fear of Turkish women and how this fear affects migrant domestics' experience of working in Istanbul.

To find a good position in this unregulated environment and to make sense of their own place in these households, the women from Gagauz Yeri spent a good deal of time trying to understand Turkish women's behavior and motives and their relationships with Turkish men. At best, most Gagauz women I spoke with perceived Turkish women as untrustworthy. Their verbal and nonverbal formalities were interpreted as "being fake." Their lack of forthrightness would "play with your mind," ruining your "morale." At worst, it could end in treachery. Deploying their gendered identities as former socialists and as Christians, the Gagauz women constructed their relationships and negotiations with their employers by activating notions of Turkish women as part of a bourgeois or "new wealthy" class and (however secular) as Muslim. Some Gagauz women I spoke with critiqued Turkish

---

my child at my sister's and we go out to a disco together. My sister looks at me strangely, but I don't see the problem. If she wants to get dressed up and feel womanly, what's the problem with that?"

women on the basis of what they observed were their lack of mothering skills and work experience. Others, who had personal relationships with men in Turkey, added to these charges critiques of Turkish women as girlfriends or wives. Stesha's view of Turkish women, for instance, was formed from the perspective of a woman who had been married to a Gagauz man and now is married to a Turkish man. Oksana too had been married, to a Russian, but now has a relationship with a married Turkish man; still other Gagauz I came to know are girlfriends of single men in Turkey. Many women from Gagauz Yeri also learned about local working-class women's views and relations with men from the "women's shows" (*kadın programlari*) on television, where working-class Turkish women would appear to narrate abuse by their husbands or fathers and ask for retribution.

The image of Turkish women that emerges among women from Gagauz Yeri from these sources and in these contexts is that of women of low cultural capital who are unappreciative of the excellent treatment they receive from men in Turkey. Local men are perceived as taking full responsibility (*sahibleniyorlar*) for their girlfriends and wives. They work hard, do not drink, and provide money and material things for them—unlike "ours" (*bizimkiler*, or men from Gagauz Yeri). Migrant women sympathize with men mostly because of what they perceive as the failures of Turkish women. Extrapolating from their experiences with their employers and from the images on television, Gagauz women see most local Turkish women as lazy: they do not work and do not care for their husband or children sufficiently, or they do so in the wrong way. By comparison with a a woman's life in Gagauz Yeri, most Turkish housewives are perceived as having it easy, enjoying nice homes, household appliances, and people to cook and clean and take care of their children. Dussa expressed surprise at Turkish women employers' lack of domestic skill; many say, humorously, that the women of the house call an electrician to change a light bulb or throw things away instead of mending them. Even those things that Turkish women are seen to do well, such as cooking complex dishes, are regarded as silly, superfluous skills. For instance, Dussa reported, "Here [in Gagauz Yeri], we don't have time to decorate our food; we eat for sustenance, whereas Turkish women, who have money, don't work, so they have time for things like that." The woman Dussa and Angela worked for, they told me, did not even do that much; she just sat around and watched television all day and was not even concerned with her children: "She let us run the house entirely!" They expressed shock at how uncaring mothers in Turkey seemed to be. Stesha too described how the woman she worked for would come home from work, give her baby some little attention, but then get impatient and say "Stesha—take her, will you?" Stesha whispered to me what she had thought to herself at the time: "Wow. I've never seen mothering like this!"

As wives, Turkish women were generally viewed as uncaring and hard on their husbands. Oksana, whose lover was a married doorman for one of the apartment buildings in the *site* where she worked, put it this way: "You see how they are closed up on the outside? [referring to the veil that some, mostly working class, women in Turkey wear]. That is how they are on the inside, too!" And, Stesha and Oksana noted, Turkish women are ignorant of and uptight about sexuality, whereas, as Stesha said, "We are more relaxed." Even if sometimes Stesha and Oksana felt that "all Turkish men think about is sex," they often expressed sympathy for them. They saw men's relationships with Turkish women as lacking in love, romance, and sex, a result, in their view, of arranged, early marriages and Islamic ideas about women's sexuality. Whatever the truth or reason for women's behavior in Turkey, the Gagauz women I spoke with interpreted it as jealousy they had to suffer on a daily basis because, as opposed to women in Turkey, women from Gagauz Yeri were deemed high in cultural capital: more skilled, educated, and attractive, and better mothers, wives, and lovers. Nonetheless, some, like Natalia, noted that they respected those Turkish women who worked outside the home. This exemplifies the way that their differences from Turkish women were often discussed, and how these differences helped this particular transnational labor market function. Ideas about gender and class, but also about ethnicity/race and religion, and a socialist and rural work ethic constructed the gendered moral economies of these now migrant worker-mothers.

These women negotiate the boundaries between working for the money or for more compassionate reasons and between domestic worker and mother, daughter, or wife inside their work households, a situation common to domestic workers worldwide but interpreted in particular ways here, and agitated by the representation of Moldovans as hardworking, modern, educated, and cultured women of easy virtue but high cultural capital and the representation of Turks as having low cultural capital. The ambiguous position they find themselves in makes them vulnerable to exploitation inside these households. But even on their days off, they cannot relax, because they are in constant fear of harassment and deportation. Even so, just as they do inside the household, these migrant workers find ways to act outside it, and exercise some agency, through their gendered interpretations and practices.

Days Off

The day off provides some refuge from disciplinary measures inside the household, but it has its own challenges (for other examples, see Constable 1997a; Yeoh and Huang 1998). Here, the representation of Moldovans as put-together and modern blends with the sexuality of the natashas—that is, gendered notions and labors are conflated—to make them vulnerable to certain exploitations, but also to provide them with a route to security on their days off. As a general rule, it is not uncommon to sexualize racialized migrant domestics. The difference here is that the domestic's race, whiteness, is highly valued while nevertheless being sexualized. We see these dynamics play out on domestic workers' days off. In recent years, groups of women from the former Soviet Union and Eastern Europe have congregated on their days off in various parks around Istanbul, some on the European side, others on the Asian side. Still others know friends or family who have married and settled here, and go stay with them. A few pool their resources to rent their own place. And, like Natalia, some also have to go to Laleli at least sometimes to send or receive goods from home.

Oksana, Stesha's friend and a domestic worker who works in the *sité* where Stesha lives, was grateful to have Stesha's place to stay. I spent several Sundays with them there. Oksana would come over to visit Stesha, whose husband often was away or working on Sunday. On the Sundays I visited, we watched television, drank and ate foods sent to them from home, and made food that was familiar to them from Moldova. Oksana would process her week with Stesha, who was a sympathetic listener. They would both complain about the women in Turkey they had to deal with—Oksana about her employer and Stesha about her colleagues at her place of work (she worked for her husband as a salesperson of textiles). They both talked a lot about their daughters. Oksana worried that without her paycheck, her teenage daughter, whom she had left with her ex-husband and family in Ukraine, would not be taken care of. Both she and Stesha had given their daughters cell phones to call them, and they complained that the daughters abused the privilege, and it was getting costly. Stesha bought things for her daughter and on a regular basis sent packages of clothes and food, only to have her daughter complain that she had sent dried fruit instead of Pringles potato chips and her mother complain that Stesha bought too many clothes for her daughter and instead should pay a visit—and that the refrigerator she bought them on her last visit was too small. Oksana and Stesha also celebrated Moldovan holidays together: the first day I visited them was the Orthodox New Year. Even though Stesha had converted to Islam to marry her Turkish husband, she still celebrated Christmas, and even had a small fake Christmas tree. Many women I knew doing elder care on the European side also frequented the Orthodox churches there on their days off. In addition to services, these churches would allow the women to spend their days on the church grounds, where they would be safe from the police.

Although some domestic workers spent their free days safely in places like this, many also continued to spend some time in and around Laleli. Whether they liked it or not, Laleli was still the place where on Sundays, traditionally the day off for domestic workers, hundreds of migrant women from formerly socialist states gathered. To cater to them (and others), on some Sundays, unregistered local male small traders set up street bazaars to sell wool sweaters and cotton jogging suits, sneakers, and other items, even fruit, filling the roads from Laleli to the official tourist sites. Migrant women would flock to Laleli from all over Istanbul—by boat, tramway, bus, and foot—to gather, eat, drink, and socialize with friends, family, and boyfriends; call home from pay phones; inquire about new jobs at the employment agencies; shop at the stores and bazaars; send goods home; or pick up packages from the minibuses that go back and forth weekly between Laleli and their hometowns. Serving as a borderland (see Yükseker 2004), Laleli is both on the sidelines and at the center, constructed by the new mobilities between Turkey and the formerly socialist world. It is a space of shifting identities, currencies, languages, labors, and strategies of survival, and a marketplace for the circulation of marginal peoples, goods, and ideas about gender, class, and sexuality.

The meeting spot for the women is usually at the lots used by the minibuses that travel between Turkey and various formerly socialist republics. Two gravel parking lots in Laleli are temporary home to anywhere from five to fifteen minibuses traveling to and from Moldova. They park with their rear doors open and facing each other. When I peeked inside, most buses looked almost full, and packages spilled out onto the ground near the doors, where the driver usually stands. On one of the open rear doors, marked by hand on brown cardboard, are listed the towns and cities visited by the particular minibus: usually at least ten stops. A minibus driver I interviewed, himself from the Gagauz town of Beşalma, whom Stesha and her mother Rosa from Comrat employ to send packages back and forth, is in Turkey every two weeks and back in Gagauz villages for the alternating two weeks (see figures 4.1 and 4.2). Many women stand around the buses, wrapping

Figure 4.1. View of the village of Beşalma, 2004. Photograph by the author.

the various items they have bought for their family—clothes, toys, letters, and money—into plastic bags tightly bound into a ball about one foot in diameter. Some items are larger—housewares such as ironing boards, even wheelchairs.

The prices for transport vary according to size and contents. If an item is newer or bigger, it is more expensive, as the taxes at the border vary accordingly. A small package of Pampers diapers, for instance, costs about US$5, while a medium-sized package of old clothes might cost US$10. If sending money, a woman is charged about 2 percent (Western Union, while fast and guaranteed, charges 10 percent). Whether or not items are exported for sale, these women are encouraged to say the items they are sending are personal, old items—hand-me-downs from their employers, or winter clothes they no longer need—to keep their costs down. But if the package is opened and found to be different at the border—new clothes, or even money—however, the driver must cover the difference, and then demand reimbursement from his customers. Some workers can send on credit, but the minibus drivers take several different currencies as well. The driver I spoke with explained that most people were sending packages to Moldova but that

Figure 4.2. View exiting Beşalma, 2004. Photograph by the author.

some items, such as wine, cognac, or vodka, were sent from Moldova to Istanbul. Stesha received her stock of foods, including *gretchka* (buckwheat), particularly good vinegar for borsch, and letters with pictures from home. Another woman I knew received a certain type of fish eaten on holidays, a local cognac, and moonshine made in her village. In this kind of unregulated environment, trust and security are forged through personal gendered relationships between minibus drivers, domestics, and merchants.

In the spring of 2002, I spent most Sundays in Laleli with Tatya's sister, Sveta, and her two friends, Irina and Vasilyeva. Sveta met Irina, who is Ukrainian, because they worked in the same neighborhood and rode the same bus to Laleli every Sunday. Vasilyeva was a childhood friend of hers from Congaz. All of these women worked as caretakers for the elderly in and around the area of Şişli, Nişantaşi, and Osmanbey. One Sunday, around Orthodox Easter in 2002, after picking up the fish and vodka that Irina's family had sent, we went to a local café about a block from the minibuses. This was one of two regular haunts for this group of three women and others, many of them from the former Soviet Union and Eastern Europe. Local men shuttled in and out. The menus were in pictures because of the variety of languages spoken.

For many women, finding a place to spend the day off is difficult, as they do not want to spend a lot of money. A constant argument with the waiter at this cafe, for instance, was over whether we were buying a meal there or not: usually we brought our own food, and he would not give us eating utensils until we ordered something. These women could not sit somewhere or even stand still for very long, and definitely not if they were alone, as they would be harassed. In another example of these women's mobility, they had to keep moving from place to place in this neighborhood, from minibuses to cafés, shops, bazaars, parks, and churches, out of fear of having to spend money (in a café or shop), being hassled by men, or being picked up by the police. As Tatya once said—and this was a typical comment in all my interviews—one of the hardest things about working in Turkey was that "we hide" (*saklaniyoruz*).

This scene in Laleli takes place within thirty yards of the local police station, which perches above one of the main streets of Laleli, up a set of fifty steps. Police raids were frequent in 2002 and, by the looks of a less populated Laleli in 2005, effective. When I returned to this place three years later, I found that many women, like Natalia, avoided hanging around there at all. They had found other places to be, with friends or family, in other neighborhoods, and even in apartments of their own, that did not expose them to police harassment and exploitation.

In both 2002 and 2005, I witnessed police take women into their cars and drive off, or stop them in the street. I heard many stories of run-ins and near misses with police, of being picked up by them; sent to the "foreigner's office" for deportation; or suffering extortion, harassment, or even rape. Even if the police simply brought the migrant back to her workplace, sometimes employers, fearing extortion or retribution from the police themselves, would not admit that she worked there. Several times, while going to Laleli with Sveta and her friends, we got off at an earlier or later stop to avoid the police, who were waiting for undocumented migrant women at the Laleli bus stop or tramway. Another Sunday, as we stood around in the parking lot, a police car drove up and blared its siren just for a short moment—a second or so. The entire crowd of women jumped and began walking away quickly en masse. I was pushed along with them, until we scattered to different areas of the neighborhood. As I looked back before turning off the street, a street merchant with a cart of fruit exclaimed to me: "They are here, sister! [*Geldiler abla!*]." He was likely selling things without a permit. The police, I noticed, did not arrest anyone this time but simply, I think, wanted to scare the women. The common vulnerability and marginality in this neighborhood bind the women and men here together.

There was a lot of discussion among women from Gagauz Yeri about how the police could recognize a woman from Eastern Europe or the former Soviet Union. Women I knew cited their physical features, especially light eyes or hair, or a slender body type (even though, especially for Gagauz, they all look very different, some having these features but many not). Some said it was what they wore or a special hoop style and color of gold earring. They also are frequently seen, at least in this neighborhood, to be carrying around big shopping bags. As I watched and walked with these women day by day, I discovered another reason why they are recognizable: because of the way they look in another sense, not as how others see them visually. The women from Gagauz Yeri actually look around and *at* people, or not, with their eyes. Sometimes smiling at men, sometimes defensive and fearful, their gaze is very different from the gaze of a local working-class woman, who would not look a man in the eye, and if avoiding them would do so with their eyes set downward (in a performance of meekness, shyness, or humility), not by looking above or away defiantly or proudly, as I saw many women from the former Soviet Union and Eastern Europe do.

To get by in this environment, the women I came to know, who worked primarily as domestic workers, used combinations of affection, sexual intimacy, and sympathy with men, all gendered efforts, to their advantage. For Sveta and her friends, for instance, a flirtation could help lower the cost of a sweater for her husband, better secure a letter with money sent home to her child, or make a local ally to rely on in the police raids. Other women tried to make extra cash on their days off by selling goods or services. All tried not to spend their own money. Sveta and her friends secured the latter by having generous local boyfriends who paid for food, drink, and goods. I witnessed one male friend financially compensate Vasilyeva when the police extorted her. These boyfriends (*arkadaş*, meaning "friend" in Turkish but used to indicate a clear romantic or sexual interest) were often drawn from the local Laleli merchants mentioned in Deniz Yükseker's (2004) analysis. They were marginal working-class entrepreneurs, some Kurdish, who were themselves savvy in dealing with the injustices of the Turkish state and with the difficulties of migration, and thus were sympathetic of the harassment these vulnerable women faced not only at the hands of Turkish police but also from mainstream Turkish middle- and upper-class prejudices. Thus, many things drew these men to these women, including gendered ideas about protecting them and pity for them as migrants who were separated from their families and working hard to make money for their children. In play here are views of these women as "liberal" and "modern" in terms of their sexuality, but also empathy with their common situation of police harassment because of their marginal, migrant status and activities in the informal economy.

For the women, these relationships were not just a means to an economic end. From what I could gather, many women developed sincere affectionate relationships with these men. They saw their boyfriends as good men who sought to take care of (*sahib olmak*) the women in their lives. And just as inside the household, so too here, in the streets on the women's day off, such arrangements indicate how conflated the affective, sexual, and economic become in these relationships of exchange in a transnational migrant labor market. Some of the Gagauz women who worked as domestics acted as traders, and some had sex with men away from their working households in exchange for favors, money, or affection. Some of these women participated in more than one type of work; others did not. Some considered caretaking houses and people, trading, and sex all to be forms of work; others did not. The experiences of Gagauz women with Turkish boyfriends support Banu Nilgün Uygun's (2004) assertion that sexual relations with local men are conceived as part of various "sexscapes" instead of "sex work" (see also Brennan 2004; Demirdirek and Whitehead 2004). These relations are one strategy among many that are activated to survive and advance in this ill-defined, unregulated, and undocumented transnational labor market. It may help to secure a business relation or a safe route home to their children and husband; it may help them save money to send home; or it may generally make them feel safer and less alone in a hostile and foreign environment. So, even though women from Gagauz Yeri suffer from being conflated with the infamous natashas, here as well as in the households they work in, they can also use these perceptions, their reputed attractiveness and liberal sexual mores, playing on the sympathy and desire of men and women in Turkey and at times even using sex itself, to lessen their vulnerability as undocumented migrant workers. In this way, they are not clearly victims but are asserting some form of agency and power in this vulnerable situation.

Migrant Women, Agency, and Labor

The above description of the gendered moral economies of domestic work on the job and off supports the existence of a complex and nuanced labor situation in which women hold varying degrees of agency in engaging in various types of gendered labor, which occur alongside varying types and exploitation. Even though migrant domestic work constitutes the bulk of female labor from Moldova in Turkey, the foremost institution dealing with migration in the region, the IOM, focuses almost exclusively on the exploitation involved in the forced prostitution of Eastern European and Russian women, a large percentage of whom is said to be Moldovan. These women are presented as young (aged eighteen to twenty-four), innocent victims of an illegal network of criminal traffickers who intend to use them as "sex slaves." Particularly at IOM-Turkey, these women are also represented as poor mothers trying to earn money for their children (IOM 2005). This representation forms part of a wider "discursive verbosity" about trafficking in women that Jacqueline Berman identifies (2003; see also Bernstein 2008; Zheng 2008a, 2008b; Brennan 2008; Shah 2008; Agustin 2008; Musto 2008; Plambech 2008). In the newspaper and nongovernmental representations Berman scrutinizes, trafficking is presented in sensationalist language meant to alarm audiences with frightening statistics and horrifying individual cases. Furthermore, gender and race are conflated with innocence: because they are white women, they are posed as being forced into prostitution. There is no panic about the trafficking of African women for prostitution, for instance, even though, as one long-standing IOM-Turkey employee (against the views of most of his colleagues) ironically pointed out to me, there are clearly many African women in desperate straits in Istanbul "who will sell their bodies for a bite of bread." In IOM's 2002 campaign materials, however, the traffic involved "naive Slavic women" and "stupid girls" in a "new white slave trade" of "trafficked sex slaves."

Such representations pose work as forced or voluntary, and these representations overlap with ideas about the reasons for Eastern European women's migration as opposed to the migration of other people or in other areas of the world. These categorizations lead organizations and states to set policies to help white migrant women from the former Soviet Union and Eastern Europe who are perceived as passive victims in need of assistance, and ignore women from other regions who may choose to go abroad to work (even as sex workers) or may be differently exploited, such as the domestic workers described here. It is not only the IOM but also policymakers, scholars, police officers, employers, and the migrant women themselves who distinguish those who engage in sex work from those who do not. For instance, Natalia complains that 10 percent of the women are "like that," implying that "the rest of us aren't," and I heard similar assertions from Stesha, Tatya, and others. Some employers and even police officials at the Ankara headquarters I spoke with claimed that the Moldovan domestic workers are "loyal" (*sadik*), and IOM-Turkey officials consider them a "different group" (*çevre*) from sex workers altogether.

However, if we look at recent ethnographic and other qualitative sociological analyses, research that takes into account the perspective of the women themselves, a different picture emerges that conceptualizes sex differently, as part of a continuum of exchanges that are both economic and affective. First, women from the former Soviet Union and Eastern Europe who participate in sex work for money in Laleli are not all trafficked. Based on participant observation in Laleli, interviews with three women sex workers from the former Soviet Union, and several bartenders, clients, and other workers in the area, Leyla Gülçür and Pinar Ilkkaracan assert that most migrant sex workers in Turkey are commuters from the former Soviet Union who work voluntarily and individually for economic survival. They point out that while prostitution is legal in Turkey, migrant sex work is not. Migrant women sex workers face various vulnerabilities. The women interviewed by Gülçür and Ilkkaracan did not complain about criminal traffickers, who, according to the sex workers, initially may have had a role in their presence there but later had no influence over their comings and goings. What they did face, however, was regular harassment by local men and the police. The latter threaten deportation and extort these women for what amounts to about 10 percent of their weekly wages (Gülçür and Ilkkaracan 2002).

Second, as we saw with the role that sex and sexuality plays for tourist-traders and domestic workers, what constitutes sex work is not always clear. Even while admitting that tourist-trade work and sex work are conflated in practice, both Deniz Yükseker and Idlikó Bellér-Hann (and most social scientists) categorically separate out sex workers from tourist-traders. For Yükseker, sexual relations help economic trade relations, but sex work is different altogether; for Béller-Hann, tourist-trading is simply a ruse, a cover for sex work. But in her ethnographic account, "Being a 'Natasha'," Uygun (2006) argues for a different conception of the work involved in marketing sex, and a broader conception of these women's aims. She asserts that "sex work" is not a good term to cover the range of practices taking place in this context. Uygun argues that women from the former Soviet Union in Turkey "assume[d] roles vis-à-vis men that included that of the wife, the mistress, and the prostitute. Central to all of these relationships was the exchange of material benefits in the form of money, food, housing, etc. . . . and sexual/affective services" (2006, 34). Uygun's research thus moves us to question the category of sex work as distinct from the activities and roles of a wife, girlfriend, or lover. She encourages us to think instead in terms of Denise Brennan's conceptualization of various transnational sexual-economic relationships as "sexscapes" (2004; see also Constable 2003; Bloch 2003; Agustin 2007). Here, whether as "work" or in personal relationships, providing sex and affection are operationalized as strategies for many different women to survive in uncertain economic situations. Such analyses help us recognize the fluidity expected in all women's labors, as opposed to the strict divisions between them we find in most social science categorizations and in those espoused by organizations such as the IOM.

The representation of the natasha, the desire for her caretaking and possibly sexual services, and the fluidity of the affective and economic practices in the above accounts are paralleled in domestic workers' practices inside and outside their places of work. From what I witnessed, from the experiences recounted to me and described here, as well as from what is available in other research, in Laleli's marketplace, sexuality and affection are commodities traded not only by sex workers and not only for money. This is not to say that some women do not refuse to use their sexuality to gain advantage: like Natalia, many simply decide to stay away from Laleli altogether. Nor is it to say that no one is coerced into sex work, as the cases of trafficking make obvious. It is, however, clear that separating female workers from the former Soviet Union and Eastern Europe into categories of tourist-traders, sex workers, or domestic workers does not adequately represent the range of gendered labor practices, experiences, or exploitations in Turkey.

It is important to develop a more nuanced sense of the continuum of practices and agency of sex workers, tourist traders, girlfriends, wives, lovers, caretakers, and domestic workers, one that admits the affective and economic dimensions of the gendered moral economies in all these exchanges. What is evident from my research is that relations and exchanges of all kinds between men and women in Laleli, and between the employer and employee, both on and off the job, are valued not only for the economic benefits but for the affective ones too. Although employers demand caring and pay for it, domestic workers also seek demonstrations of caring from employers, making their interactions a two-way gendered moral economy. A reliance on both types of exchanges marks the unregulated market for domestic workers in Istanbul and the benefits and pitfalls of employment as a domestic there.

The insight into women's labor and agency gleaned from these data is that separating out women's migrant labors in terms of agency and even ethnicity or race and religion, as the IOM does, obscures the fact that all women from the former Soviet Union and Eastern Europe in Turkey are in a similar situation. Like other migrant women, they cobble together various kinds of work and strategies to get by. Grouping by factors such as race, religion, or agency also obscures the fact that women from this region are in a situation similar to that of other undocumented migrant women. Categorizing migrant women according to assumptions about the type of labor they do, the agency they hold, their citizenship, ethnicity, race, and religion, disguises how their strategies for survival and advancement are prompted not only by the fall of communism but also by the mechanics and common effects of neoliberalism on "global women," whether those women are from Gagauz Yeri, the global south, a third-world state, or a former colony (Ehrenreich and Hochschild 2002).

To summarize, there are particularities to the Gagauz experience of domestic work in Turkey, but they also share many similarities with other instances of migrant labor. Their moral economies are tinged by their socialist past and by the high cultural capital they hold, but such moral economies are not limited to postsocialist cases (Nare 2011; Lan 2006a). Like other migrant workers, women from Gagauz Yeri are downwardly mobile in some ways. Their expressions of similarity or even superiority to their employers work to assuage the loss of status. It is important to note here that such sentiments are not deployed solely for instrumental purposes. As we hear in their own words, it is much more complicated than that.

Conventional notions of gender, class, race, and sexuality are resisted in some ways and reproduced in other ways in migrant domestic workers' interpretations of the challenges of, expectations of, and compensation for their work. They make sense of Turkish households and their conflated roles within them through shifting gendered moral economies, and this reasoning helps this transnational labor market function. In illuminating subjective accounts, we can better understand how women may implicate themselves voluntarily and strategically in gendered categories and in neoliberalism and how this voluntary implication can sometimes work to their disadvantage.

Migrant domestics and their female employers in Turkey share experiences of exploitation in the patriarchal neoliberal capitalist system, which continues to uphold women primarily as caretakers and sets them up to blame other women, not men, for their dual, even triple, burdens. We hear this as much when Turkish employers accuse migrant workers of being out to bed their husbands and take over their homes as when Gagauz women accuse Turkish women of being bad mothers, wives, lovers, and workers.

The migrant domestics, however, are clearly in more dire straits. Unlike their employers, Gagauz workers in Turkey cannot work and mother in their home nation-state. This has economic and emotional costs. Further, it demonstrates yet another form of inequality between women domestics and their women employers (Parrenas 2012; see also Lan 2006b; Romero 2006). Moreover, in this case, because Gagauz women's work in Turkey is undocumented, there are even more costs, such as their curtailed ability to question or resist the conditions of their employment. It is vital to understand the workings of gendered moral economies like these, which drive this market, in order to understand migrant women's various exploitations, agency, and power.

Having returned to Moldova and Turkey twice in the early to mid-2000s, I can attest to some changes that occurred in this migration from 2002 to 2005 and from 2005 to 2009. In recent years, women from Gagauz Yeri who commute for work have become more adept at negotiating their lives in Istanbul. They keep abreast of the visa regime, sharing information with each other frequently. They handle their own passport and travel arrangements. Most now take one of two flights to Istanbul on regular airlines, avoiding the two-day boat trip and the complicated bus routes through several countries. For their employment, most inquire into the details of the job: whether they are expected to cook, clean, iron, or wash windows in addition to caretaking; what the employer's schedules are like; and, if it is elder care, whether they are expected to live alone or with others. If there is a man in the house, regardless of his marital status, many domestic workers are concerned about sexual harassment and will not take the job. Many request locks for their doors. In such situations, they also might try the job out to see whether the wife is the jealous type. Many have cell phones of their own. For elder care, an invalid's weight and ability to take care of his or her own "bathroom business" are also concerns. Moreover, to avoid exploitation outside the workplace, many, like Natalia, avoid Laleli altogether.

Migrant domestic workers from Gagauz Yeri typically leave Turkey anywhere from six months to a year after they arrive. They leave because of their longing for a home visit, issues of visas and fines, the demands of their husbands and families, flight from "bad people," lack of success in finding a new job, or because they are outright deported by police. Some return to Istanbul; others swear they will never come back.

By now, vast numbers of Gagauz mothers are absent from their village homes. Great anxiety has arisen over their behavior abroad, their absence from their families, and how they use their new wealth at home. What greets them on their return is blame for social disorder in their villages and in Moldova. The IOM also makes these accusations. The organization responds to migrant women's complex situations with policies and initiatives that rely on the same gendered ideas of class, citizenship, race, ethnicity, and religion. Thus, shifting gendered moral economies are as relevant to understanding the policy response to this migration as it is to understanding women migrants' and employers' engagement in it.

Chapter 5

Managing Migration

Migrant labor from Gagauz Yeri has prompted panic over the potential for dissolving families and orphaned children, and the blame has fallen especially on the shoulders of migrant worker-mothers. This anxious tenor also resonates in intergovernmental organization (IGO), nongovernmental organization (NGO), and governmental policy responses to migration from Moldova. This is true particularly of the International Organization for Migration (IOM), an IGO funded primarily by the United States and the European Union (EU) that is the foremost institution dealing with migration in Moldova and in Europe more broadly. The IOM was the final site I investigated in the social field of transnational labor circulating from Moldova to Turkey and back. As at the other sites, here too we find gendered moral economies expressed and constituted that do not necessarily work in the best interests of women migrants. In both its Moldovan and Turkish offices, the IOM gathers a wealth of data on this migration pattern. In addition to trying to assist migrants, IOM staff disseminate knowledge about migration in media campaigns to raise public consciousness about the plight of migrants.

These efforts have focused almost exclusively on countering trafficking in women from Moldova to Turkey. Profiling a typical victimized migrant woman and her criminal traffickers, they make a particular argument for the appropriate policy response to this migration: imprison traffickers and repatriate and rehabilitate victims. For the latter, they have created a trafficking hotline and women's shelters. Yet little effort has been expended on identifying and addressing the root economic causes of trafficking and on creating jobs for women at home, let alone on addressing other migrant labor exploitations such as those described by the migrant women themselves.

In 2002 and again in 2004–5, I approached the IOM to discuss migration and migrant domestic work in Turkey. After introducing myself and explaining my research, I faced stunned faces and dropped jaws. One staffer I interviewed, Iris, gasped in surprise: "There really *is* domestic work in Turkey?" Most staffers believed that the idea that such work existed at all was a ruse employed by traffickers to lure ignorant women into sex work in Turkey.[1] Moreover, their data did not distinguish between Moldovan populations in terms of either ethnicity or the variety of migration routes they take. This situation was beginning to change somewhat in 2004–5, when IOM staff found themselves scrambling to locate victims for their well-funded countertrafficking programs. At that point, they sought out Contact, a small, three-person NGO based in Comrat, the capital of the Gagauz Yeri autonomous region, to identify victims of trafficking and to conduct countertrafficking activities in Gagauz Yeri. Yet most of the individuals that Contact eventually identified were not victims of sex crimes or forced migration, but were former migrant domestic workers.

IOM-Moldova admits that since 2002, the total number of women victims of trafficking has decreased consistently. That the number of trafficked women falls far short of estimates is true for other countries as well. A 2007 *Washington Post* article noted that in 2000, an estimated 50,000 women were being trafficked to the United States every year (Markon 2007). In 2004, this figure was revised to an estimated 14,000 to 17,000 women and girls every year. Countertrafficking programs have been widely funded to stop trafficking in the United States and elsewhere, but from 2000 to 2007,

---

[1] In a set of early cases described in the previous chapter, it may have been true that some women who traveled to Turkey through contacts with a particular agency were duped by the lure of migrant domestic work and then trafficked into sex work, but I was unable to independently verify this. In any case, as we see in this book, domestic work is readily available.

fewer than two hundred individual victims per year had been identified (Markon 2007).² Despite declining numbers, many argue that trafficking persists and has gone deeper underground, and that better-funded counter-trafficking projects are vital. Because of the flawed data and biases, this supposition is difficult to verify and the projects are difficult to justify. The numbers that are available reflect generalizations based on very few documented cases (Tyldum and Brunovskis 2005). Moreover, according to the women's studies scholar Jennifer Lynne Musto, even these documented cases are flawed by law enforcement practices that identify victims based on "ideological biases against immigrants in general and prostituting immigrants in particular" (2008, 9; see also Godziak and Collett 2005). A 2009 IOM report recognized the problem of bias, admitting that the focus on sex trafficking in women posed a problem to the IOM's conceptualization of what constituted illegal migration by women, and to finding solutions to the exploitation of migrants more broadly (Kontula and Saaristo 2009). Indeed, the absence of an accurate accounting of victims of trafficking prompted a self-evaluation process for the IOM-Moldova's mission.

My initial interaction with the IOM staff in Moldova and Turkey led to a longer conversation over time regarding their assumptions about why women go to Turkey, the effects of migration on women migrants and their families, and the appropriate policy response to it. I had many questions. When undocumented voluntary migrant domestics shuttling to Turkey account for a large portion of migration from Moldova (and many of them are from Gagauz Yeri), why did IOM activities overlook them? And when IOM staff got over their shock that some success stories actually existed for migrant mothers and their families, why was this migration pattern still greeted with great unease? Further, with the low numbers of victims of sex trafficking identified, why did the IOM insist on continuing to focus on the lot of women trafficked for sex work? This is not to diminish the horrors or the reality of sex trafficking; even if there are only a few victims, it is a crime that demands criminal investigation and victim retribution and rehabilitation. Yet why did the IOM focus on this particular crime at the cost of ignoring the plight of other migrants, many of whom were being exploited and in need of assistance?

---

²For a discussion of this problem as part of a longer piece on the IOM's countertrafficking efforts and the conservative (even evangelical Christian) politics of these efforts, see William Finnegan's informative essay in the *New Yorker* (2008).

As it turns out, a basic ideological flaw wrapped in a faulty concept underlay the IOM's response. IOM staff, despite their vast education and skills and despite having their own revised data on migrants, still managed to miss—and even to dismiss—key dynamics of women's migrant labor because of their assumption that Moldovan women would go abroad to Turkey only if they were forced or duped. The intersection of these ideological notions of gender, migration, and agency in this context prevented the IOM from making its mark and helping migrant women from Moldova. To understand this failure, in this chapter I examine what the IOM does focus on and deconstruct its notions of gendered culpability and responsibility. With what considerations, under what structural conditions (including the funding priorities and influence of the United States and the EU), are these projects conceived, negotiated, and implemented? What politics, what new stratifications, are being created through them? I propose that IOM campaigns and their interpretation by local elites charged with their implementation are representative of new gendered moral economies that help individual IOM migration managers understand and justify new stratifications in a rapidly changing Moldovan society.[3] These local, moral notions are at the root of the problem, but they coincide with neoliberal shifts in governance that affect women globally. These shifts focus responsibility for change and the welfare of populations not on the state or collective action but on the moral behavior of individuals.

My conclusion supports that of anthropologists of former socialist states who have argued that gender is a key cultural form through which new political-economic regimes are legitimized (Gal 1994b; Gal and Kligman 2000a, 2000b; Wedel 2001; Rivkin-Fish 2005; Evans, Henry, and Sundstrom 2006; Hemment 2004, 2007; for postcolonial contexts, see Mohanty 2003). Moving forward from these efforts, I show how a new migration regime is emerging in this region, one that is neoliberal and highly gendered in its effects.

To do so, I also draw on scholarship on the unintended effects of countertrafficking campaigns. The social scientist Jacqueline Berman has analyzed the discourse of countertrafficking campaigns in Europe and shown how panics over the trafficking of women in Eastern Europe in the early 2000s

---

[3] The campaign materials and narratives described and analyzed here were collected through a combination of interviews with IOM staff members in Turkey and Moldova, written and web-based policy materials, and participant observation. The latter involved observation and sometimes participation in countertrafficking and other campaigns and observation and participation in the day-to-day operations of the IOM office, particularly in Chişinău, the capital of Moldova.

provided the rationale for a new, more forceful performance of EU statecraft (2003). Many others have shown how, in the US context (and especially during the George W. Bush administration), the moral panic over trafficking links countertrafficking programs to antimigration agendas concerned with border security and with "policing non-procreative sex on a global scale" (Soderlund 2005, 79; see also Luibhéid 2002; Chapkis 2003; Shah 2008). As Musto explains:

> NGOs must align their internal policies and philosophies with the views of their funders, namely, the US government. In so doing, they must implicitly distinguish between voluntary economic migrants and involuntarily trafficked persons (read women trafficked for sexual exploitation) where the latter are given shelter and protection and the former are arrested and deported. (2008, 10)

In a similar vein, Denise Brennan has pointed out that the focus on funding countertrafficking efforts and on helping women and girl victims has undermined efforts by undocumented workers, whether trafficked or not, to organize for their human and worker rights (2008).

The above works analyze US and EU policies in various contexts, but a story just beginning to be told is how these panics and projects targeting migrant women, whether funded by or influenced in other ways by US or EU policies, take root in particular national contexts in Eastern Europe and the former Soviet Union.[4] This chapter marks the beginning of an exploration of that story in Moldova through critical discourse analysis and an ethnographic examination of countertrafficking and other migration management initiatives. Caroline Humphrey's work on tourist-traders offers some insight into these processes in the region (2002). She argues that the regulation of migrant trading by the Russian state constructs a new Russian citizen that excludes certain ethnicities. Trading by certain ethnic groups—often those from central Asia—is devalued and delegitimized, while "Russian" goods and merchants are upheld as legitimate. Following these analyses, I explore how the IOM discriminates legitimate from illegitimate migration from Moldova in its campaigns, and how gender works in this subjectification. I explain here how and why men and women migrants and different migrant routes are differently valued and targeted for regulation by the

---

[4] Susan Dewey (2008) tells part of this story in comparing countertrafficking programs in Bosnia, Armenia, and India.

IOM. I hope to discern what IOM discourses and interventions accomplish, what concerns they displace, and what effects they have on women workers in Moldova.

In Moldova and Turkey, the subject of trafficked women is discussed and solutions to trafficking are produced (while other victims, problems, and solutions are erased) through a negotiated process involving research on trafficking, as reflected in campaign materials, but also through the local reasoning of the Moldovan elites implementing these projects. Attending to elites' roles is important because, as David Mosse puts it, we have to assume the following:

> International policy regimes do not simply arrive, but are produced by intermediary actors, frontline workers ... who translate abstract global policy into their own ambitions, interests and values. These actors are both objects and agents of global policy, charged with bringing about the new normative/legal and administrative orders, imposing definitions which categorize people, making them into proper consumers, clients, users or patients. (2005, 20)

From the perspective of these front-line workers, US and EU policies and attitudes about migration, sexual commerce, and borders are being exported through funding initiatives. As these policies are increasingly appropriated and applied throughout the world (Shah 2008, 2014; Bernstein 2008; Mahdavi 2011), it is important to recognize that they are refracted through local political and economic debates and local gendered moral economies. We need to see not only how larger processes are manifested in different sociocultural contexts (Dewey 2008) but also how they are specifically interpreted in discrete locales. Doing so allows the agency of local actors to emerge more clearly and helps us understand how ideas and policies are localized.

In this chapter, I deploy ethnographic techniques to illustrate how knowledge about migrant women's problems and solutions to them are produced through the dissemination of neoliberal policy ideals directed by a global development agenda based in the West, and also through local considerations and ideas about gender, ethnicity, class, and urbanity. In Moldova, the panic over the symbolically charged site of women's sexuality and mobility and the projects such panic subsequently spawns provide a rich mine from which elite women working at the IOM extract concerns about local gendered moral economies in a state of flux. They take moral stances regarding ways of making a living and regarding gender and labor roles in a changing market-oriented and neoliberalizing economic and social environment. These conventional categories (similar to those expressed by women from Gagauz Yeri in previous chapters) deem certain types of migrations and certain desires for wealth and worldliness appropriate only to certain migrants, sexes, or classes, or only if they are realized by means of journeys taken on certain migration routes.

These local narratives have gendered effects that coincide with those of global neoliberalism and Western funding priorities that focus on countering sex trafficking and prostitution. The effect of these campaigns is to prevent *all women* from migrating abroad. In so doing, they ignore the structural problems of joblessness and poverty in Moldova and the importance of working to women, particularly mothers. Ideas about gender (and issues of class, urbanity, and ethnicity) in the IOM's discourse play a key role in structuring politics and legitimating certain elites and agendas. From different locations (official documentation and agendas at IOM headquarters and regional offices at IOM-Moldova and IOM-Turkey) and through different campaigns over time, IOM profiles of gendered victims and culprits permit or legitimate certain political and economic policies and imaginings and dismiss others.

Here, after giving a short history of the IOM, I detail the shifting gendered assumptions and effects of three consecutive IOM-Moldova projects in the 2000s ("You Are Not a Commodity," "Smart Migration," and "Migration Management") and, briefly, one out of IOM-Turkey ("Have You Seen My Mother?"). I then analyze the assumptions about the moralities of women's mobility in these campaigns and elite narratives, as well as in wider migration management initiatives. I conclude by examining the effects of these gendered moral economies on women migrants.

Although IOM projects categorize women as passive victims of economic transformations, in its later campaigns the IOM recognized that migrants are also now the primary *agents* for economic development in Moldovan communities (as we heard women migrants themselves assert in earlier chapters). However, in new "migration management" plans this positive, active role for the migrant is reserved for men, while women migrants continue to be represented as victims and are encouraged to stay home. In this, these projects continue to collude with the feminization of the private realm and the masculinization of the public sphere in Moldova, as has been the effect of state processes in other formerly socialist settings (Gal 1994b; Gal and Kligman 2000b; Pine 2002). The gendered moral economies at work here also justify new stratifications taking root in Moldova; between NGO elite women and other women in Moldova, between those who are encouraged to migrate ("opportunity-driven migrants") and those whose migrations are negatively marked ("desperation-" or "poverty-driven" migrants); between those who go to Russia and those who work in Turkey; and between male migrants and female migrants. I show here, as others have, that these policies align with antimigration agendas, but I also point out that they particularly target women's, not men's, mobility.[5] I explain here the effects of these dynamics on the Gagauz case in particular.[6]

IOM Campaigns

The IOM was established in 1951 to help relocate individuals who had been displaced during and after World War II, and as such is a classic Western Cold War institution.[7] The organization became concerned with both gender

---

[5] That some forms of economic migration—here, men's—is actually encouraged in this case seems a peculiarity of a "migrant-giver" nation and distinguishes the policies in Moldova from those enacted in the United States or the EU, discussed in other analyses above.

[6] The following narratives and project information were collected in 2004–5 in both Moldova and Turkey. I interviewed six IOM-Moldova officials (the transitional chief of mission, the countertrafficking project manager, the Better Borders project manager, the national outreach coordinator, the psychiatrist of the IOM-Moldova– and La Strada–run shelter for victims of trafficking, and the media campaign manager). I also met a group of twelve youth (college student) volunteers for IOM, one of whom was Gagauz. The IOM-Moldova volunteer coordinator, Lena, herself a college student, was my translator for interviews with those who did not speak English, and also translated website and print materials for me. I conducted participant observation in a countertrafficking presentation targeted to an audience of ten high school students. During the Turkish portion of my research project, I spent one week at IOM-Turkey's Ankara office, where the countertrafficking activities were based. Even this Turkish office was very Moldova-oriented: the chief of mission for IOM-Turkey was formerly chief of mission at IOM-Moldova, and the "transitional" chief of mission at IOM-Moldova, who had taken her place, had also recently moved to work at IOM-Turkey as the countertrafficking media consultant. I interviewed four people at the IOM-Turkey offices (chief of mission, countertrafficking media consultant, and two different countertrafficking project managers). With respect to other organizations, I interviewed one IREX employee who was project manager for a countertrafficking project that had concluded; the assistant director of the Moldovan Migration Department; and three project managers at Contact, an NGO partnered with IOM-Moldova that dealt with countertrafficking in Gagauz Yeri. Besides the interviews, I spent time with most of these individuals informally and would check in with them if I was in Istanbul and Chișinău, respectively. At that time and since then, I also have tracked IOM activities through its websites and publications (IOM 2003, 2004, 2005, 2007, 2010).

[7] The IOM's main mission, according to its constitution, is to assist in the "operational challenges of migration management," advance a better understanding of migration, assist in social and economic development through migration, and better the lives of migrants. Originally called the

issues and countertrafficking in Eastern Europe in the mid-1990s. These efforts are funded primarily by the EU and Sweden and supported by the United States. Even if not directly funded by the United States, NGOs and IGOs in Moldova are influenced by US concerns over sex trafficking, concerns that emerged particularly during the George W. Bush administration. The US Trafficking Victims Protection Act, initially passed in 2000, set up a three-tier system to monitor individual states' progress in countertrafficking; this system is still in place, and ranks countries accordingly.[8] According to Musto, concern with sex trafficking is tied to the faith-based conservative position that reduces all sex work to forced prostitution; if an organization takes an ideologically more nuanced position on the latter, its funding is cut (2008, 8). Countertrafficking programs are part of the IOM's broader "Regulating Migration" program theme and focus on (1) the prevention and greater awareness of trafficking, (2) the prosecution of criminals, and (3) the rehabilitation of victims of trafficking.[9] As analyzed by Berman,

---

Intergovernmental Committee on European Migration, its history includes assistance to Czech refugees in Hungary; assistance to Jews fleeing the Soviet Union; and the relocation of refugees from Vietnam, Laos, and Cambodia. In 1980, it was renamed the Intergovernmental Committee on Migration to reflect its increasingly global concerns, and in 1989 it became the IOM. Since the end of the Cold War, its activities have included helping refugees from Iraq and providing assistance to those displaced in Chechnya and in the former Yugoslavia. The concerns with trafficking began in southeast and east Asia and in Central America, two places where Western military interventions had taken place and where international development efforts were already focused. Concerns over trafficking in eastern and central Europe and the former Soviet Union soon followed. The full members of the IOM now include many eastern and central European states, while Russia, Bosnia and Herzegovina, Estonia, Macedonia, Turkey, and Turkmenistan are only observing members. Full members in eastern and central Europe include Albania, Armenia, Azerbaijan, Bulgaria, Croatia, the Czech Republic, Hungary, Kyrgyzstan, Latvia, Lithuania, Moldova, Poland, Romania, Serbia and Montenegro, Slovakia, Slovenia, and Ukraine. According to Musto, perspectives on the type of exploitation that trafficking constitutes vary among NGOs and IGOs. She argues that the IOM views trafficking as a human rights issue (as opposed to a those who see it as a migration or a sexual labor issue, those holding abolitionist or neoabolitionist perspectives who see it as an issue of slavery, and those who see it as a religious, faith-based issue) (2008, 7).

[8] For further analysis of the Trafficking Victims Protection Act, see Wendy Chapkis (2005).

[9] The IOM accepts the definition of trafficking as stated in the Protocol to Prevent, Suppress and Punish Trafficking in Persons, especially Women and Children supplementing the UN Convention Against Transnational Organized Crime. Here, trafficking is understood as "the recruitment, transportation, transfer, harboring, or receipt of persons, by the threat or use of force, by abduction, fraud, deception, coercion or the abuse of power or by the giving or receiving of payments or benefits to achieve the consent of a person having control over another person for the purpose of exploitation." Exploitation involves "prostitution of others or other forms of sexual exploitation, forced labor or services, slavery or similar practices to slavery, servitude, or the removal of organs." In the UN definition, trafficking is distinguished from smuggling activities, which serve only to secure a financial reward for the smuggler for procuring illegal entry into a state. The

these kinds of countertrafficking programs and the "discursive verbosity" about trafficking in media accounts of the 1990s represented young white females as purely naive victims of racially marked (often Balkan) criminal networks (2003). They focused on criminalization and security issues and tended to disregard the issues of poverty that prompted these problems. These reductionist tendencies are reflected in countertrafficking programs in other states as well (Dewey 2008; Bernstein 2008; Zheng 2008b; Brennan 2008; Mahdavi 2011).

These priorities were represented in the IOM-Moldova 2002 campaign "You Are Not a Commodity." The campaign was part of the IOM's wider countertrafficking activities and involved opening a trafficking hotline and a local shelter for repatriated victims of trafficking. Women were posited in the campaign to be victims of traffickers, who were individuals involved in criminal networks taking advantage of economic transformations under way in formerly socialist states. In other words, women were symbolically treated as commodities in a new criminal economy burgeoning alongside market capitalism. The goals of the campaign were to prevent women from leaving, to imprison criminals, and to repatriate victims. The 2002 "You Are Not a Commodity" Moldovan campaign was centered at the IOM office in Romania, and so the campaign materials were only in the Romanian language (figure 5.1).

By 2004, the IOM had opened an independent Moldovan mission. Government offices in Moldova were often stuffy, modernist, dark, and drab, with old furniture and computers, reflecting the government's poverty. But international NGO and IGO offices like the IOM were fast-paced, colorful, sleek, and bright, and housed the latest technology, reflecting their Western funding. The IOM was full of frenetic energy, reminiscent of a New York marketing firm, and was staffed by highly ambitious and well-educated individuals (whether local or Westerners) who spoke several languages (most

---

IOM accepts this UN definition, but its own definition of trafficking is broader and overlaps with smuggling at times: "Trafficking occurs when a migrant is illicitly engaged (recruited, kidnapped, sold, etc.) and/or moved, either within national or across international borders; and when intermediaries (traffickers) during any part of this process obtain economic or other profit by means of deception, coercion and/or other forms of exploitation under conditions that violate the fundamental human rights of migrants." In the detailing of this definition, "recruited," "deception," and "exploitation" are taken to be conditions of both legal and illegal migration and are defined very broadly as things that also occur "within the wider context of irregular migration." In this definition of trafficking, the IOM admits that the range of services considered trafficking, the reasons individual migrants may seek them out, and the conditions of migration—legal or illegal—all vary. This definition also allows, however, for a wider definition of who a trafficker might be.

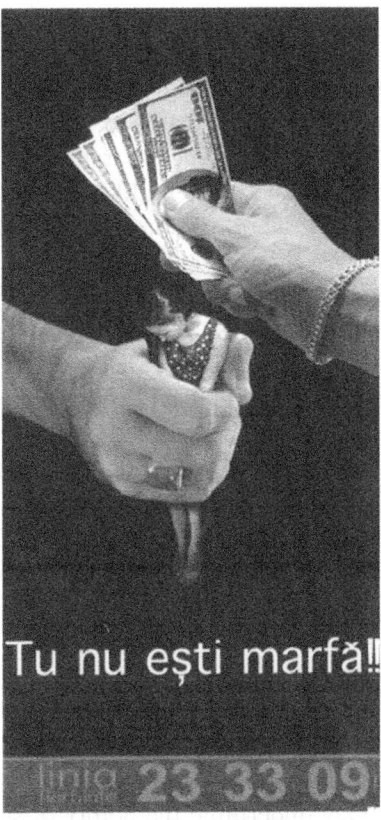

Figure 5.1. Branding image for the IOM "You Are Not a Commodity" campaign, 2002. This image is from the cover of a pamphlet.

included English among them). Glossy campaign photos lined the walls; staff gathered nearby at an in-house (on the same floor) café and gossiped. The cafeterias people frequented on their lunch hour were expensive by national standards but were also cleaner and served better food. They were open only to other NGO and IGO staff in Chişinău, a community of a few hundred people, many of whom knew each other professionally and personally. The chiefs of mission of both IOM-Moldova and IOM-Turkey were individuals from Europe and the United States, but otherwise the offices were staffed by local elites. Most of the people employed by or volunteering at IOM-Moldova were Moldovan, although some were part of a Russian-speaking elite. There were no individuals from Gagauz Yeri, except one young woman volunteer.

By this time, the "You Are Not a Commodity" campaign and related countertrafficking activities had come under widespread criticism among scholars and activists working with migrant women. They pointed out that while some women were forced to go abroad, the majority were migrating voluntarily and for a variety of jobs, such as trade or domestic work, or even for sex work, and that men and women alike were falling into conditions of trafficking that involved labor exploitation other than sexual exploitation (see, e.g., Wijers 1998; Kempadoo and Doezema 1998; Ehrenreich and Hochschild 2002; Berman 2003; Brennan 2004, 2008; Global Movement against Migration Control 2004; Sharma 2005; Soderlund 2005; Markon 2007; Dewey 2008; Bernstein 2008; Cheng 2008, 2010; Shah 2008; Plambech 2008; Briones 2008; Mahdavi 2011). Ethnographers and others who work with migrant sex workers pointed out that migrants often know the risks of trafficking but are willing to take those risks because of widespread poverty and joblessness, issues that the campaigns like those conducted by the IOM ignored (Gülçür and Ilkkaracan 2002; Keough 2003, 2004; Agustin 2007; Zheng 2008b). As a result of ignoring these issues and projecting women instead as simple victims, Susan Dewey argues, NGOs like the IOM draw on

> sexist stereotypes that separate women into categories of guilt and innocence; they deeply disadvantage women who do not fit the narrow set of criteria devised by international organizations, governments, and aid agencies and they may undermine the ability of such groups to implement real change in women's lives. (2008, 6)

When I returned to the IOM in the fall of 2004, I found that the IOM's own assessments of its programs supported such insights, and as a result, the organization had begun a new campaign. Alexei, a recent graduate of the Department of Communication at the University of Moldova and IOM-Moldova's national outreach coordinator, described to me how IOM had switched from what he called the "negative" message of the "You Are Not a Commodity" campaign to a more "positive" campaign, "Smart Migration," in 2003–4 (figure 5.2). Alexei explained that in interviews with women who called the trafficking hotline and those who had been assisted at the IOM's shelter for victims of trafficking, women did not identify as victims at all. In fact, it was increasingly recognized that women were choosing to go abroad voluntarily. According to recent IOM statistics, although 65 percent of these women thought they were going abroad for "low-risk" work such as construction or domestic work, up to 35 percent knew that they would be expected to do a "high-risk" job such as begging, dancing, or sex work. Moreover, many had been what the IOM called "retrafficked." In other words, after escaping a trafficking situation, they chose to go abroad again under similar conditions, thinking they would not be trafficked this time. Why would they agree to do this? New data in IOM materials suggested that a combination of poverty, experiences of sexual and domestic abuse, psychological trauma, and lack of education made women desperate to go abroad and even endure abusive situations. It was also pointed out in these materials that many of these women (33 percent) were mothers seeking a way to support their children.[10] Moreover, campaign materials admitted to a new profile of the "trafficker." These newer materials pointed out that most recruiters were local women acquainted with the potential victim and not, as former materials had emphasized, foreigners from the Balkans or Turkey. The profile of the victims had also diversified. New data noted that men, boys, and older women were also trafficked for enslavement as beggars, construction workers, or domestics.

Of the migrant domestic workers, most cited by the organization Contact as trafficked were women from Gagauz Yeri. In fact, adding these women helped the organization justify its mission. Were it not for the fifty migrant domestics identified as victims of trafficking in 2004, the IOM beneficiary numbers would have fallen drastically short of the IOM's target. A lack of beneficiaries of the programs would have made it difficult to gain further funding for the IOM-Moldova countertrafficking campaigns. Funding was a deep concern, as it was the basis not only for the projects but also for the staff's jobs and salaries (see Dewey 2008). Lana, the IOM-Moldova countertrafficking manager, admitted to me that they were scrambling to find women "victims." The only way to reach substantial numbers was to include the fifty Gagauz women who had gone to Turkey to work as domestics—women who were not necessarily sexually abused.

A new migration website set up by the IOM in the fall of 2004 also acknowledged the diversity of migration situations and exploitations. The narratives on the website included those concerning five migrants, four of

---

[10] These materials came out in 2005, after I wrote a report for the IOM detailing some aspects of my research in 2005. My findings that many women migrating to Turkey were mothers looking for work may have influenced this particular spin on the issue of trafficking as well. Yet how they used this information is telling: they did not campaign for more jobs for working mothers at home but deployed ideas of desperate mothers as victims to gain sympathy for victims profiled in their countertrafficking campaigns.

Figure 5.2. Branding image for the IOM "Smart Migration" campaign, 2004. The image was used on a number of things, including posters. This image is from a business card–sized flyer. The back presents contact information for the trafficking hotline and a migration information telephone number.

whom were men: two had good experiences working abroad, one was left unpaid, and one was killed by his employer. The fifth narrative focused on a woman who had been tricked into thinking that there was good work abroad and then trafficked. In addition to acknowledging new profiles of traffickers and victims, the realization of the voluntary nature of migration, even for sex work, while not surprising to social scientists studying this phenomenon, was the most difficult challenge to the IOM-Moldova countertrafficking campaign and its ideological assumptions about female victims, traffickers, and the nature of trafficking. Yet proscriptions from IOM headquarters and funders who required data reflecting that the campaigns had achieved results forced them to change their tone, if not their underlying beliefs.

To address the new data, and in an attempt to find more individuals to assist, the IOM changed its language and purported role. The organization now presented its primary role as that of educator for a disorganized woman migrant, who was no longer called a victim but was now a beneficiary of IOM assistance. The goal was to teach women and the wider public about the dangers of trafficking and to offer information about legal migration in order to make women into capable decision makers—to help them make good choices.

Alexei went on to explain how the new "visibility campaign" for "smart migration" used modern marketing techniques such as cross-promotion in traditional (print, radio, television) and new (Internet) media to get its message across. The targets of these campaigns thus were complex and included potential and repatriated women victims, the general public, and particularly youth, but the campaigns were also directed at donor states and organizations. The main tool of the "Smart Migration" campaign was the 2002 film *Lilya 4-Ever*. This tool, he said, offered the IOM a "brand" ("Lilya 4-Ever") for its "products" (i.e., the campaigns), which was useful in competing for funding among the NGO community.

Directed by the Swede Lukas Moodysson, the film (purportedly based on a true story) tells how a teenage girl in a poor "unidentified part of the former Soviet Union" is abandoned by her mother, who moves to America with her lover. Lilya first seeks help from her aunt, but instead of helping, her aunt repossesses Lilya's mother's house from Lilya, leaving the young girl on the street. Lilya then approaches social services, which do not respond to her plight. Her situation at school deteriorates. Then she is convinced by a classmate to prostitute herself to Westerners at a local disco. After her friend too betrays her, Lilya turns to a young local man she meets at the disco, who promises to take her to Europe for a job. She agrees. After entering the "unidentified country in Western Europe," she is locked in a room and forced into work as an unpaid prostitute: she is trafficked.[11] The film is incredibly sad, brutal, and traumatizing for viewers; certainly it gets the audience's attention focused on the dire situation of trafficked young women.

According to Alexei and others, the IOM uses this film to push the audience to better understand trafficking as the IOM sees it. The IOM and formerly trafficked, repatriated women are cast literally as angels who can save victims. After the screening, a half-hour interactive presentation takes place, with IOM staff leading a discussion based on a pamphlet they created titled *Yes or No*, which aims to educate viewers on how to know whether they are being trafficked, how to avoid it, and information on legal migration to Russia and Turkey, among many other places, for students, au pairs, and workers (IOM 2004) (figure 5.3). At this time, they also pass out information about their migration website (www.migratie.md) and the Moldova

---

[11] On the *Lilya 4-Ever* website, one can learn that Lilya is from Estonia and is trafficked to Sweden. The Swedish International Development Cooperation Agency was also funding IOM-Moldova's campaign, and the former chief of mission at this site, who was also chief of mission in Turkey in 2005, was herself Swedish. This particularism is interesting insofar as a virulently antiprostitution brand of feminism is touted in Sweden.

trafficking hotline. In the summer of 2004, they took this show on the road. They rented a minivan with a crew of about ten volunteers, all elite students from Chişinău (many of whom were in media studies), who traveled to cities and towns in Moldova that had been identified as trafficking sites. The idea behind the crew of youth volunteers was to create a network of individuals who would then distribute information to their peers. These elite volunteers were not just the disseminators, then, but also the targets of the campaign.

The information given in the pamphlets, on the website, and in my interviews with IOM staff in 2004 reflected a modified profile of the trafficking criminal and victim, but in a way that shifted the focus of blame for trafficking from the former to the latter. The victim still was presented as a young woman, if a modified one who had voluntarily gone abroad seeking a better life. IOM materials continued to emphasize why and how she made bad choices out of naïveté. Significantly, instead of targeting the criminality of the trafficker, the newer profiles even more than the previous campaign targeted the faulty psychology of the young woman victim. This young woman victim of *sexual* exploitation was highlighted as most at risk, even though the materials also stated that victims were diverse in terms of age, sex, and degree and type of work and exploitation. Similarly, the statistical diversity is belied by the campaign's prime case: Lilya, the most compelling

Figure 5.3. Cover of the pamphlet *Yes or No*, used to help publicize the IOM "Smart Migration" campaign, 2004. The image shows material from the 2002 film *Lilya 4-Ever*. The pamphlet text reads, "You deserve to know all the answers!"

and dramatic example of trafficking. Finally, the IOM contended that the organization was simply preparing women to make their own good choices through providing material with correct information—even though they clearly thought that migration was the wrong choice.

The materials offered were supposed to give information about how to migrate abroad legally, such as what information to know about your destination and the dangers to be aware of in advertisements for jobs, au pair situations, or marriage abroad. Yet these materials portrayed migration as a formidable task. One could not help but be entirely overwhelmed by the legal hoops one would have to jump through and the financial burdens it would take to work abroad legally. The only logical conclusion one could come to was "don't go—you are better off staying home." This also is the lesson learned in *Lilya 4-Ever* (see also Dewey 2008). The film even suggests that women should choose a more traditional route to happiness: becoming a wife to a local man. In one scene, Lilya and a local friend, a boy, play house: The boy pretends out loud, "I have come home from work and you have cooked the bread." This scene upholding "traditional" gender roles is reinvoked in Lilya's nostalgic reminiscences at the end of the film; it is the choice she has forsaken for the riches and better life of the West. The IOM campaign projected an image of itself as offering information and a model for smart migration, but in fact it was biased toward women staying home. Although IOM materials and staff claimed that they wanted not to address women as victims but to empower them to make their own choices, in fact they had made the choice for them already. The campaign even promoted being a good domestic housewife as the best alternative to the risks of migrant work.

These profiles, scenarios, and emphases were obvious in the IOM-Turkey campaign as well, which also used *Lilya 4-Ever* in 2004 to underscore these points. In Moldova, mothers who leave their children to go abroad are warned about the dangers of trafficking not only to the daughters they leave behind but also to themselves. In the case of Turkey, these mothers are emphasized even more. In an advertisement that promoted a Turkish IOM countertrafficking hotline in early 2005, Moldovan children are quoted asking, "Where is my mother?," and saying, "I need her" (see www.countertrafficking.org). According to IOM-Turkey countertrafficking staff, these stories are targeted to potential male clients in Turkey in order to gain sympathy for the situation of the foreign woman (a difficult task in a migrant host country, particularly one in which popular representations of the natasha are not sympathetic). Again, seeing them as "desperate mothers," it seems, is one side of the coin; the other represents them as young, uneducated, perhaps previously sexually abused, psychologically damaged, weak women who made bad choices to leave their children and will silently endure many hardships.

The "Smart Migration" and "Where Is My Mother?" campaign materials hold most of same assumptions of the previous "You Are Not a Commodity" campaign about naive young women who need help. The IOM is positioned as educator and savior. The only logical and moral choice offered to women in this scenario is to stay home: "smart migration" means no migration at all. This is not to say that this is not the best choice for some women; some are uneducated, ignorant of the dangers of trafficking; and I even found many to be oddly trusting of strangers whom they came across, particularly men in Turkey. This campaign can serve to educate these women; in many cases, perhaps it is better for them to stay home. Nonetheless, as we saw in previous chapters, with no work at home, many women find good employment abroad that allows their families to thrive back in Moldova. These jobs allow women new opportunities and freedoms, demonstrating their agency and power. The IOM campaigns are blind to this dimension of migrant labor in many ways. The IOM encourages women to stay home, but they do not offer them alternatives to work and advancement at home.

A gendered moral economy of transnational labor is constituted through these campaigns. Like the discourses of blame in local Gagauz communities illustrated in chapter 1, IOM discourses also place blame for local social disorder on women and justify the feminization of the private realm in this post-Soviet context. Although there are some consistencies between these and previous campaigns, the "Smart Migration" campaign has a different conceptualization of who is to blame for trafficking: instead of targeting the criminality of the foreign male trafficker, the new capitalist economy, or even a local woman trafficker, it blames the faulty psychology of women who chose to go abroad. In turn, changing women's psychology becomes the solution to trafficking. Scholars have associated such shifts in the design of global development projects targeting women in this region with a neoliberal governmentality that focuses culpability on individual psychology over broader economic or political injustices (Rivkin-Fish 2005; Hemment 2007).[12] This forms an integral part of the gendered moral economies of these campaigns.

---

[12] Julie Hemment's (2007) work in Russia on how violence-against-women campaigns target women offers insight on this point of how NGO campaigns focusing on women may represent women's defective psychology as part of the source of their troubles, as opposed to looking to

This discourse analysis so far has focused on the IOM's official stance as reflected in the organization's printed and online materials and media representations. The tensions and consistencies involved in the shift in economic regime to a neoliberal one emphasizing the private market and personal responsibility rather than state welfare are reflected as well in the priorities identified by the IOM headquarters and the concerns of those charged with implementing these priorities, the countertrafficking staff at IOM-Moldova and IOM-Turkey.

The Morality of Women's Mobility

This shift in blame that now sees women themselves as responsible for the problem of trafficking is also present in the narratives of those implementing countertrafficking campaigns. Their discursive practices draw on local gendered moral economies that blame the ignorance of local rural women for social disorder. I interviewed two women employees who worked at the IOM and one who worked at another NGO. A wider range of interactions took place at the IOM, after I observed a presentation to an IOM targeted audience, or while eating lunch or chatting with staff at the in-house café.

I would characterize the employees' response to the shift in campaign strategies as sounding two main notes. First, after their initial disbelief in their own new data and my research, which showed that women's voluntary migration to Turkey actually existed, they expressed unease and continued frustration with women who chose to go abroad. For them, if the problem of trafficking was not an issue of rural young women *ignorant* of trafficking risks, then it was an issue of women making *immoral* decisions to work abroad. The second note verbalized many of the same understandings of class, urbanity, and upward mobility as were expressed in the narratives of the women of Gagauz Yeri in previous chapters. It was not only that women, in particular mothers, were leaving, but that women of a certain place in this society were seeking to move up in the world that occasioned controversy. This gendered moral economy regarding female migrant laborers from Moldova to Turkey, like that of the community members in Gagauz Yeri, focused on the need and responsibility of mothers to be at home with their children.

---

political-economic determinants of exploitations. For narratives of personal responsibility (as opposed to the state's or the economy's instability as responsible) in new discourses on Russian reproductive health, see Michele Rivkin-Fish (2004, 2005).

As we walked to the NGO/IGO staff cafeteria in Chişinău one day, I spoke with Anca, an NGO official, a twenty-something, university-educated Moldovan who grew up in rural Moldova but now lived in the capital. She explained to me how her father was left unemployed after 1999 and that her mother, who took on the responsibility of supporting her family, did so through any kind of work she could find *within* Moldova. Anca and others like her with whom I spoke could understand how women might be duped by stories of good jobs, good money, and a better life to go abroad and then end up trafficked, but they were frustrated by the fact that such women would keep trying, and even more by the success stories of women who worked abroad. Among this set of Moldovan women working at IGOs, there was great resistance to, and at times even denial of, the idea that there were good jobs in Turkey for women. When pressed, Anca admitted that underemployment and underpayment are key problems in Moldova and are why women seek work abroad, but she still found it frustrating that they would leave their families to go to Turkey to work as domestics. She saw these women as participating in a vicious cycle of naïveté. During this informal conversation, the following picture emerged as Anca's view of the typical scenario: a young couple gets married and has a child, but they do not have enough to buy a house, so without even trying to make it in Moldova, they leave their children with their parents and go abroad. They may come back with money to buy a house, but they do not have enough to fill it with anything and have forgone their employment opportunities at home, so they have to go abroad again. And while there, they get used to "drinking coffee and smoking cigarettes." In the end, they are not capable of living in their village.

As with Anca, when I told Iris about my research, she was shocked to hear that domestic work actually existed in Turkey, assuming that this was just a traffickers' ploy. Iris was another university-educated Moldovan woman, an official involved in IOM campaigns against trafficking in women. She did not always agree with the language or goals of the "Smart Migration" campaigns. This was evident when she rolled her eyes at the idea of calling the women at the shelter "beneficiaries" of IOM aid, instead of the victims she clearly felt they were. The fact that women might be making choices to go to Turkey voluntarily and that such a choice might be based on sound information, secure and trustworthy kin and friendship networks, and even knowledge and experience was a challenge to her line of thought. Narratives like hers were infused with a strain of culpability that focused particularly on uneducated village women (not men), and especially mothers, who chose to migrate for a better, worldlier life. For Iris, as for Anca, the problem of trafficking came down to one of women making not only uninformed but also immoral choices to go abroad. I talked with Iris one evening after she had given one of her many presentations of the film *Lilya 4-Ever* as part of the IOM's "Smart Migration" countertrafficking campaign. For her, the family of the victim, particularly the mother, was to blame: "I don't know if it is in our culture, or what," she explained, "but our mothers leave their children." Whereas the question-and-answer period which Iris ran after the screening focused on Lilya's choices to stay or go, here Iris pointed to the voluntary female migrant in the film, the mother, as the ultimate culprit and her daughter as her victim.

These narratives reflect some of the same ideas as those held in Gagauz Yeri (and even Turkey) about the place of women from Gagauz Yeri. In this and other elite narratives, I found that mothers (not fathers) who migrated for work to provide a better life for their families were blamed for social disorder in Moldova. They were seen as transgressors not only of geographic boundaries but also of local moral codes that policed the economic, social, and physical mobility of women. Anca's views coincided with IOM projects and gendered neoliberal tenets that devolved responsibility to individual women, but they did not necessarily descend from such neoliberal priorities, and they included a view of all migrant women (not just trafficked ones), particularly mothers.

To understand her views, we have to take into account the dissemination of funds and funding priorities that contribute to isolating trafficking victims as the only women migrants worthy of assistance, but we also need to be attentive to the local contexts and stratifications within the former Soviet republics and Moldova. First, as Michele Rivkin-Fish discusses in her ethnography of women's health in post-Soviet Russia, low birth rates in the Soviet and now former Soviet space have long been blamed on "selfish" and "ignorant" women (2004, 2005). This discourse of blame for a demographic crisis provides one of the contexts in which finding a mother's psychology at fault for social disorder and trafficking becomes a compelling narrative. There is also, as Rivkin-Fish (2005) and Julie Hemment (2007) point out, an inherent distrust of public, state-run initiatives for women in the post-Soviet space, a distrust that legitimates a new personal and individual locus for change. In the elite Moldovan reactions to the success of women migrants from Gagauz Yeri, we must also take into account assumptions about the backwardness of Gagauz as opposed to other regions of Moldova. Gagauz communities in Moldova are perceived by NGOs to be more "traditional" than other Moldovan communities in terms of gender relations, and thus the women are deemed particularly susceptible to domestic abuse. Also, domestic abuse was considered more pronounced in Gagauz Yeri. Some Gagauz women migrants acknowledged that migration is sometimes a response to domestic abuse, but this should not be taken to mean that this is peculiar to the Gagauz case. From what I witnessed in and outside of Gagauz homes, women from Gagauz Yeri were not more vulnerable to men's abuse than other women in Moldova. I would suggest we take into account the negative images of the Gagauz in Moldova to understand these representations. As discussed previously, to whom the Gagauz belong—Central Asian Turks, Turkey, Bulgaria, Russia, Moldova—has long been in question here. For Moldovans, Gagauz inhabit a liminal identity with regard to the key divide of European civilization and Oriental barbarism (which in this case means both Islamic Oriental and Russian Oriental) and are thus associated with these "others." This thrusts them into ambiguous alignment with Turkey or with Russia and supports distrust of them as some sort of fifth column in Moldova. Thus, migrant women from Gagauz Yeri are taken to be especially backward, and one of the signs of backwardness is low status and abuse of women. Such images are of long standing in European views of rurality and savagery.

Another thing to consider as structuring these professional women's perspectives on voluntary women's migration is that even though the women who worked at the IOM and other NGOs were part of an elite, they themselves had few opportunities to go abroad. When they did travel, they had to do so legally, which was difficult. They envisioned their own migration as a different "opportunity-driven" pattern. Thus their anger and frustration might also be understood as a response to the threat that lower-class, village women—Gagauz, at that—were granted these opportunities to be "worldly." To them, it was appropriate for informed, educated women to go abroad to work legally; they had the means and the smarts to do so (even though here too, trafficking was sometimes feared). But as for other women, particularly uneducated villagers—what were they doing going abroad? Perhaps some of these elite women had hopes of gaining positions that allowed them to travel and even marry and settle abroad. I know that Anca often asked me about my own travels. I had recently come back from a conference in Vienna, and she thought longingly of going there herself someday.[13] Could this impression also be left over from Soviet times, when only the con-

---

[13] For more on the upward mobility of postsocialist women, see Kristen Ghodsee's analysis of the case of Bulgarian women (2005).

nected, the well-educated, and the skilled were allowed to travel abroad? Yet even in that era, the act of going abroad was transgressive. Only those citizens who were party members and who pledged that their sole purpose in going abroad was to spread communism were allowed to exit the country. There is a still a certain sense here that those who leave have somehow sold out. All of these local gendered moral economies structure and help these elites make sense of women's migrations from Moldova. Countertrafficking programs embolden these moral economies.

Lana, head of countertrafficking at IOM-Moldova, was also frustrated by female migrant success stories and frankly did not believe that many of them really existed. She thought women were either so traumatized or stupid that they did not know they were victimized or were too proud to admit it. For her, it was not only that ignorant villagers had success stories but that some of her peers were also going abroad to work illegally. Lana said she had a friend who went to Egypt to do consumption, by which she meant sitting with clients at restaurants, dancing with them, and entertaining them so they would buy drinks. She had returned with money, new jewelry, and an Egyptian husband. But Lana suspected that her friend had not told the truth about the exploitations she suffered to gain these rewards. She described seeing pictures of such women doing "consumption"—and how, if you look at their faces when they are dancing with clients, "they look dead." In the end, she told me, her friend returned to Moldova for good, divorced the foreigner, and married a Moldovan man. This ending confirmed for Lana that it was not morally legitimate to seek out a better life abroad.

Similarly, one of the IOM volunteers I came to know, Alisa, a young woman from Gagauz Yeri, had a Turkish male suitor who flew her to Turkey for weeks at a time to visit him. She did not tell a lot of people about this, but not because they would worry that she would be trafficked. Her reticence was more because she knew she would be greeted with a combination of jealousy (of the money and travel) and disdain (of a woman who would be with a Turkish man to get money and to travel). Alisa responded to my concerns that she might be exploited by her suitors by saying that she was in control of these men. She told me stories of how she heartlessly manipulated them to give her money. And she insisted that she was not forced into any situation of sexual or physical harm. Travels like Alisa's were considered success stories for educated women, let alone for uneducated villagers, but ones that came at the cost of violating loyalties to conventional moral codes.

According to Lana, finding work or a husband abroad was considered a route to success for an educated woman, but such upper-class success stories set a bad example to uneducated young village girls. Those things were not deemed appropriate desires for a villager and could put them in danger. One young woman from Gagauz Yeri also demonstrated this distinction. Her reason for going abroad was not because she desperately needed the money but instead because she wanted to "see the world," and if this meant starting as an au pair in Turkey, where she was promised $800 a month since she knew English, that was okay with her. This kind of opportunity-driven reasoning was seen as appropriate for youth, even female youth, in some ways, but not for young mothers. At the same time, it was rife with anxieties over wanting too much.

These conventional categories deem certain types of migrations and desires for wealth and worldliness as appropriate only to certain types of women. They show the development of new stratifications between women migrants; distinctions between "opportunity-driven" and "desperation-driven" migrants that work with old and new ideas about class and urbanity as well as ethnicity in Moldova to construct this gendered moral economy. These notions help elite women grapple with, and find their own place in, a rapidly changing socioeconomic environment. At the same time, such gendered moral economies, combined with IOM campaigns (even if in tension with them sometimes) and donor frameworks, blame migrant women, especially mothers, for the problem of social disorder and trafficking and ignore the common underlying economic causes of both. This latter point came out in women's narratives in Gagauz Yeri, and it emerged as well in the villagers' responses to the IOM's "Smart Migration" campaign.

Responses to the IOM's Smart Migration Campaign

Allegiances to funder priorities were reflected in IOM campaigns in Moldova, both because such a posture would secure funding (and salaries for employees) (see Musto 2008; Dewey 2008) and because in many senses, these priorities aligned with local elites' beliefs about women. NGOs and the funding community were thus among the targets of the campaign. Yet the people who were intended to benefit the most from it were the youth of Moldova, particularly uneducated young women. Even so, many elite students were also targeted in the hope that the word would spread more generally and they could act as good models to others.

Iris invited me to a screening and discussion of *Lilya 4-Ever* with a group of elite high school students. The students spoke English and, as they told me with evident pride, volunteered at many different NGOs. After this screening, Iris asked the students to tell her who they thought was to blame for Lilya's situation. For their initial round of answers, they responded in English, and then they continued the discussion in Moldovan and Russian. Afterward, Iris and I discussed their responses. It might not be surprising, since the campaign and the film itself lead one to blame the victim, and IOM staff also see women as to blame, that students saw Lilya herself responsible for her situation. "She should've stayed in school," one remarked; "She could've gotten a job," another said; and still another: "She should've known better." The secondary culprit was her mother, according to the group. After that, discos where prostitution was allowed were blamed, and then the failure of social services.

Iris was disappointed by their responses and said she found them cruel not to see how it was Lilya herself who was the victim. Iris, I recall here, blamed Lilya's mother and family for her fate. She said that this harsh blaming of the victim was peculiar to elite groups like this one: since they could not relate to a poor girl, they could not sympathize with her. Yet when I asked about the response of villagers (as opposed to elites) to the campaign when it was taken across the country in the minivan over the summer, she sighed and explained that they were not incredibly moved by the victimization of the trafficked girl, either. Some of them appreciated the information, but villagers were impressed most by the amount of money spent on the campaign materials, video equipment, movie, computers, and the minivan itself (a Mercedes). They were also impressed by the well-dressed, well-educated youth who could afford to do unpaid internships for the campaign. Why, these villagers asked, did you not spend that campaign money on giving us jobs instead? This sentiment echoes the economic concerns expressed in the narratives of Gagauz Yeri related earlier in the book. It is an especially salient objection here, since those campaigns were finding it difficult to identify many actual victims of sex trafficking.

Even though the IOM admitted that poverty was the main reason for trafficking in women, the "Smart Migration" campaign, like the "You Are Not a Commodity" campaign, focused on disseminating information instead of on job creation as a means of prevention. I asked the IOM staff about this odd emphasis, and several pointed to some limited job training programs for repatriated victims of trafficking (part of their reintegration process) and even more limited programs at the preventive stage for "at-risk" populations. For both programs, they worked with the Ministry of Labor, Family, and Social Protection and other local NGOs that were trying to create jobs in

Moldova. Yet, that one-third of the population (half of the working population) took care of their needs by working abroad was taken to be something they could not change. Job-creation programs were small and few and far between. Even if jobs were created, they often paid too little to live on, as the average monthly income at this time was about $30 (Government of the Republic of Moldova 2004; World Bank 2004, 2005; IOM 2005). Several IOM staff pointed out that donors' funding priorities precluded them from focusing on poverty at home: Most donors, they claimed, do not fund at-risk populations but only victimized ones, and it was hard to find funding for the general economic and social dislocation that caused trafficking and other exploitations. It was even harder to find funding for nonfemale victims of trafficking, Lana claimed. When I walked into my interview with her, she was on the phone trying to find help for a male victim of forced labor who had been trafficked to Russia. She expressed her frustration to me that they could not help this man and that their aid was only for women victims, whom they were having trouble finding. Lana likened the IOM to doctors who give medicine for symptoms of the flu but cannot provide flu shots to prevent it. "If people have their own money to get a flu shot, then they can do it!" Other than IGOs, NGOs, and wealthy individuals, IOM staff thought that outside investment might help. Yet, as Lana pointed out, it angers her that European companies are applauded for "bringing jobs" to Moldova by locating their factories there, when in fact they benefit greatly from cheap Moldovan labor as they pay Moldovans only slightly above the existing average wage. This does not alleviate local poverty but only perpetuates global inequity.

What about seeking assistance from the Moldovan state? When I put this question to IOM staff, they all answered, as Iris summarized, "It is corrupt and poor. There is no hope there." This comment goes straight to the heart— or lack thereof—of the neoliberal moral economy in Moldova. The lack of expectations of the state excuses it from the obligation of job creation and thus colludes with neoliberal rationales that place greater burdens for social welfare on individuals. In this case, the blame is gendered, and focused particularly on mothers, who were perceived to hold primary responsibility for social disorder.

Because of the problem of the lack of victims and thus the lack of proven results, countertrafficking campaigns were becoming harder to fund at the IOM, though they were still very active. In the meantime, since 2005, IOM agendas have moved to better understand the economic role that migrant workers play in development in Moldova and have funded projects to assist some migrant workers. Where do female migrants fit into these campaigns and the new "migration and development nexus?" In comparing these campaigns in this broader context, I demonstrate even more deeply the gendered effects of IOM projects.

Migration Management

The "Smart Migration" campaign, even though it advanced information about legal travel abroad as an alternative to undocumented migration and trafficking, really colluded in keeping women at home, even if they did not have jobs and were unable to survive or advance without them. Yet lately, alongside these agendas, IOM-Moldova is also increasingly recognizing that efforts to stem migration are breaking under the very economic constraints that the commuter women in this book face: there are no jobs and social services in Moldova, and many people live below the poverty line. As a result, women, including many mothers, continue to go abroad to work despite the risks to themselves or their daughters left at home. Moreover, many women do find well-paying jobs in decent conditions and manage to mother transnationally; they represent very real success stories. The international development community and the IOM are beginning to take note of this, especially as migrant remittances roll in.

These remittances are considerable. This was indicated in the Kiel Institute Report, an extensive survey research report on migration in Moldova funded by the IOM, which was unveiled at IOM-Moldova on the first "Migrants' Day," December 18, 2006 (Lücke, Mahmoud, and Pinger 2007). According to this report, in 2005, remittances constituted up to US$1 billion, or 30 percent of gross domestic product (up from only 5 percent in 1997) and contributed up to 50 percent of each migrant worker's household budget. Some 85 percent of households surveyed said that their incomes had increased as a result of their migration (although 28 percent said that the absence of parents for the children left behind was a problem). Indeed, the report admitted that 40 percent of the migrants are heads of households and their average age is thirty-five. The report offered the following recommendation:

> Because of the large role of remittances in reducing poverty at the household level, policies should not focus on migration prevention, but rather on helping migrants to maximise the gains from migration.

It also recommended the legalization of illegal migrant labor routes that are the most prosperous in terms of remittances.

The Kiel Institute Report recommended that such legal opportunities not encourage migrant laborers to emigrate permanently, since this would deter remittances. Very few migrants, only 13 percent, plan to stay abroad, according to the report, and it should stay that way. Addressing concerns that Moldova could become a nation without people, the Kiel report suggested that Moldova is and should remain a nation of migrants—a "diaspora." Full membership in another nation-state, it is argued, prevents individuals from investing in their country back home—thus ending migrant remittances and the benefits to migrant workers' communities and the Moldovan economy. They are encouraged to remain commuters, and the state is encouraged to work with host countries to create guest worker systems whereby migrants would not gain residence or family reunification rights in the host society but would instead continue to invest in their home societies. The report suggested that migrants might have to pay income taxes in the host country, but it also urged that Moldova "should strive for bilateral agreements that give migrants the choice of paying Social Fund contributions on legal income from abroad in Moldova" while also avoiding "double taxation" of remittances, which would drive the money underground. Finally, it suggested that Moldova create strong links with the diaspora to "increase the likelihood of a migrant returning to MD [Moldova] for good." Such efforts would involve creating advice centers in host countries. The report suggested in particular that Moscow, as the place where most migrants go, would be a great place to start.[14]

Since late 2005 or so, the main headquarters of the IOM has been touting migration as a tool for development—something referred to as a "migration-development nexus" in the development community. This campaign continues to encourage migrant labor as opposed to focusing on job creation at home, and thus, like the countertrafficking campaigns, is aligned with and influenced by neoliberal structural adjustment policies. The IOM's main office is now trying to encourage IOM-Moldova to admit that migrant labor is a reality and necessity, and to refrain from trying to prevent it. As an

---

[14] The new focus on remittances has also received attention from scholars. Savitri Taylor's take on it is similar to the Kiel Institute Report's positive notion of remittances as a route to development (2005). Madeleine Wong (2006) offers an interesting gendered scalar analysis of the meaning of remittances. She details how women migrants' gendered obligations to remit their wages involve varying degrees of agency and contestation, but sustain the transnational family socially and economically nonetheless. Finally, Ester Hernandez and Susan Bibler Coutin (2006), also considering the social costs of remittances, question whether or not remittances are "cost-free" as many economists claim. They are interested in how this encouragement of remittances plays into (or resists) neoliberalism.

alternative, the IOM advocates constructing a system to capture the incomes remitted by migrants to their families as a tool for community and national development, rather than focusing on the difficult task of creating jobs at home.

The "Smart Migration" model—emphasizing getting information before a woman leaves—works to legitimate women staying home, as above analyzed. In contrast, recent materials coming out of the IOM-Moldova office explain that, as part of this "Migration Management" project, IOM-Moldova is supporting new state-run legal labor migration programs. In 2006, one guest worker–style program sent laborers to the Czech Republic, and another offered cultural training for five hundred female Moldovan citizens to work in Italy as domestic workers. In fact, legal migrant domestic work sometimes is perceived in these new campaigns as a good alternative to counter women's undocumented migration abroad. At the annual Human Rights Film Fest in Istanbul in January 2005, a film titled *Have You Seen My Mother?* by a Swedish journalist depicted how a woman trafficked to Turkey for sex work was later rehabilitated and eventually found a legal job working as a caretaker for an elderly woman in Italy. IOM-Turkey and the Turkish Ministry of Labour and Social Security for elderly care in Turkey are also proposing such a program.

Such projects are a way to control migration by allowing the Moldovan economy to benefit from the remittances of migrants and overriding the need to create jobs or provide social services at home, and thus are in line with International Monetary Fund and World Bank dictates. It seems that the state no longer has a stake in employing people in Moldova. It does, however, have an interest in "ordering" the disorganized and undocumented nature of such movements of people and wages and in ensuring that these individuals do not migrate abroad permanently.

The geographic routes that these migration and development campaigns focus on reveal their gendered dynamics. Istanbul holds fourth place as a destination for migrant labor from Moldova, especially for women. Yet, because the Kiel report organized the data according to *regions* that individuals migrate to—countries of the Commonwealth of Independent States (CIS), EU/Israel, and "other"—instead of according to individual cities or countries, and because in this categorization Istanbul falls into the "other" region (which holds the least number of migrant laborers), the route from Moldova to Turkey becomes a less important target for the "migration and development" campaign. Interestingly, the most significant problem with migration, according to this report, is no longer the trafficking of Moldovan women to Turkey for sexual exploitation but problems with wages not being paid to migrant laborers and getting hassled by local authorities in CIS nations such as Russia and Ukraine. These latter are routes taken primarily by men. In terms of its concerns with the wider exploitations of migrant laborers in general, this campaign is a beneficial development for migrants of all kinds. Yet the kind of exploitation acknowledged here seems limited almost exclusively now to men. Women migrants and their exploitations are still noticed only when they are sexual in nature. That they may have other types of exploitations, such as the work-related ones detailed in chapter 4, is not acknowledged. Men who might be forced or duped into being trafficked, let alone sexually abused, are also largely invisible.

This narrative of migration is one example of how new actors, such as IGOs, are influencing shifting state processes in a formerly Soviet state. In Moldova, the image of disorderly migrant labor gives IGOs like the IOM, and even the Moldovan state itself, reason to intervene (or not) in particular ways through regulations: a reason for statecraft, much as Berman (2003) argues is the case for the regional EU. It also works to uphold old stratifications and to construct new ones. The Kiel report represents a new, positive view of the potentials of migrant labor. In a general sense, then, this shifts the value of migrations from Moldova from a negative image (even if such negative views are still represented in the IOM and NGO staff narratives regarding the "Smart Migration" campaign) to a positive one (in IOM headquarters' materials online and in funded research reports like the Kiel report). With these shifts come some tensions between the priorities of IOM headquarters and the concerns of IOM-Moldova and IOM-Turkey staff on the ground.

Yet we can see here a general trend, especially in official documentation from IOM headquarters and influential more and more in the local IOM-Moldova office. In the emergent gendered moral economies of the IOM, migrant subjects have been transformed from victims of economic change to agents for economic development. The disorderly migrant in question at the IOM has traditionally been a woman (or even a girl), whether she is in danger (as in the 2002 "You Are Not a Commodity" campaign) or just in need of some guidance (as in the 2004 "Smart Migration" model). Constructions of commuter women as bad mothers, supported by information campaigns around the country and at border crossings that target young migrant women, surveil and restrict women's movements. Countertrafficking projects continue to pose migrant women as victims (whether of international criminal networks or of their own unstable psyches) forced to migrate abroad by others or by their own desperation. But new IOM migration management plans seek to prioritize migrant laborers—and their remitted earnings—as key agents in the transition from poverty to economic development for individual nation-states. This dynamic is particular to the workings of migration policy in migrant-sending nations.

The migration management campaign, which emerged after the countertrafficking one, represents the development of a new gendered moral economy. Now, the "disorderly migrant" has shifted from being represented primarily as a female victim of trafficking to being seen as a male worker and remitter of wages. The effect of these campaigns, then, is to prevent further female migration to Turkey in any form while legalizing and regulating migration to CIS and the EU, which predominantly are routes taken by males, particularly in the Gagauz instance. With the targeting of certain routes for certain types of migration regulation—preventing some migration and encouraging others—male and female migration is differently legitimated as well. Thus, ideas about gender in IOM countertrafficking campaigns, of women as victims or as the main culprits of social disorder, work to uphold these shifts. Again, women, and especially mothers, seem able to work abroad legitimately only if they are desperate. Yet such migration management programs cast desperate women as either naïve or psychologically faulty for going abroad, whereas men are able to work abroad legitimately if they are advancing themselves.

This new gendered moral economy affects male and female roles as wage earners for their households in Moldova. It creates opportunity for men, as traditional providers, and restricts women's ability to fulfill such a role. It curtails the women whom we have met in this ethnography from becoming the global worker-mothers they seek to be, limiting their roles to the private realm at home in Moldova. Men are thus positioned to be sole agents of community development and change in Moldova. Moreover, these gendered discursive practices of migrant labor deny a space for undocumented women migrants to address exploitations other than those that are sexual in nature, whereas men migrants can address issues such as unpaid wages or other work-related problems, and be heard.

It will be interesting to follow the effects of the regulation of these routes on Gagauz and other migrant labor–sending areas in the future and to see whether regulation actually does provide sufficient incentive for women to stay home while men go to work abroad. This discursive analysis, along with the ethnographic investigation into IOM staff perspectives, points to the questions we need to ask of future policy campaigns and proposed solutions to the variety of exploitations involved in undocumented migrant work. More ethnographic work at the site of implementation could reveal more clearly how much of what we know about trafficking and migration is a reflection of a locally negotiated process involving certain gendered constructs and constraints. The analysis I have provided also moves us toward a better understanding of these migrations and the best policy solutions to them.

It seems clear that in the absence of jobs becoming more available at home, migrant labor will continue to be a way of life in Moldova. Key to the fair and effective management of migration is recognizing and legitimating the voluntary migrations by men and by women for different kinds of work (whether construction work, domestic work, trading, or sex work) that help families and communities. And this recognizing and legitimating should be done while simultaneously preventing and prosecuting all the various types of exploitations that men and women incur in both undocumented and documented migrations, not only sexual exploitation but also other labor exploitations. We must ensure that presumptions about the appropriate roles, labors, and representations of men and women and of culprits and victims—these gendered moral economies—do not prejudice understandings of the problems of migrants and policy solutions to their exploitations, and do not contribute to the feminization of the private realm in this region. As it stands, by upholding the function of women as primarily mothers and nurturers, the IOM campaigns foreclose thinking about women as providers for their families, as well as the exploitations—other forms of trafficking in women—that they face regularly simply as poor women.

Conclusion

"Driven" Women

This book has looked at the gendered moral economies at multiple sites where mobile women workers from Gagauz Yeri have been constrained or uplifted by gendered ideas and practices in Moldova and Turkey and state and nongovernmental organization policies. From this exploration, what can be concluded, not only about the effects on women and families of migrating for work in an era of global neoliberalism, but also about gendered mobilities and agency more generally?

The women from Gagauz Yeri who commute to Turkey to work are actually continuing to express and act on values derived from an earlier socialist worker-mother model and ideals (the alternative would be to remain at home and lose the worker role). Yet even when those women try to function according to those worker-mother ideals, their migrant domestic work and their experiences abroad eventually prompt new desires for consumer goods, a revision of the gendered obligations to their families, new labor relationships that differ from those of the socialist state, and new expectations of their home country. This development is in keeping with one of Pierre

Bourdieu's classic tenets: namely, that individual actions may be motivated by traditional or conventional attitudes (the individuals may be trying to act as previous generations did), but because of the march of time (and in this case the women's movements over space) the actions do not—and cannot— mean the same thing that they did for previous generations. Bourdieu refers to this dynamic as the "Don Quixote" effect (1984). In fact, individuals who desire to "stay the same" as previous generations often must make deliberate changes to their current practices. Thus, these migrant women workers may have the intention of fulfilling their roles as socialist worker-mothers, but their practices and the conditions of their work align them as well with the global neoliberal capitalist structures and values of the contemporary era, not with the socialist past.

In the course of these transformations and movements, they gain and lose power in various ways. Compared with the powerful effects of global neoliberalism on their villages and towns, and in contrast to the powerful position of their employers and the International Organization for Migration (IOM), these migrant women's power is negligible. All of these forms of power and their limitations are important to understanding this case, the processes of change, and women's intentionality in it. Whereas Bourdieu too often leaves power out of the equation (see Ortner 1996), this book, with its foucauldian and feminist concerns, has attempted to place it front and center. I have tried to illuminate what kind of power and agency the main actors in the social field of women's transnational labor hold, the varying degrees and forms of that power, and how the women may or may not enact agency.

Understanding the meanings of the individual actions, agency, and power that inform migrant women's lives is particularly important if we are to create policies to help them. To do so, we need ethnographic studies conducted at both the source and the destination of migration. We cannot understand these new moral economies without understanding the reasoning of women based on their experiences in Moldova and in Turkey. Moreover, without research in Turkey, IOM-Moldova could not possibly understand how to help migrant women who go there, whether or not the women are coerced into making the move. Multisited ethnography is thus key to good migration policymaking.

This book has outlined gendered moral economies at various sites, illustrating different cultural notions of gender, class, ethnicity, race, religion, rurality or urbanity, and culturedness to better understand the on-the-ground rationales for and effects of this gendered migrant labor. These rationales complicate any simple view of the migration of women from the former

Soviet Union and Eastern Europe. In their stories and explanations we find meanings "beneath and beyond" the political-economic structures and neoliberal gendered hegemonies that inform women's lives (Ortner 1996, 146). It is clear from these narratives that women leave to go abroad to raise themselves up, to gain opportunities, as much as they do so out of a need to help their families rise out of poverty. Nonetheless, in many senses, migrant domestic work does not lead to a transformation of traditional gendered hegemonies, even though such a change would benefit women and families. We have seen that mobile working women's narratives may align them with the gendered logics of neoliberal global capitalism, on the one hand, and with the limitations set by social norms in their communities on the other. Yet women's narrative justifications, which recruit ideas of gender informed by such hegemonies, also gain them access to work, wealth, and worlds to which they would not normally have had access, and expand their freedoms in some ways. They gain the freedom to think of themselves, and to live beyond the conceptual and physical confines of the societies into which they were born, even if only temporarily.

Key to understanding these transformations and continuities detailed in this book was capturing the shifts in gendered moral economies over time for four sets of actors: the transnational laborers from Gagauz Yeri, their communities back home, the Turkish households in which they worked, and finally the IOM staff. Aligning with and affecting these shifting gendered moral economies are transformations in the global political economy. Supported by International Monetary Fund and World Bank structural adjustment policies, this new political economy forces a formerly socialist state to be more concerned with security than with providing jobs and welfare for its citizens (processes that new IOM priorities in Moldova legitimate). This change in priorities emphasizes personal responsibility over a state's role in the welfare of its citizens. Transformations in these various discourses and practices regarding women and gender are best conceptualized, I have suggested, as a social field of shifting values, or gendered moral economies, of transnational migrant labor under conditions of global neoliberalism. This social field conditions and is conditioned by the gendered moral economies of migrant labor by Gagauz migrant domestics, Turkish employers, Gagauz communities at home, and the wider international policymaking community in Moldova, particularly the IOM.

In all of these sites, women are defined as "driven," whether by ambition or by desperation. In Istanbul, women from the former Soviet Union and Eastern Europe are represented as desirable as domestics because they are seen as educated, hardworking, and modern. Yet these very characteristics position them as too desirable to be a domestic—for they are driven by desperation—and leads to others (mostly female employers) suspecting that they are women angling for more. They are sometimes accused of using their position as a stepping-stone toward bigger and better things, a better job or a better husband. Thus, they are also seen as desiring too much for a domestic—for they are driven by too much ambition—and as wanting too much from their life and not knowing their "place." Both representations qualify them as women whose desires for upward mobility are inappropriate either because of the assumed desperate routes they take to achieve their goals (monetizing sexuality, working as a domestic) or because of their station as domestic workers and their assumed working-class and rural status. In Moldova, similar accusations abound, even if they often take a form peculiar to former socialist sensibilities about women. In Moldova, at the sending end, migrant women are accused of being bad mothers and disloyal wives who have abandoned their children and husbands because they want too much. "Too much" can mean a Turkish husband and a better life abroad, but it can also mean overconsumption inappropriate for their households, such as bigger weddings for their children and a higher status for their family, which could be achieved through sending their children to university or building a larger house. In Moldova too, then, migrant women are represented as driven—by ambition. These gendered moral economies work to police these women's sexuality, physical mobility, and ambitions to move up in the world.

At the IOM, especially among the staff, we find similar representations, and the IOM staff narratives have consequences for aid targeted to women migrants. If a woman is seen as driven by desperation and is sexually victimized by traffickers as a result, she is regarded as a legitimate recipient of sympathy and assistance. However, women who are driven by the ambition to work abroad for a better life, who may also be exploited in their workplaces (either sexually or in terms of working conditions), are left to fend for themselves. As one IOM-Moldova employee said, with a shrug, "They are on their own." In IOM staff narratives, as in those of community members left behind in Gagauz Yeri, the women who left Gagauz Yeri because they wanted to better their lives were not perceived as deserving of pity and were mostly derided for leaving their children. The *way* that a woman is driven, then, makes all the difference. In the IOM "You Are Not a Commodity" campaign, a mobile worker is seen as driven in the sense of being *forced by* traffickers against her will; as such, she is morally clean and worthy of assistance. New IOM projects recognize the agency of women in choosing to leave for work abroad, yet even these representations position women as forced by other factors: "driven" by poverty and desperation, naïveté, and a faulty psychology. In emergent IOM discursive practices, such "desperation-driven" migration is being marked negatively and is associated with migrant labor routes taken by women, whereas "opportunity-driven" migrant labor is marked positively and associated with routes taken by men.

At all these sites—in Gagauz villages, in Moldova, in Istanbul, and at the IOM—women were seen as legitimately migrating to work abroad only if they were forced to through the victimization of traffickers or by poverty. Even if they are driven by poverty, their migrant labor is seen as inappropriate because of their roles as mothers. Sometimes the driven-by-desperation narrative can even be compelling for migrant women themselves. Migrant women argue that they go for their children, and we have no reason to doubt this is true. Yet this narrative is also a performance of cultural competence, a legitimate argument for seeking to work abroad. The driven quality of women permeates the gendered moral economies that make up the social field of values of this transnational labor.

The representation of the difference in legitimacy of geographic and social mobility for men and women coincides with that in other cases of migrant domestic work (see in particular Parrenas 2005). There are many particularities to the Moldovan case, but only some of them involve Gagauz women's identity as citizens of a former Soviet republic. Their experiences, as we have seen, are both more particular and more general than would support simply chalking them up to the women's status as "postsocialist." We should also remember that panics about trafficking in women—panics over women's bodies, bondage, and freedom—are to some degree consistent over time. At other historical moments in different geographies (such as the United States at the turn of the twentieth century), trafficking in women became an important social issue. Even in Eurasia, the anthropologist Seteney Shami points to the phenomenon of Circassian women slaves in the Ottoman Empire and explains how that practice informs current women's diasporic return to Circassia (2000). Implying the consistencies in these narratives, Shami seems to argue that trafficking is in some sense simply part of the condition of being a woman.[1] Yet there are also particular politics that the issue of trafficking in women tap into at particular moments and in particular geographies.

---

[1] For the attention given to such Circassian women in the West, see Charles King (2008).

The local gendered explanations used to understand and categorize women's migrant labor at these various sites must be analyzed critically, as I hope I have gone some way toward doing, and can also help us critique theoretical categorizations of labors, agency, and gender. The separation of opportunity-driven from desperation-driven migrant labor in the different narratives summarized above is paralleled in social science studies that differently value economic practices in formerly socialist states (Smith and Stenning 2006). In the case of migrant laborers, these values—the "moral economies of postsocialism," as Adrian Smith and Alison Stenning call them—are marked by, and work through, discursive practices connected to gender. This is true not only for women from formerly socialist states but for the wider field of women's migrant labor. As discussed in chapter 4, migrant sex work is separated from other types of women's labor, such as trade and migrant domestic work. Differing notions of agency are applied to these different kinds of work: whereas sex workers are viewed as forced by traffickers into mobility, other types of laborers are seen as forced by economic necessity. What I have argued in this case of women's migration is that the agency associated with certain labors is distinguished by the ethnicity and race of a woman as well: white women (here, from the former Soviet Union) are seen as particularly victimized. Clearly, some postsocialist white women really are sexually victimized and trafficked in this horrific manner, and this practice should be stopped. However, research on the ground with women migrants, like that presented in this book, shows that most situations of women's migrant labor are much more complex: the women are victimized, sometimes by traffickers, sometimes by men, sometimes by other women. Their exploitation may be sexual, but it is also possible, and perhaps more likely, that it is economic, based in class and labor relations and complicated by citizenship, race, ethnicity, and especially gender. In fact, as Gayle Rubin argued decades ago, women are exploited just because they are *women*: as members of kinship systems, worldwide they are trafficked as wives, exchanged by men (1975). However, it is also apparent from ethnographic accounts of women migrants that the women themselves are equally caught up in a variety of these types of exchanges, voluntarily engaging in migration and labors of various kinds and exchanging their work for different forms of reward.

Although the emphasis by some scholars on women being driven primarily by economic desperation is an important counterpoint to the discourse of trafficking that envisions all women as being forced to go abroad by traffickers, this perspective also limits an understanding of women's agency. There is no doubt that migrant domestics' lives are marked by great economic injustice and that many of their own actions and narratives unintentionally support such injustice. Yet describing their lives only in terms of economic dictates does not do justice to their creativity and vitality, to their ability to create meaning in their lives with great agility, even in rapidly and drastically changing times. It is in this meaning-making that human agency resides.

In this book, I have not questioned the root, the underlying structure, of women's oppression so much as I have tried to describe, interpret, and analyze a particular case of it. As in Sherry Ortner's work, this book has also explored the "cultural meanings and structural arrangements that construct and constrain [women's] agency and that limit the transformative potential of all [such] intentionalized activity" (Ortner 1996, 2). Yet the issue of the similarity in the representations of migrant women at various sites—and all women's similar oppressions—cannot be denied, and concerns over wider structural oppression have guided this analysis as well.

I came to the topic of Gagauz migrant labor from my experience studying the gendered moralities of women in a very different cultural context, while plumbing the arguments between secularists and Islamists over veiling in Turkey. Yet time and again, while speaking with the migrant Gagauz women or reading the literature on migrant women in different regions, I was struck by the similarities in the discourses on women. In both Turkey and Moldova, for instance, anxieties regarding modernity—whether that means secularism (as in the case of Turkey) or marketization (in the case of Moldova)—take on different patterns but seem to be drawn with the same pen. Representations of women as "driven" are relevant not only to these Gagauz women but also to Turkish women who choose to work outside the home or are seen as too ambitious. I note this here to point out that images of driven women and their agency inform a great deal of different cultural contexts.

To understand women's oppressions in all these contexts, we must look to the intersection of gender and political economy. In the case of domestic work in particular, and as demonstrated at multiple points in this book, the overlapping subjugations associated with capitalism and patriarchy are linked in lockstep. I believe, with Nancy Fraser, that "the dream of women's emancipation is harnessed to the engine of capitalist accumulation" (2009, 111), and that one way to fight for it is by "decentering wage work and valorizing unwaged activities, especially the socially and economically necessary carework performed by women" (105). Whether migrant domestics from Moldova will take up this struggle or related ones remains to be seen.

To be sure, their physical, economic, and social mobility and the freedom to see themselves as both mothers and workers are a first step in the process.

This book has illuminated women's views of their roles as worker-mothers in migrant labor situations, their experiences of that migrant labor, and what it might have meant and now means to be a worker-mother under socialism. There are certainly some questions left to answer. More in-depth research in Moldova could reveal more of the specifics of the experiences of being a mother and a worker there, how the particular configurations of kinship affect these dual roles, and how socialism and neoliberal capitalism have configured family relations in Moldova. More research on worker-mothers' potential mobilization for their rights and the limits to such efforts could allow us to analyze their ability to overcome the exploitations they face inside and outside the family and workplace. As it stands, the exploration in this book, as Aihwa Ong notes of her own study, provides a picture that is "incomplete, fraught with ambiguity, and shifting perceptions, the way life is experienced by people who live outside of ethnographic texts" (1987, 216).

Gender hegemonies are always partial. Even though women may work within dominant gendered paradigms that circumscribe their roles and status, as ethnographic feminist research shows, they are always working against the limits placed on them in one way or another, whether or not they understand it as "resistance." This applies as much to women conditioned by formerly socialist gender hegemonies as to those conditioned by capitalist ones. Even if those resistances are then co-opted by other systems of oppression, at the very least we can be sure that new systems are just as incomplete as the previous ones and just as likely to change over time. I have found some hope in Ortner's analytical tilt. Power, through the economic and discursive effects of global economic neoliberalism and women's oppression, can be forceful. However, the great variability in ways of life and in individual understandings of them will provoke instability in overlapping subjugations. In the image or experience of alternatives, however brief, moments of disorder will arise to provide some hope.

Bibliography

Abbott, Pamela. 2007. "Cultural Trauma and Social Quality in Postsoviet Moldova and Belarus." *East European Politics and Societies* 21 (2): 219–58.
Abu-Lughod, Lila. 1990. "The Romance of Resistance: Tracing Transformations in Women." *American Ethnologist* 17:41–45.
———. 1991. "Writing against Culture." In Fox, *Recapturing Anthropology*, 137–62.
———. 1999a. "Comments on 'Writing for Culture.'" *Current Anthropology* 40:s13–15.
———. 1999b. "The Interpretation of Culture(s) after Television." In *The Fate of "Culture": Geertz and Beyond*, edited by Sherry Ortner. Berkeley: University of California Press.
Adak, Hülya and Altınay, Ayşe Gül. 2010. "Guest Editors' Introduction: At the Crossroads of Gender and Ethnicity: Moving beyond the National Imaginaire." *New Perspectives on Turkey* 42:9–30.
Adams, Kathleen M., and Sara Dickey, eds. 2000. *Home and Hegemony: Domestic Service and Identity Politics in South and Southeast Asia*. Ann Arbor: University of Michigan Press.
Agustin, Laura. 2007. *Sex at the Margins: Labour Markets and the Rescue Industry*. London: Zed Books.

———. 2008. "Sex and the Limits of Enlightenment: The Irrationality of Legal Regimes to Control Prostitution." *Sexuality Research and Social Policy* 5 (4): 73–86.
Akalin, Ayşe. 2007. "Hired as a Caregiver, Demanded as a Housewife: Becoming a Migrant Domestic Worker in Turkey." *European Journal of Women's Studies* 14 (3): 209–25.
Akçapar, Sebnem Koser. 2006. "Conversion as a Migration Strategy in a Transit Country: Iranian Shiites Becoming Christians in Turkey." *International Migration Review* 40 (4): 817–53.
Altınay, Ayşe Gül. 2004. *The Myth of the Military-Nation: Militarism, Gender, and Education in Turkey*. New York: Palgrave Macmillan.
Andall, Jacqueline, ed. 2003. *Gender and Ethnicity in Contemporary Europe*. New York: Berg.
Anderson, Bridget. 2000. *Doing the Dirty Work: The Global Politics of Domestic Labour*. New York: Zed Books.
———. 2002. "Just Another Job? The Commodification of Domestic Labor." In Ehrenreich and Hochschild, *Global Woman*, 104–14.
———. 2007. "A Very Powerful Business: Exploring the Demand for Migrant Domestic Workers." *European Journal of Women's Studies* 14 (3): 247–64.
Anderson, Elizabeth. 2005. "Backward, Forward, or Both? Moldovan Teachers' Relationship to the State and the Nation." *European Education* 37 (3): 53–67.
Anthias, Floya, and Gabriella Lazaridis. 2000. "Introduction: Women on the Move in Southern Europe." In *Gender and Migration in Southern Europe: Women on the Move*, edited by Floya Anthias and Gabriella Lazaridis, 1–14. Oxford: Berg.
Appadurai, Arjun. 1988. "Putting Hierarchy in its Place." *Cultural Anthropology* 3(1): 36–49.
———. 1991. "Global Ethnoscapes: Notes and Queries for a Transnational Anthropology." In Fox, *Recapturing Anthropology*, 191–238.
Arat, Yeşim. 1994. "Women's Movement of the 1980s in Turkey: Radical Outcome of Liberal Kemalism?" In *Reconstructing Gender in the Middle East: Tradition, Identity, and Power*, edited by Fatma Müge Göçek and Shiva Balaghi, 100–12. New York: Columbia University Press.
Babb, Sarah. 2005. "The Social Consequences of Structural Adjustment: Recent Evidence and Debates." *Annual Review of Sociology* 31:199–222.
Bakan, Abigail B., and Daiva K. Stasiulis. 1997a. "Negotiating Citizenship: The Case of Foreign Domestic Workers in Canada." *Feminist Review* 57 (1): 112–39.
———. 1997b. *Not One of the Family: Foreign Domestic Workers in Canada*. Toronto: University of Toronto Press.
Bellér-Hann, Ildikó. 1995. "Prostitution and its Effects in Northeast Turkey." *European Journal of Women's Studies* 2 (2): 219–35.
Berdahl, Daphne. 1999. *Where the World Ended: Re-unification and Identity in a German Bordertown*. Berkeley: University of California Press.
Berdahl, Daphne, Matti Bunzl, and Martha Lampland, eds. 2000. *Altered States: Ethnographies of Transformation in Eastern Europe and the Former Soviet Union*. Ann Arbor: University of Michigan Press.
Berman, Jacqueline. 2003. "(Un)Popular Strangers and Crises (Un)Bounded: Discourses of Sex-Trafficking, the European Political Community, and the Panicked State of the Modern State." *European Journal of International Relations* 9 (1): 37–86.

Bernstein, Elizabeth. 2008. "Introduction to Special Issue: Sexual Commerce and the Global Flow of Bodies, Desires, and Social Policies." *Sexuality Research and Social Policy* 5 (4): 1–5.
Bloch, Alexia. 2003. "Victims of Trafficking or Narratives of Postsoviet Entrepreneurs? Entertainers in Turkey." *Canadian Women's Studies* 22 (3.4): 152–58.
Borneman, John. 2009. "The Fieldwork Encounter, Experience, and the Making of Truth: An Introduction." In *Being There: The Fieldwork Encounter and the Making of Truth*, edited by John Borneman and Abdellah Hammoudi, 1–24. Berkeley: University of California Press.
Bourdieu, Pierre. 1984. *Distinction: A Social Critique of the Judgment of Taste*. Cambridge, MA: Harvard University Press.
———. 1993. *The Field of Cultural Production: Essays on Art and Literature*. Edited by Randal Johnson. New York: Columbia University Press.
———. 1998. *Outline of a Theory of Practice*. Cambridge: Cambridge University Press.
Brennan, Denise. 2004. *What's Love Got to Do with It? Transnational Desires and Sex Tourism in the Dominican Republic*. Durham, NC: Duke University Press.
———. 2008. "Competing Claims of Victimhood? Foreign and Domestic Victims of Trafficking in the United States." *Sexuality Research and Social Policy* 5 (4): 45–61.
Brettell, Caroline. 1982. *We Have Already Cried Many Tears: Portuguese Women and Migration*. Cambridge: Schenkman.
———. 2003. *Anthropology and Migration: Essays on Transnationalism, Ethnicity, and Identity*. Walnut Creek, CA: AltaMira Press.
Bridger, Sue, and Frances Pine, eds. 1998. Introduction to *Surviving Postsocialism: Local Strategies and Regional Responses in Eastern Europe and the Former Soviet Union*, 1–15. London: Routledge.
Briones, Leah. 2008. "Beyond Trafficking, Agency, and Rights: A Capabilities Perspective on Filipina Experiences of Domestic Work in Paris and Hong Kong." *Wagadu: A Journal of Transnational Women's and Gender Studies* 5:50–72.
Bruno, Marta. 1997. "Women and the Culture of Entrepreneurship." In Buckley, *Postsoviet Women*, 56–74.
Buckley, Mary, ed. 1997. *Postsoviet Women: From the Baltic to Central Asia*. Cambridge: Cambridge University Press.
Buğra, Ayşe, and Çaglar Keyder. 2003. *New Poverty and the Changing Welfare Regime in Turkey*. Ankara: UNDP.
Buijs, Gina, ed. 1993. *Migrant Women: Crossing Boundaries and Changing Identities*. Oxford: Berg.
Burawoy, Michael, and Katherine Verdery. 1999. Introduction to *Uncertain Transitions: Ethnographies of Change in a Postsocialist World*, 1–17. Lanham, MD: Rowman & Littlefield.
Butler, Judith. 1992. "Contingent Foundations." In *Feminists Theorize the Political*, edited by Judith Butler and Joan W. Scott, 3–21. New York: Routledge.
Çağlar, Ayşe. 1995. "German Turks in Berlin: Social Exclusion and Strategies for Social Mobility." *Journal of Ethnic and Migration Studies* 21 (3): 309–23.
Carter, Donald Martin. 1997. *States of Grace: Senegalese in Italy and the New European Immigration*. Minneapolis: University of Minnesota Press.
Chakrabarty, Dipesh. 2000. *Provincializing Europe: Postcolonial Thought and Historical Difference*. Princeton, NJ: Princeton University Press.

Chang, Grace. 2000. *Disposable Domestics: Immigrant Women Workers in the Global Economy.* Cambridge, MA: South End Press.
Chang, Kimberly, and Julian McAllister Groves. 2000. "Neither 'Saints' nor 'Prostitutes': Sexual Discourse in the Filipina Domestic Worker Community in Hong Kong." *Women's Studies International Forum* 23 (1): 73–87.
Chapkis, Wendy. 2003. "Trafficking, Migration, and the Law: Protecting Innocents, Punishing Immigrants." *Gender and Society* 17:923–37.
———. 2005. "Soft Glove, Punishing Fist: The Trafficking Victims Protection Act of 2000." In *Regulating Sex: The Politics of Intimacy and Identity*, edited by Elizabeth Bernstein and Laurie Schaffner, 51–65. New York: Routledge.
Cheng, Sealing. 2008. "Muckraking and Stories Untold: Ethnography Meets Journalism on Trafficked Women and the U.S. Military." *Sexuality Research and Social Policy* 5 (4): 6–18.
———. 2010. *On the Move for Love: Migrant Entertainers and the U.S. Military in South Korea.* Philadelphia: University of Pennsylvania Press.
Chin, Christine B. N. 1998. *In Service and Servitude: Foreign Female Domestic Workers and the Malaysian "Modernity" Project.* New York: Columbia University Press.
Cole, Jeffrey. 1997. *The New Racism in Europe: A Sicilian Ethnography.* New York: Cambridge University Press.
Collins, Patricia Hill. 1990. *Black Feminist Thought: Knowledge, Consciousness, and the Politics of Empowerment.* Minneapolis: University of Minnesota Press.
Constable, Nicole. 1997a. *Maid to Order in Hong Kong: Stories of Filipina Workers.* Ithaca, NY: Cornell University Press.
———. 1997b. "Sexuality and Discipline among Filipina Domestic Workers in Hong Kong." *American Ethnologist* 24 (3): 539–58.
———. 1999. "At Home but Not at Home: Filipina Narratives of Ambivalent Returns." *Cultural Anthropology* 14 (2): 203–28.
———. 2002. "Filipina Workers in Hong Kong Homes: Household Rules and Relations." In Ehrenreich and Hochschild, *Global Woman*, 115–41.
———. 2003. *Romance on a Global Stage: Pen Pals, Virtual Ethnography, and "Mail Order" Marriages.* Berkeley: University of California Press.
———. 2004. *Cross-Border Marriages: Gender and Mobility in Transnational Asia.* Philadelphia: University of Pennsylvania Press.
Coşar, Simten, and Metin Yeğenoğlu. 2011. "New Grounds for Patriarchy in Turkey? Gender Policy in the Age of AKP." *South European Society and Politics* 16 (4): 555–73.
Danış, Didem. 2006. "Waiting on the Purgatory: Religious Networks of Iraqi Christian Transit Migrants in Istanbul." European University Institute Working Paper RSCAS 2006/25. Florence: Badia Fiesolana, European University Institute, Robert Schuman Centre for Advanced Studies.
Danış, Didem, and Ayşe Parla. 2009. "Nafile soydaşlık: Irak ve Bulgaristan Türkleri örneğinde göçmen, dernek ve devlet" [Ethnic brotherhood in vain: Migrant, association and state in the case of Turks from Iraq and Bulgaria]. *Toplum ve Bilim* [Society and science], 114:131–58.
Demirdirek, Hulya. 2001. "(Re)making of a Place and Nation: The Gagauz of Moldova." PhD diss., University of Oslo.

Demirdirek, Hulya, and Judy Whitehead. 2004. "Introduction: Sexual Encounters, Migration, and Desire in Post-socialist Context(s)." *Focaal: European Journal of Anthropology* 43:3–13.

Dewey, Susan. 2008. *Hollow Bodies: Institutional Responses to Sex Trafficking in Armenia, Bosnia, and India.* Sterling, VA: Kumarian Press.

Diner, Çağlar, and Şüle Toktaş. 2010. "Waves of Feminism in Turkey: Kemalist, Islamist and Kurdish Women's Movements in an Era of Globalization." *Journal of Balkan and Near Eastern Studies* 12 (1): 41–57.

du Plessix Gray, Francine. 1989. *Soviet Women Walking the Tightrope.* New York: Doubleday.

Eder, Mine, and Özlem Öz. 2010. "From Cross-border Exchange Networks to Transnational Trading Practices: The Case of Shuttle Traders in Laleli, Istanbul." In *Transnational Communities: Shaping Global Economic Governance*, edited by Marie-Laure Djelic and Sigrid Quack, 57–81. Cambridge: Cambridge University Press.

Eder, Mine, Andrei Yakovlev, Ali Carkoğlu, and Kiren Chaudry. 2002. "Redefining Contagion: Political Economy of Suitcase Trade between Turkey and Russia." IREX Project, Final Report. Washington, DC: International Research and Exchanges Board (IREX). August.

Ehrenreich, Barbara, and Arlie Russell Hochschild, eds. 2002. *Global Woman: Nannies, Maids, and Sex Workers in the New Economy.* New York: Metropolitan Books.

Erden, Atilla, Melvut Ozhan, Piri Er, and Doğanay Cevik. 1999. *Gagauz halk kültürü* [Gagauz folk culture]. Ankara: T. C. Kultur Bakanligi.

Erel, Umut. 2009. *Migrant Women Transforming Citizenship: Life Stories from Britain and Germany.* Farnham, UK: Ashgate.

Ergul, Baybora. 2002. "Hala Moldovyali Hizmetciniz Yok Mu?" [You still don't have a Moldovan maid?] *Tempo* 4 (737): 34–36.

Evans, Alfred B. Jr., Laura A. Henry, and Lisa McIntosh Sundstrom. 2006. *Russian Civil Society: A Critical Assessment.* Armonk, NY: M. E. Sharpe.

Faier, Lieba. 2009. *Intimate Encounters: Filipina Women and the Remaking of Rural Japan.* Berkeley: University of California Press.

Finnegan, William. 2008. "The Countertraffickers: Rescuing the Victims of the Global Sex Trade." *New Yorker*, May 5.

Foucault, Michel. 1980. *Power/Knowledge: Selected Interviews and Other Writings, 1972–1977.* New York: Pantheon.

Fox, Richard G., ed. 1991. *Recapturing Anthropology: Working in the Present.* School of American Research Advanced Seminar Series. Santa Fe, NM: School of American Research Press.

Fraser, Nancy. 1997. "Introduction." In *Justice Interruptus: Critical Reflections on the "Postsocialist" Condition*, edited by Nancy Fraser, 1–8. New York: Routledge.

———. 2006. "After the Family Wage: A Postindustrial Thought Experiment." In Zimmerman, Litt, and Bose, *Global Dimensions of Gender and Carework*, 304–10.

———. 2009. "Feminism, Capitalism, and the Cunning of History." *New Left Review* 56 (March–April): 97–119.

Gal, Susan. 1994a. "Feminism and Civil Society." In *Transitions, Environments, Translations: Feminisms in International Politics*, edited by Joan Wallach Scott, Cora Kaplan, and Debra Keates, 21–29. New York: Routledge.

———. 1994b. "Gender in the Post-socialist Transition: The Abortion Debate in Hungary." *East European Politics and Societies* 8 (2): 256–86.
Gal, Susan, and Gail Kligman, eds. 2000a. *The Politics of Gender after Socialism: A Comparative Historical Essay*. Princeton, NJ: Princeton University Press.
———. 2000b. *Reproducing Gender: Politics, Publics, and Everyday Life after Socialism*. Princeton, NJ: Princeton University Press.
Gamburd, Michele. 2000. *The Kitchen Spoon's Handle: Transnationalism and Sri Lanka's Migrant Housemaids*. Ithaca, NY: Cornell University Press.
Gardner, Andrew. 2010. *City of Strangers: Gulf Migration and the Indian Community in Bahrain*. Ithaca, NY: Cornell University Press.
Geertz, Clifford. 1973. "Thick Description: Toward an Interpretive Theory of Culture." In *The Interpretation of Cultures: Selected Essays*, edited by Clifford Geertz, 3–30. New York: Basic Books.
———. 1983. "'From the Native's Point of View': On the Nature of Anthropological Understanding." In *Local Knowledge: Further Essays in Interpretive Anthropology*, edited by Clifford Geertz. New York: Basic Books.
Ghodsee, Kristen. 2005. *The Red Riviera: Gender, Tourism, and Postsocialism on the Black Sea*. Durham, NC: Duke University Press.
Gibson-Graham, J. K. 1996. *The End of Capitalism (As We Knew It): A Feminist Critique of Political Economy*. Cambridge, MA: Blackwell Publishers.
Glick-Schiller, Nina, Linda Basch, and Cristina Szanton Blanc. 1994. *Nations Unbound: Transnational Projects, Postcolonial Predicaments, and Deterritorialized Nation-States*. London: Routledge.
Glick-Schiller, Nina, Ayşe Çaglar, and Thaddeus Buldbransen. 2006. "Beyond the Ethnic Lens: Locality, Globality, and Born-Again Incorporation." *American Ethnologist* 33 (4): 612–33.
Glick-Schiller, Nina, Boris Nieswand, Günther Schlee et al. 2003. "Pathways of Migrant Incorporation in Germany." In *Max Planck Institute for Social Anthropology Report 2002–2003*. Halle: Max Planck Institute for Social Anthropology.
Global Movement against Migration Control. 2004. "Stop IOM." http://www.noborder.org/iom/index.php (accessed 2010).
Goddard, Victoria, Josep Llobera, and Cris Shore. 1994. *Anthropology of Europe: Identity and Boundaries in Conflict*. Oxford: Berg.
Godziak, Elzbieta M., and Elizabeth A. Collett. 2005. "Research on Human Trafficking in North America: A Review of the Literature." *International Migration* 43(1/2): 99–128.
Goldman, Wendy. 1991. "Working-Class Women and the 'Withering Away' of the Family: Popular Responses to Family Policy." In *Russia in the Era of the NEP: Explorations in Soviet Society and Culture*, edited by Sheila Fitzpatrick, Alexander Rabinowitch, and Richard Stites, 125–36. Bloomington: Indiana University Press.
Government of the Republic of Moldova. 2004. "Economic Growth and Poverty Reduction Strategy Paper (2004-6)." http://www.worldbank.org/md.htm (accessed spring 2005).
Grewal, Inderpal, and Caren Kaplan, eds. 1992. *Scattered Hegemonies: Postmodernity and Transnational Feminist Practice*. Minneapolis: University of Minnesota Press.
Guenther, Katya. 2010. *Making Their Place: Feminism after Socialism in Eastern Germany*. Stanford, CA: Stanford University Press.

Gülçür, Leyla, and Pinar Ilkkaracan. 2002. "The 'Natasha' Experience: Migrant Sex Workers from the Former Soviet Union and Eastern Europe in Turkey." *Women's Studies International Forum* 25 (4): 411–21.
Güngör, Harun, and Mustafa Argunsah. 2002. *Gagauz Türkleri: Tarih, dil, folkor ve halk edebiyati* [Gagauz Turks: History, language, folklore and folk literature]. Ankara: T. C. Kultur Bakanligi Yayinlari 2934.
Gupta, Akhil, and James Ferguson. 1992. "Beyond 'Culture': Space, Identity, and the Politics of Difference." *Cultural Anthropology* 7 (1): 6–23.
———, eds. 1997. *Culture, Power, Place: Explorations in Critical Anthropology*. Durham, NC: Duke University Press.
Hann, C. M., ed. 2002. *Postsocialism: Ideas, Ideologies and Local Practices in Eurasia*. London: Routledge.
Hansen, Karen Tranberg. 1992. *African Encounters with Domesticity*. New Brunswick, NJ: Rutgers University Press.
———. 1997. *Keeping House in Lusaka*. New York: Columbia University Press.
Haraway, Donna. 1988. "Situated Knowledges: The Science Question in Feminism and the Privilege of Partial Perspective. *Feminist Studies* 14 (3): 575–99.
Hardt, Michael, and Antonio Negri. 2001. *Empire*. Cambridge, MA: Harvard University Press.
Harvey, David. 2005. *A Brief History of Neoliberalism*. New York: Oxford University Press.
Hemment, Julie. 2004. "The Riddle of the Third Sector: Civil Society, International Aid, and NGOs in Russia." *Anthropological Quarterly* 77 (2): 215–41.
———. 2007. *Empowering Women in Russia: Activism, Aid, and NGOs*. Bloomington: Indiana University Press.
Hernandez, Ester, and Susan Bibler Coutin. 2006. "Remitting Subject: Migrants, Money, and States." *Economy and Society* 35 (2): 185–208.
Herzfeld, Michael. 1987. *Anthropology through the Looking-Glass: Critical Ethnography in the Margins of Europe*. Cambridge: Cambridge University Press.
———. 2004. *The Body Impolitic: Artisans and Artifice in the Global Hierarchy of Value*. Chicago: University of Chicago Press.
———. 2005. *Cultural Intimacy: Social Poetics in the Nation State*. London: Routledge.
Hirsch, Jennifer S. 2003. *A Courtship after Marriage: Sexuality and Love in Mexican Transnational Families*. Berkeley: University of California Press.
Hochschild, Arlie Russell. 2002. "Love and Gold." In Ehrenreich and Hochschild, *Global Woman*, 190–206.
Hondagneu-Sotelo, Pierrette. 2001. *Domestica: Immigrant Workers Cleaning and Caring in the Shadow of Affluence*. Berkeley: University of California Press.
———. 2002. "Blowups and Other Unhappy Endings." In Ehrenreich and Hochschild, *Global Woman*, 55–69.
Hondagneu-Sotelo, Pierrette, and Ernestine Avila. 1997. "I'm Here, but I'm There: The Meanings of Latina Transnational Motherhood." *Gender & Society* 11 (5): 548–71.
Houston, Christopher. 2002. "Legislating Virtue, or Fear and Loathing in Istanbul?" *Critique of Anthropology* 22 (4): 425–44.
Huang, Shirlena, Leng Leng Thang, and Mika Toyota. 2012. "Transnational Mobilities for Care: Rethinking the Dynamics of Care in Asia." *Global Networks* 12 (2): 129–34.

Humphrey, Caroline. 2002. *The Unmaking of Soviet Life: Everyday Economies after Socialism*. Ithaca, NY: Cornell University Press.
İçduygu, Ahmet. 2006. "Labour Dimensions of Irregular Migration in Turkey." Robert Schuman Research Report. Florence: European University Institute, Robert Schuman Centre for Advanced Study.
İçduygu, Ahmet, and Kemal Kirişci. 2009. *Land of Diverse Migrations: Challenges of Emigration and Migration in Turkey*. Istanbul: Bilgi University Press.
İçduygu, Ahmet, and Deniz Yükseker. 2010. "Rethinking Transit Migration in Turkey: Reality and Representation in the Creation of a Migratory Phenomenon." *Population, Space and Place* 18 (4): 441–56.
International Organization for Migration (IOM). 2003. *Migration Management: Moldova*. Geneva, Switzerland: IOM. http://publications.iom.int/bookstore/free/Moldova_Migration2003.pdf.
———. 2004. *Changing Patterns and Trends of Trafficking in Persons in the Balkan Region*. IOM Counter-Trafficking Service Working Paper, July. Geneva, Switzerland: IOM. http://publications.iom.int/bookstore/free/Changing_Patterns.pdf.
———. 2005. *Migration and Remittances in Moldova*. Report prepared by CBS-AXA Consultancy for IOM-Moldova; European Commission Food Security Programme Office in Moldova; and International Monetary Fund Office in Moldova. Chişinău: IOM. http://www.iom.md/materials/6_migration_remittances.pdf.
———. 2007. *Migration As It Is: An Overview of Migration in the Republic of Moldova*. Chişinău: IOM. http://iom.md/materials/brochures/10_migration_as_it_is_eng.pdf.
———. 2010. Countertrafficking.org (accessed July 17, 2010).
Kabachnik, Peter, Magdalena Grabowska, Joanna Regulska, Beth Mitchneck, and Olga V. Mayorova. 2013. "Traumatic Masculinities: The Gendered Geographies of Georgian IDPs from Abkhazia." *Gender, Place & Culture* 20 (6): 773–93.
Kadıoğlu, Ayşe. 1994. "Women's Subordination in Turkey: Is Islam Really the Villain?" *Middle East Journal* 48 (4): 645–60.
Kalaycıoğlu, Sibel, and Helga Rittersberger-Tılıç. 2000. *Evlerimizdeki gündelikçi kadınlar: Cömert "abla"ların sadık "hanım"ları* [Women laborers in our house: Generous "sisters" and loyal "ladies"]. Istanbul: Su Yayınları.
Kandiyoti, Deniz, ed. 1991. *Women, Islam, and the State*. Philadelphia: Temple University Press.
———. 1997. "Gendering the Modern: On the Missing Dimensions in the Study of Turkish Modernity." In *Rethinking Modernity and National Identity in Turkey*, edited by Sibel Bozdoğan and Reşat Kasaba, 113–32. Seattle: University of Washington Press.
Kaneff, Deema. 2002. "The Shame and Pride of Market Activity: Morality, Identity, and Trading in Postsocialist Rural Bulgaria." In Mandel and Humphrey, *Markets and Moralities*, 33–52.
Kaplan, Ceren, Norma Alarcon, and Minoo Moallem, eds. 1999. *Between Woman and Nation: Nationalisms, Transnational Feminisms, and the State*. Durham, NC: Duke University Press.
Karanastas-Radova, O. K. 2004. "Tuna Ötesi göçmenleri ve Gagavuzlar: 19. Yüzyıl sonlari–20. yüzyıl başları" [Beyond the Danube immigrants and Gagauzia: Late 19th and early 20th centuries]. Trans. M. Musaoğlu. Ankara: Türk Dünyası Yazarlar ve Sanatçılar Vakfi.

Kaşka, Selmin. 2006. *The New International Migration and Migrant Women in Turkey: The Case of Moldovan Domestic Workers.* MiReKoc Research Project. Istanbul: Koç University.

Kempadoo, Kamala, and Jo Doezema, eds. 1998. *Global Sex Workers: Rights, Resistance and Redefinition.* New York: Routledge.

Keough, Leyla. 2003. "Driven Women: Reconceptualizing Women in Traffic through the Case of Gagauz Mobile Domestic Laborers in Istanbul." *Anthropology of East European Review* 21 (2): 73–80.

———. 2004. "Mobile Domestics and Trafficking Discourse in the Margins of Europe." *Focaal: European Journal of Anthropology* 43:14–26.

———. 2006. "Globalizing 'Postsocialism': Mobile Mothers and Neoliberalism on the Margins of Europe." *Anthropological Quarterly* 21 (3): 431–61.

Keyder, Çaglar, ed. 1999. *Istanbul: Between the Local and Global.* Lanham, MD: Rowman & Littlefield.

Kideckl, David, ed. 1995. *East European Communities: The Struggle for Balance in Turbulent Times.* Boulder, CO: Westview Press.

King, Charles. 2000. *The Moldovans: Romania, Russia, and the Politics of Culture.* Stanford, CA: Hoover Institution Press.

———. 2008. *The Ghosts of Freedom: A History of the Caucasus.* Oxford: Oxford University Press.

Kirişci, Kemal. 2000. "Disaggregating Turkish Citizenship and Immigration Policies." *Middle Eastern Studies* 36 (3): 1–22.

———. 2005. "A Friendlier Schengen Visa System as a Tool of 'Soft Power': The Experience of Turkey." *Europe Journal of Migration and Law* 7:343–67.

Kligman, Gail. 1998. *The Politics of Duplicity: Controlling Reproduction in Ceausescu's Romania.* Berkeley: University of California Press.

Knorr, Jacqueline, and Barbara Meier, eds. 2000. *Women and Migration: Anthropological Perspectives.* New York: St. Martin's Press.

Koffman, Eleonore. 1999. "Female 'Birds of Passage' a Decade Later: Gender and Immigration in the European Union." *International Migration Review* 33 (2): 269–99.

Koffman, Eleonore, Annie Phizacklea, Parvati Raghurma, and Rosemary Sales. 2000. *Gender and International Migration in Europe: Employment, Welfare, and Politics.* New York: Routledge.

Konstantinov, Yulian. 1996. "Patterns of Reinterpretation: Trader-Tourism in the Balkans (Bulgaria) as a Picaresque Metaphorical Enactment of Post-Totalitarianism." *American Ethnologist* 23 (4): 762–82.

Konstantinov, Yulian, Gideon M. Kressel, and Trond Thuen. 1998. "Outclassed by Former Outcasts: Petty Trading in Varna." *American Ethnologist* 25 (4): 729–45.

Kontula, Anna, and Elina Saaristo. 2009. *Countering Trafficking in Moldova.* Chişinău: IOM.

Krummel, Sharon. 2012. "Migrant Women: Stories of Empowerment, Transformation, Exploitation, and Resistance." *Journal of Ethnic and Migration Studies* 38 (7): 1175–84.

Kuehnast, Kathleen, and Carol Nechemias. 2004. *Postsoviet Women Encountering Transition: Nation Building, Economic Survival, and Civic Activism.* Washington, DC: Woodrow Wilson Center Press; Baltimore, MD: Johns Hopkins University Press.

Kurti, Lazlo, and Juliet Langman, eds. 1996. *Beyond Borders: Remaking Cultural Identities in the New Eastern and Central Europe*. Boulder, CO: Westview Press.
Ladwig, James. 1994. "For Whom This Reform? Outlining Educational Policy as a Social Field." *British Journal of Sociology of Education* 15 (3): 341–63.
Lan, Pei-Chia. 2002. "Among Women: Migrant Domestic Workers and Their Taiwanese Employers across Generations." In Ehrenreich and Hochschild, *Global Woman*, 169–89.
———. 2006a. *Global Cinderellas: Migrant Domestics and Newly Rich Employers in Taiwan*. Durham, NC: Duke University Press.
———. 2006b. "Maid or Madam? Filipina Migrant Workers and the Continuity of Domestic Labor." In Zimmerman, Litt, and Bose, *Global Dimensions of Gender and Carework*, 346–59.
———. 2010. "They Have More Money, but I Speak Better English! Transnational Encounters between Filipina Domestics and Taiwanese Employers." *Identities* 10 (2): 133–61.
Lass, Andrew. 1999. "Portable Worlds: On the Limits of Replication in the Czech and Slovak Republics." In Burawoy and Verdery, *Uncertain Transitions*, 273–300.
Ledeneva, Alena. 1998. *Russia's Economy of Favours: Blat, Networking, and Informal Exchange*. Cambridge: Cambridge University Press.
Lemon, Alaina. 1998. "Your Eyes Are Green Like Dollars: Counterfeit Cash, National Substance, and Currency Apartheid in 1990s' Russia." *Cultural Anthropology* 13 (1): 22–55.
Levitt, Peggy, and Sanjeev Khagram, eds. 2007. *The Transnational Studies Reader: Intersections and Innovations*. London: Routledge.
Levitt, Peggy, and Nina Glick-Schiller. 2004. "Conceptualizing Simultaneity: A Transnational Social Field Perspective on Society." *International Migration Review* 38 (3): 1002–39.
Lilya 4-Ever. 2002. Lukas Moodysson, dir. 109 min. Sonnet Films. Sweden/Russia.
Lovell, Terry. 2003. "Resisting with Authority: Historical Specificity, Agency, and the Performative Self." *Theory, Culture, and Society* 20 (1): 1–17.
Lücke, Matthia, Toman Oma Mahmoud, and Pia Pinger. 2007. *Moldova: Migration and Remittances*. Kiel: Kiel Institute for the World Economy.
Luibhéid, Eithne. 2002. *Entry Denied: Controlling Sexuality at the Border*. Minneapolis: University of Minnesota Press.
Lutz, Helma. 2007. "Domestic Work." Editorial. *European Journal of Women's Studies* 14 (3): 187–92.
Lutz, Helma, and Khalid Koser. 1998. *The New Migration in Europe: Social Constructions and Social Realities*. London: MacMillan.
Mahdavi, Pardis. 2011. *Gridlock: Labor, Migration, and Trafficking in Dubai*. Stanford, CA: Stanford University Press.
Mahler, Sarah, and Patricia Pessar. 2006. "Gender Matters: Ethnographers Bring Gender from the Periphery toward the Core of Migration Studies." *International Migration Review* 40 (1): 27–63.
Mandel, Ruth, and Caroline Humphrey, eds. 2002. *Markets and Moralities: Ethnographies of Postsocialism*. New York: Berg.
Mansoor, Ali, and Bryce Quillin. 2007. *Migration and Remittances: Eastern Europe and the Former Soviet Union*. Washington, DC: World Bank.

Marcus, George E. 1995. "Ethnography in/of the World System: The Emergence of Multi-sited Ethnography." *Annual Review of Anthropology* 24: 95–117.
Markon, Jerry. 2007. "Human Trafficking Evokes Outrage, Little Evidence." *Washington Post*, September 23.
McClintock, Ann, Aamir Mufti, and Ella Shohat, eds. 1997. *Dangerous Liaisons: Gender, Nation, and Postcolonial Perspectives*. Minneapolis: University of Minnesota Press.
McMurray, David A. 2001. *In and Out of Morocco: Smuggling and Migration in a Frontier Boomtown*. Minneapolis: University of Minnesota Press.
Migration Policy Centre. 2013. *MPC - Migration Profile: Moldova*. June. Florence: European University Institute. http://www.migrationpolicycentre.eu/docs/migration_profiles/Moldova.pdf.
Mills, Mary Beth. 1999. *Thai Women in the Global Labor Force: Consuming Desires, Contested Selves*. New Brunswick, NJ: Rutgers University Press.
———. 2003. "Gender and Inequality in the Global Labor Force." *Annual Review of Anthropology* 32:41–62.
Misra, Joya. 2003. "Caring about Care." *Feminist Studies* 29 (2): 387–477.
Misra, Joya, Jonathan Woodring, and Sabine N. Merz. 2006. "The Globalization of Carework: Immigration, Economic Restructuring, and the World-System." *Globalizations* 3 (3): 317–32.
Modood, Tariq and Pnina Werbner, eds. 1997. *The Politics of Multiculturalism in the New Europe: Racism, Identity, and Community*. New York: Palgrave.
Mohanty, Chandra Talpade. 2003. *Feminism without Borders: Decolonizing Theory, Practicing Solidarity*. Durham, NC: Duke University Press.
Momsen, Janet Henshall, ed. 1999. *Gender, Migration, and Domestic Service*. New York: Routledge.
Moors, Annelies. 2003. "Migrant Domestic Workers: Debating Transnationalism, Identity Politics, and Family Relations: A Review Essay." *Society for Comparative Study of Society and History* 45 (2): 386–94.
Morokvasic, Mirjana. 1991. "Fortress Europe and Migrant Women." *Feminist Review* 39 (1): 69–84.
———. 1993. "In and Out of the Labor Market: Immigrant and Minority Women in Europe." *New Community* 19 (3): 459–83.
Mosse, David. 2005. "Global Governance and the Ethnography of International Aid." In *The Aid Effect: Giving and Governing in International Development*, edited by David Mosse and David Lewis, 1–36. London: Pluto Press.
Musto, Jennifer Lynne. 2008. "The NGO-ification of the Anti-Trafficking Movement in the United States: A Case Study of the Coalition to Abolish Slavery and Trafficking." *Wagadu: A Journal of Transnational Women's and Gender Studies* 5:7–20.
Nare, Lena. 2011. "The Moral Economy of Domestic Care Labor: Migrant Workers in Naples, Italy." *Sociology* 45 (3): 386–412.
Negri, Antonio, and Michael Hardt. 2000. *Empire*. Cambridge, MA: Harvard University Press.
Nieuwenhuys, Céline, and Antoine Pécoud. 2007. "Human Trafficking, Information Campaigns and Strategies of Migration Control." *American Behavioral Scientist* 50 (12): 1674–95.

Nuhoğlu-Soysal, Yasemin. 1994. *Limits of Citizenship: Migrants and Postnational Membership in Europe.* Chicago: University of Chicago Press.
Oishi, Nana. 2005. *Women in Motion: Globalization, State Policies, and Labor Migration in Asia.* Stanford, CA: Stanford University Press.
Öncü, Ayşe. 1997. "The Myth of the 'Ideal Home': Travels across Cultural Borders to Istanbul." In Öncü and Weyland, *Space, Culture and Power*, 56–72.
Öncü, Ayşe, and Petra Weyland, eds. 1997. *Space, Culture and Power: New Identities in Globalizing Cities.* London: Zed Books.
Ong, Aihwa. 1987. *Spirits of Resistance and Capitalist Discipline: Factory Women in Malaysia.* New York: State University of New York Press.
———. 1999. *Flexible Citizenship: The Cultural Logics of Transnationality.* Durham, NC: Duke University Press.
Onica, Cristina. 2008. "Women's Migration from Postsoviet Moldova: Performing Transnational Motherhood." Master's thesis, Central European University.
Ortner, Sherry. 1996. *Gender Matters: The Politics and Erotics of Culture.* Boston: Beacon Press.
———. 1999a. Introduction to *The Fate of "Culture": Geertz and Beyond*, edited by Sherry Ortner, 1–13. Berkeley: University of California Press.
———. 1999b. "Thick Resistance: Death and the Cultural Construction of Agency in Himalayan Mountaineering." In *The Fate of "Culture": Geertz and Beyond*, edited by Sherry Ortner, 136–63. Berkeley: University of California Press.
Özbay, Ferhunde. 1999. "Gendered Space: A New Look at Turkish Modernisation." *Gender and History* 11 (3): 555–68.
Özyeğin, Gul. 2001. *Untidy Gender: Domestic Service in Turkey.* Philadelphia: Temple University Press.
———. 2002. "The Doorkeeper, the Maid, and the Tenant: Troubling Encounters in the Turkish Urban Landscape." In *Fragments of Culture: The Everyday of Modern Turkey*, edited by Deniz Kandiyoti and Ayşe Saktanber, 43–72. New Brunswick, NJ: Rutgers University Press.
Palmer, Phyllis. 1989. *Domesticity and Dirt: Housewives and Domestic Servants in the United States, 1920–1945.* Philadelphia: Temple University Press.
Pantiru, Maria Cristina, Richard Black, and Rachel Sabtaes-Wheeler. 2007. *Migration and Poverty Reduction in Moldova.* Working Paper C10. Brighton: University of Sussex, Development Research Center on Migration, Globalisation, and Poverty.
Parla, Ayşe. 2001. "The 'Honor' of the State: Virginity Examinations in Turkey." *Feminist Studies* 27 (1): 65–88.
———. 2007. "Irregular Workers or Ethnic Kin? Post-1990s Labour Migration from Bulgaria to Turkey." *International Migration* 45 (3): 157–81.
———. 2009. "Remembering across the Border: Postsocialist Nostalgia among Turkish immigrants from Bulgaria." *American Ethnologist* 36 (4): 750–67.
———. 2011. "Undocumented Migrants and the Double Binds of Rights Claims." *Differences: A Journal of Feminist Cultural Studies* 22 (1): 64–89.
Parla, Ayşe, and Zeynep Ülker Kaşlı. 2009. "Broken Lines of Il/Legality and the Reproduction of State Sovereignty: The Impact of Visa Policies on Immigrants to Turkey from Bulgaria." *Alternatives* 34:203–27.
Parrenas, Rachel Salazar. 2000. "Migrant Filipina Domestic Workers and the International Division of Reproductive Labor." *Gender and Society* 14 (4): 560–80.

———. 2001. *Servants of Globalization: Women, Migration, and Domestic Work.* Stanford, CA: Stanford University Press.

———. 2005. *Children of Global Migration: Transnational Families and Gendered Woes.* Stanford, CA: Stanford University Press.

———. 2008. *The Force of Domesticity: Filipina Migrants and Globalization.* New York: New York University Press

———. 2012. "The Reproductive Labor of Migrant Workers." *Global Networks* 12 (2): 269–75.

Patico, Jennifer. 2005. "To Be Happy in a Mercedes: Tropes of Value and Ambivalent Visions of Marketization." *American Ethnologist* 32 (3): 479–96.

———. 2010. "Kinship and Crisis: The Embedding of Economic Pressures and Gender Ideals in Postsocialist International Matchmaking." *Slavic Review* 69 (1): 16–40.

Peleah, Mihail. 2007. "The Impact of Migration on Gender Roles in Moldova." *Development and Transition* 8 (December). www.developmentandtransition.net.

Pelkmans, Mathijs. 2006. *Defending the Border: Identity, Religion, and Modernity in the Republic of Georgia.* Ithaca, NY: Cornell University Press.

Pesmen, Dale. 2000. "Do Not Have 100 Rubles, Have Instead 100 Friends." In *Russia and Soul: An Exploration*, edited by Dale Pesmen, 126–45. Ithaca, NY: Cornell University Press.

Pessar, Patricia, and Sarah J. Mahler. 2003. "Transnational Migration: Bringing Gender In." *International Migration Review* 37 (3): 812–46.

Phillips, Sarah. 2008. *Women's Social Activism in the New Ukraine: Development and the Politics of Differentiation.* Bloomington: Indiana University Press.

Pine, Frances. 2002. "Retreat to the Household? Gendered Domains in Postsocialist Poland." In Hann, *Postsocialism*, 95–113.

Plambech, Sine. 2008. "From Thailand with Love: Transnational Marriage Migration in the Global Care Economy." *Wagadu: A Journal of Transnational Women's and Gender Studies* 5:33–48.

Pletsch, Carl E. 1981. "The Three Worlds, or the Division of Social Scientific Labor, circa 1950–1975." *Comparative Studies in Society and History* 23 (4): 565–90.

Raghuram, Parvati. 2012. "Global Care, Local Configurations: Challenges to Conceptualizations of Care." *Global Networks* 12 (2): 155–74.

Raijman, Rebecca. 2012. "Foreigners and Outsiders: Exclusionist Attitudes towards Labour Migrants in Israel." *International Migration* 51 (1): 136–51.

Ries, Nancy. 1994. "Burden of Mythic Identity: Russian Women at Odds with Themselves." In *Feminist Nightmares: Women at Odds*, edited by Susan Ostrov Weisser and Jennifer Fleischner, 242–68. New York: New York University Press.

———. 2002. "'Honest Bandits' and 'Warped People': Russian Narratives about Money, Corruption, and Moral Decay." In *Ethnography in Unstable Places: Everyday Lives in Contexts of Dramatic Political Change*, edited by Carol J. Greenhouse, Elizabeth Mertz, and Kay B. Warren, 276–315. Durham, NC: Duke University Press.

Rivas, Lynn May. 2002. "Invisible Labors: Caring for the Independent Person." In Ehrenreich and Hochschild, *Global Woman*, 70–84.

Rivkin-Fish, Michele. 2004. "Change Yourself and the Whole World Will Become Kinder: Russian Activists for Reproductive Health and the Limits of Claims Making for Women." *Medical Anthropology Quarterly* 18 (3): 281–304.

———. 2005. *Women's Health in Postsoviet Russia: The Politics of Intervention.* Bloomington: Indiana University Press.

Rogers, Douglas. 2005. "Moonshine, Money, and the Politics of Liquidity in Rural Russia." *American Ethnologist* 32 (1): 63–81.

———. 2009. "Postsocialisms Unbound: Connections, Critiques, Comparisons." *Slavic Review* 69 (1): 1–15.

Rollins, Judith. 1985. *Between Women: Domestics and Their Employers*. Philadelphia: Temple University Press.

Romero, Mary. [1992] 2002. *Maid in the U.S.A.* New York: Routledge.

———. 2006. "Unraveling Privilege: Workers' Children and the Hidden Costs of Paid Childcare." In Zimmerman, Litt, and Bose, *Global Dimensions of Gender and Carework*, 307–29.

Rouse, Roger. 1996. "Migration and the Social Space of Postmodernism." In *In Between Two Worlds: Mexican Immigrants in the United States*, edited by David G. Gutiérrez, 247–263. Wilmington, DE: Scholarly Resources.

Rubin, Gayle. 1975. "The Traffic in Women: Notes on the 'Political Economy' of Sex." In *Toward an Anthropology of Women*, edited by Rayna R. Reiter, 157–210. New York: Monthly Review Press.

Ruble, Blair. 2005. *Creating Diversity Capital: Transnational Migrants in Montreal, Washington, and Kyiv*. Washington, DC: Woodrow Wilson Center Press; Baltimore, MD: Johns Hopkins University Press.

Ruble, Blair, and Cynthia Buckley, with Erin Trouth Hoffman. 2008. *Migration, Homeland, and Belonging in Eurasia*. Washington, DC: Woodrow Wilson Center Press; Baltimore, MD: Johns Hopkins University Press.

Ruble, Blair, and Nancy Popson. 2000. "Kyiv's Nontraditional Immigrants." *Postsoviet Geography and Economics* 41 (5): 365–68.

Sanjek, Roger, and Shellee Colen, eds. 1990. *At Work in Homes: Household Workers in World Perspective*. Washington, DC: American Anthropological Association.

Sassen, Saskia. 1998. *Globalization and Its Discontents: Essays on the Mobility of People and Money*. New York: New Press.

———. 2000. "Women's Burden: Counter-Geographies of Globalization and the Feminization of Survival." *Journal of International Affairs* 53 (12): 503–24.

Shah, Svati P. 2008. "South Asian Border Crossings and Sex Work: Revisiting the Question of Migration in Anti-Trafficking Interventions." *Sexuality Research and Social Policy* 5 (4): 19–30.

———. 2014. *Street Corner Secrets: Sex, Work, and Migration in the City of Mumbai*. Durham, NC: Duke University Press.

Shami, Seteney Khalid. 2000. "Prehistories of Globalization: Circassian Identity in Motion." *Public Culture* 12 (1): 177–204.

Sharma, Nandita. 2005. "Anti-Trafficking Rhetoric and the Making of a Global Apartheid." *NWSA Journal* 17 (3): 88–111.

Silverstein, Paul. 2004. *Algeria in France: Transpolitics, Race and Nation*. Bloomington: Indiana University Press.

Smith, Adrian. 2010. "Informal Work in the Diverse Economies of 'Post-Socialist' Europe." In *Informal Work in Developed Nations*, edited by Enrico Marcelli, Colin C. Williams, and Pascale Joassart, 47–65. New York: Routledge.

Smith, Adrian, and Alison Stenning. 2006. "Beyond Household Economies: Articulations and Spaces of Economic Practice in Postsocialism." *Progress in Human Geography* 30 (2): 190–213.

Soderlund, G. 2005. "Running from the Rescuers: New U.S. Crusades against Sex Trafficking and the Rhetoric of Abolition." *NWSA Journal* 17:64–87.
Soysal, Levent. 2003. "Labor to Culture: Writing Turkish Migration to Europe." *The South Atlantic Quarterly* 102 (2/3): 491–508.
———. 2004. "Rap, Hiphop, Kruezberg: Scripts of/for Migrant Youth Culture in the WorldCity Berlin." *New German Critique* 92:62–81.
Tavcer, D. Scharie. 2006. "The Trafficking of Women for Sexual Exploitation: The Situation from the Republic of Moldova to Western Europe." *Policy Practice and Research* 7 (2): 135–47.
Taylor, Savitri. 2005. "From Border Control to Migration Management: The Case for a Paradigm Change in the Western Response to Transborder Population Movement." *Social Policy & Administration* 39 (6): 563–86.
Tekeli, Şirin. 1995. *Women in Modern Turkish Society: A Reader*. London: Zed Books.
Temkina, Anna, and Anna Rotkirch. 1997. "Soviet Gender Contracts and their Shifts in Contemporary Russia." *Finnish Review of East European Studies* 2:6–24.
Tishkov, Valery, Shanna Zayinchkovskaya, and Galina Vitkovskaya. 2005. "Migration in the Countries of the Former Soviet Union." Working Paper for Policy Analysis and Research Program of the Global Commission on International Migration. Geneva, Switzerland: Global Commission on International Migration.
Truong, Thanh-Dam. 1996. "Gender, International Migration, and Social Reproduction: Implications for Theory, Policy, Research and Networking." *Asian and Pacific Migration Journal* 5 (1): 27–52.
Tyldum, Guri, and Anette Brunovskis. 2005. "Describing the Unobserved: Methodological Challenges in Empirical Studies on Human Trafficking." *International Migration* 43 (1/2): 17–34.
Unal, Rahime Arzu. 2006. *Transformations in Transit: Reconstitution of Gender Identity among Moldovan Domestic Workers in Istanbul Households*. Masters of Arts in Sociology thesis, University of Bosphorus, Istanbul.
Urla, Jacqueline, and Jennifer Terry, eds. 1995. *Deviant Bodies: Critical Perspectives on Difference in Science and Popular Culture*. Bloomington: Indiana University Press.
Uygun, Banu Nilgün. 2004. "Post-socialist Scapes of Economy and Desire: The Case of Turkey." *Focaal: European Journal of Anthropology* 43:27–45.
———. 2006. "Being a 'Natasha': Transnationalism, Sex Work and the Political Economy of Desire in Black Sea Region." PhD diss., Duke University. ProQuest Company.
Verdery, Katherine. 1996. *What Was Socialism and What Comes Next?* Princeton, NJ: Princeton University Press.
Verdery, Katherine, and Sharad Chari. 2009. "Thinking between the Posts: Postsocialism, Postcolonialism, and Ethnography after the End of the Cold War." *Comparative Studies in Society and History* 51 (1): 6–34.
Wanner, Catherine. 2005. "Money, Morality and New Forms of Exchange in Postsocialist Ukraine." *Ethnos* 70 (4): 515–37.
Wedel, Janine. 2001. *Collision and Collusion: The Strange Case of Western Aid to Eastern Europe*. New York: Palgrave.
Werbner, Pnina. 2002. *Imagined Diasporas Among Manchester Muslims: The Public Performance of Pakistani Transnational Identity Politics*. Santa Fe, NM: School of American Research Press.

Wijers, Marjan. 1998. "Women, Labor and Migration: The Position of Trafficked Women and Strategies for Support." In Kempadoo and Doezema, *Global Sex Workers*, 69–78.
Willis, Katie, and Brenda Yeoh, eds. 2000. *Gender and Migration*. Northampton, MA: Elgar Reference Collection.
Wimmer, Andreas, and Nina Glick-Schiller. 2003. "Methodological Nationalism, the Social Sciences, and the Study of Migration: An Essay in Historical Epistemology." *International Migration Review* 37 (3): 576–610.
Wise, Amanda, and Selvaraj Velayutham. 2005. "Moral Economies of a Translocal Village: Obligation and Shame among South Indian Transnational Migrants." *Global Networks* 5 (1): 27–47.
Wolfe, Thomas. 2000. "Cultures and Communities in the Anthropology of Eastern Europe and the former Soviet Union." *Annual Review of Anthropology* 29:195–216.
Wong, Madeleine. 2006. "The Gendered Politics of Remittances in Ghanaian Transnational Families." *Economic Geography* 82 (4): 355–81.
Wood, Elizabeth. 1997. *The Baba and the Comrade: Gender and Politics in Revolutionary Russia*. Indianapolis: Indiana University Press.
World Bank. 2004. *International Development Association Country Assistance Strategy for Republic of Moldova*. ECCU2 Country Unit, Europe and Central Asia Region Report 28556-MD, November 12. Washington, DC: World Bank.
———. 2005. *Moldova: Opportunities for Accelerated Growth: A Country Economic Memorandum for the Republic of Moldova*. Poverty Reduction and Economic Management Unit Report 32876-MD, September 9. Washington, DC: World Bank.
Yavuz, M. Hakan. 2000. "Cleansing Islam from the Public Sphere (1)." *Journal of International Affairs* 54 (1): 21.
Yeates, Nicola. 2012. "Global Care Chains: A State-of-the-Art Review and Future Directions in Care Transnationalization Research." *Global Networks* 12 (2): 135–54.
Yeoh, Brenda A., and Shirlena Huang. 1998. "Negotiating Public Space: Strategies and Styles of Migrant Female Domestic Workers in Singapore." *Urban Studies* 35 (3): 583–602.
Yükseker, Deniz. 2000. "Weaving a Market: The Informal Economy and Gender in a Transnational Trade Network between Turkey and the Former Soviet Union." PhD diss., State University of New York at Binghamton.
———. 2004. "Trust and Gender in a Transnational Market: The Public Culture of Laleli, Istanbul." *Public Culture* 16 (1): 47–65.
Yurchak, Alexei. 2006. *Everything Was Forever, Until It Was No More: The Last Soviet Generation*. Princeton, NJ: Princeton University Press.
Zarembka, Joy M. 2002. "America's Dirty Work: Migrant Maids and Modern-Day Slavery." In Ehrenreich and Hochschild, *Global Woman*, 142–253.
Zheng, Tiantian. 2008a. "Anti-Trafficking, Human Rights, and Social Justice." Editorial. *Wagadu: A Journal of Transnational Women's and Gender Studies* 5:1–5.
———. 2008b. "Anti-Trafficking Campaign and Karaoke Bar Hostesses in China." *Wagadu: A Journal of Transnational Women's and Gender Studies* 5:74–92.
Zimmerman, Mary, Jacqueline Litt, and Christine Bose, eds. 2006. *Global Dimensions of Gender and Carework*. Stanford, CA: Stanford University Press.
Žižek, Slavoj. 2002. Introduction to *Revolution at the Gates: A Selection of Writings from February to October 1917 by V. I. Lenin*, edited by Slavoj Žižek. London: Verso.

Index

Page numbers in boldface refer to illustrations.

Abu-Lughod, Lila, 15, 23
activism, 28–29
affective labor: domestic work as, 103, 132; kinship terms, use of, 118, 127, 140, 153; sex work and, 169–70; Soviet *blat* economy and, 142–43; women's relationships outside of work and, 167, 170, 197–98
agency, 97; acceptance of/resistance to dominant discourses and, 47–48, 98; acceptance of/resistance to gendered moral economies and, 17–18, 33–34, 43, 97, 141–42, 208–9; construction vs. denial of, 212–14; consumerism and, 44; managing work conditions and, 139–40, 147; meaning making and, 28–29, 98; sexuality and, 167, 170; social field concept and, 10
Akalin, Ayşe, 103, 114, 119, 123n13, 128
ambition, 33; agency and, 213–14; Moldovan views of commuter mothers and, 210; Turkish views of Moldovan domestics and, 106, 126–27, 129, 130, 138, 158, 209–10. *See also* uplift and upward mobility

Ana Sozu (*Mother Tongue*, Gagauz-language newspaper), 81
Anderson, Bridget, 104
Appadurai, Arjun, 9n8, 21
Armenians, 123
Avila, Ernestine, 45

Basch, Linda, 10n9, 12–13
Belarus, 26, 79, 122
Bellér-Hann, Ildikó, 109, 111, 122, 169
Berdahl, Daphne, 88n11, 141
Berman, Jacqueline, 168, 178–79, 183–84, 204
Beşalma. *See* Gagauz Yeri
Blanc, Cristina Szanton, 10n9, 12–13
blat relations, 41–42, 142–43, 147, 154
Bose, Christine, 48
Bourdieu, Pierre, 5–6, 9–10, 15–16, 207–8
Brennan, Denise, 22, 170; on countertrafficking efforts, 179; Dominican sex worker ethnographic work, 43n, 75, 140
Brettell, Caroline, 13n13
Bruno, Marta, 59
Bulgaria, 3n3, 26, 68n16, 94, 124
Bulgarian Turks, 123–24, 125

child care: as affective labor, 127; as class of domestic work in Turkey, 114–15, 121, 123; duty descriptions, 119, 128, 131, 153; employer conflicts and, 155–56; Turkey's lack of public services, 101; working conditions and, 145
Chimpoesh, Luba, 34, 96
Chin, Christine, 104, 117
Chişinău, 29, 51, 52, 52n10, 59, 83, 89, 151, 178n3, 182n6, 185, 190, 194
class status: attitude toward trade and, 90–91; migrant work causing shifts in, 27, 46, 60–61, 70, 76, 96–97, 181–82; migration opportunities and, 6–7, 42–43, 48–49, 57; relative power and, 24; Russian language and, 78–79. *See also* elites, Moldovan; elites, Turkish; uplift and upward mobility
Commonwealth of Independent States (CIS), 49n9, 83, 203–4, 205
Comrat. *See* Gagauz Yeri
Congaz. *See* Gagauz Yeri
Constable, Nicole, 145
consumerism: as agency, 44; local (Moldovan) concerns about, 50, 62–63, 66, 67–68, 69, 71, 210; migrant work as encouraging, 19, 61–62, 207; neoliberalism and, 21, 39; women's decisions to work and, 41
"consumption" work, 111, 197
Contact (nongovernmental organization), 176, 182n6, 187
cooking (as duty of domestics in Turkey), 114, 123, 125, 128
countertrafficking campaigns, 180, 204; as detrimental to voluntary migrants, 177–79, 181; difficulty finding victims, 4, 176–77, 187, 199, 200; inability to address joblessness as cause, 176, 199–200, 202; individual responsibility focus, 189–92; security focus, 183–84. *See also* International Organization for Migration
Coutin, Susan Bibler, 202n14
cultural capital, 16, 68, 133, 138–39, 159–60, 171

daughters as migrant workers, 43–44, 46
days off, 102n1, 153, 161–67
day workers, 114
desperate mother narratives, 7; home community criticisms and, 47, 71; in IOM discourses, 205, 209; as

masking more nuanced reasons, 5, 18, 36–37, 42, 69, 70, 74, 84; perceptions of women traders and, 59; as performances of values, 3, 35–37, 211; sympathy within host country and, 73; *vs.* trafficking explanations, 212–13

Dewey, Susan, 179n4, 186

diversity: countertrafficking material and, 187–88, 190–91; within home communities, 23–24, 76–77, 86–87, 92, 98; within host communities, 24, 76–77, 105, 129; philosophical transnationalism and, 12

domestic work as women's work: countertrafficking campaign narratives and, 181, 191, 192, 201, 206; Gagauz criticisms of Turkish women and, 155–56, 158–60, 171–72; limits to women's advancement and, 47; men and, 47, 63–64; postsocialist changes and, 33, 41, 55–56, 71, 181, 192; professionalization and, 125–26, 128; socialist practices, 50; Turkish norms, 100–101, 101–2, 127, 130–31; undervaluing of work and, 19, 66, 77, 214; worldwide, 103–4

doormen, 114n10, 117, 127n14, 157, 160

duties of migrant domestics. *See* child care; cooking; elder care

education expenses as reason for migrant work, 3, 35, 36, 54, 57, 87, 89, 90, 210

Ehrenreich, Barbara, 22, 39–40, 130

elder care: as affective labor, 127; as class of domestic work in Turkey, 114–15, 121, 123; duty descriptions, 131; Turkey's lack of public services, 101; Turkish employers' preferences for migrant workers, 102; working conditions, 129, 145, 152, 153, 172

elites, Moldovan, 181–82; desires to travel abroad, 196–97; IOM countertrafficking campaigns and, 180–81, 185, 190, 195–96, 198–99

elites, Turkish, 103, 103n2: desire for domestic workers, 30–31, 103, 129; secularism among, 115, 213; *sité* description, 115–16

employment agents: fees charged, 102n1, 136; interviews of, 30; promotion of Moldovan domestics within Turkey, 102, 112–13, 120; as traffickers, 149–50, 155; as worker advocates, 148

ethnic identity, 23; ethnicities within Moldova and, 77–78, 79; migration opportunities and, 179; perceived low importance of, 10–11, 84–85, 99; in stereotypes of migrant workers globally, 103–5, 131–32; Turkish perceptions of Moldovan domestics and, 105, 115, 122–24, 125, 132. *See also* cultural capital; whiteness/Westernness of Moldovan domestics

European Union, 26, 178–79, 180, 203, 205

exploitation, 106; capitalist restructuring and, 47, 71; cultural capital of Moldovan domestics and, 133, 138–39, 160; definitions, 183–84n9, 186; diversity in, 170, 177, 187–88, 203–4, 212; gender differences and, 203–4, 205–6; minimization strategies, 50, 140–41, 147, 149–51, 172. *See also* trafficking; undocumented labor, difficulties from

factory work, 44, 47
farmwork, 49, 50, 55–56, 70, 72, 96
feminist movement in Turkey, 117
feminization of migration, 6–7, 39
feminization of the private realm, 33, 41, 181, 192, 206
Ferguson, James, 9n8
Fraser, Nancy, 19, 20, 38–39, 214
funding for IOM and other nongovernmental organizations: as cause of trafficking focus, 179, 180, 181, 183, 195; funders as campaign targets, 189, 198; lack of attention to structural problems and, 200; results focus and, 188; Sweden as source of, 183, 189n11; US or EU as source of, 175, 176–77, 178, 179, 180, 183; victims, necessity of finding and, 187, 200

Gagauz language: revived interest in, 80–82, 95–96; rurality and, 96; Russian language and, 78–79, 80–82, 96; similarity to Turkish, 3, 11, 84–85; Turkish views of, 99, 112, 122
Gagauz Yeri: as "backward," 195–96; Beşalma (village), **163**, **164**; Comrat (regional capital), 52, **80**, **81**, 82–83, 92; Congaz (village), 51–53, **54**, 87, 89; descriptions, 3, 33, 51; history, 78–79, 80–81
Gal, Susan, 41
gendered hegemonies: agency/power and, 18, 209; definitions, 17n18; as limiting to women, 43, 44, 101; as partial/unstable, 27, 28, 214; resistance to, 47, 71, 214
gendered moral economies: agency/ power and, 17–18, 33–34, 43, 97, 141–42, 208–9; complicating factors, 23–24, 27, 76, 180–82, 207; definitions, 4, 7–9, 17n18, 37; resistance to gender hegemonies and, 44; social field concept and, 10, 14, 16, 27–28. *See also* desperate mother narratives; domestic work as women's work; motherhood discourses; social disorder, blaming of commuter mothers for; socialist moralities, persistence of; stereotypes of Moldovans in Turkey; trust assessment; Turkey, Gagauz negative perceptions of; worker-mother discourse; individual responsibility
Glick-Schiller, Nina, 10n9, 12–13, 85
Global Cooperation Council countries, 101
Gülçür, Leyla, 169
Gupta, Akhil, 9n8

Hardt, Michael, 103, 132
Have You Seen My Mother? (2004 film), 203
Hemment, Julie, 192n12, 195
Hernandez, Ester, 202n14
Herzfeld, Michael, 69
Hochschild, Arlie Russell, 22, 39–40, 130
home renovations/upgrades, 3, 35, 36, 63, 86, 87–88, 90, 210
homesickness, 145
Hondagneu-Sotelo, Pierrette, 45
Humphrey, Caroline, 68n16, 179

Ilkkaracan, Pinar, 169
immaterial labor, 132. *See also* affective labor
individual responsibility: migration as faulty individual decision, 189–92, 193–95, 198, 199, 205; neoliberalism and, 2, 19, 20, 61–62, 63, 69, 72–73, 178, 200, 209
International Organization for Migration (IOM), 175–206;

criticism of policy discourse by, 34; desires of elite staff to travel abroad, 196–97; focus on women's defective psychology, 210–11; goals, 175–76, 182–83, 182n7; "Have You Seen My Mother?" campaign, 181, 191–92; history, 182–83n7; legitimate *vs.* illegitimate migration, 179–81, 198; "Migration Management" campaign, 181, 201–6; migration statistics, 49n9; "Regulating Migration" campaign, 183–84; research methods and, 6, 29, 182n6; rigid categories for sex work, 170; "Smart Migration" campaign, 181, 186–87, **188**, 189–91, 194–95, 198–201, 204; social disorder, blaming women for, 172–73, 192, 194–95, 198, 200, 205; staff and office descriptions, 33, 184–85; trafficking focus, 4–5, 22, 168, 175–77, 178, 182–84; voluntary migration and, 186–88, 193–95, 201–6; "You Are Not a Commodity" campaign, 181, 184, **185**, 186, 199, 204, 210. *See also* countertrafficking campaigns; funding for IOM and other nongovernmental organizations
intersectionality, 8, 23, 98
Iraq War (1991), 110
IREX, 30, 182n6
Islam: choice of domestic workers and, 121–22, 123–24, 125; Gagauz prejudice against, 11, 66, 85, 160; Turkey as other and, 26
Istanbul, 12; demand for migrant domestics in, 100–103, 138; descriptions, 33, 107–8, 114; images, **108**, **109**; Kurds in, 110n5; as migration destination, 203; research methods and, 29–30, 113–14; *sités*, 115–16;

tourist-trading and, 94. *See also* Laleli
Italy, as migration destination: costs to migrate, 50n; for Filipinas, 76; for men in construction industry, 2; for Moldovan women domestics, 49n9, 83–84, 203; stereotypes of domestic workers in, 104, 128, 140

Japan, 101

Khagram, Sanjeev, 12
Kiel Institute Report, 201–2, 203–4
Kirişci, Kemal, 124
Kligman, Gail, 41
Konstantinov, Yulian, 68n16, 69, 94
Kurds, 110, 115–16

Laleli: descriptions, 107–8; migrant worker avoidance of, 136, 170, 172; as migrant workers' gathering site, 161, 162–66; police harassment in, 136, 165–66; sex work in, 111, 136–37, 169, 170; tourist-traders and, 94, 110–11
Lan, Pei-Chia: class status of migrant workers, 42; cooking as domestic work, 123n13; migrant domestic work in Taiwan, 104, 105, 118, 131, 139, 154–55
Ledeneva, Alena, 143
legal migration: advocacy for, 201–2, 203; barriers to in Turkey, 101–2, 124–25, 191; commuter and employer desires for, 72, 126
Levitt, Peggy, 12, 85
Lilya 4-Ever (2002 IOM film), 189–91, **190**, 195, 198–99
Litt, Jacqueline, 48
local domestic laborers: heavy work, 102–3, 106, 119, 120, 128; state benefits and, 149n4; stereotypes of, 112–13, 125

Malaysia, 44, 104
Marcus, George, 9n8
McMurray, David, 12n13
medical expenses, 51, 54, 57, 59, 87, 93
men: migrant fathers, 36, 46–47, 89–90; in migrant representations, 181, 182n5, 205; migration destinations, 2, 83–84, 90, 204, 205; migration statistics, 2, 49n9; private realm work and, 47, 63–64; as traders, 59
Mills, Mary Beth, 22, 47; informal employment growth, 39; modernity as migration goal, 43, 44, 75
minibuses, 14, 51–52, 136, 162–64
modernity: as migration goal, 43, 44, 45, 46, 75; negative perceptions of Turkey and, 19, 76; Russia and, 96
modernity, as goal of employers: distance from "dirty" work and, 104, 116–18, 131; ethnicity preferences in domestic workers and, 99, 105–6, 119–21, 125–26, 127, 132; sexuality and, 111
Moldova: Europe and, 26; Gagauz liminal position within, 196; history of, 20–21, 38, 39–40, 78–79; lack of state power in, 200, 203, 204; language in, 77–83, 84n9; wages in, 1, 2, 49, 53–54, 57, 93, 200. See also Chișinău, Gagauz language; Gagauz Yeri; unemployment in Moldova
Moodysson, Lukas, 189
Moors, Annalies, 122
Mosque of Suleyman, 107–8, **109**
Mosse, David, 180
motherhood discourses, 35–37, 45–48, 57–59, 67–70, 71. See also desperate mother narratives; social disorder, blaming of commuter mothers for

Musto, Jennifer Lynne, 177, 179, 183, 183n7

Nare, Lena, 128, 140, 147
natashas: conflation of migrant domestic worker with, 3, 110–11, 130, 161, 167, 169–70; stereotype source, 94, 107, 108–9
nationalism, 12–13, 14
Negri, Antonio, 103, 132
neoliberalism: as cause of migration, 6, 28, 97, 202–3; countertrafficking campaigns and, 180–81, 192–93, 195; individual responsibility and, 2, 19, 20, 61–62, 63, 69, 72–73, 178, 200, 209; informal employment and, 38–39; mixing of socialist and neoliberal discourse, 24–25, 208; postsocialist context and, 20–21, 23, 24–25, 25–26, 27, 34, 40–41

Oishi, Nana, 101, 154–55
Ong, Aihwa, 43–44, 47, 75, 214
Onica, Cristina, 84n9
Ortner, Sherry, 17n18, 28, 98, 213, 214
Özbay, Ferhunde, 117, 118
Özyeğin, Gul, 118

Parrenas, Rachel Salazar: Filipina migrant domestics, 46–47, 64, 73, 75–76; global care circuit, 42; home community perspective, 12n13
particularities, 23–24, 27, 76–77, 154. See also diversity
Patico, Jennifer, 13n13
Pesmen, Dale, 143
physical labor, 66, 68, 85, 91–92, 146
postsocialism, 19–27, 212; definitions, 19–21, 38–39; as moral concept, 25–26; neoliberal transitions and,

20–21, 23, 24–25, 25–26, 27, 34, 40–41; overdetermination of socialist past, 22–23, 98; private realm changes and, 33, 41, 55–56, 71, 181, 192; transnationalism and, 34. *See also* socialist moralities, persistence of

"ready" work, 151
religion, 11, 26, 122, 123, 124, 162
remittances: of daughters, 43; as goal of migration, 67, 85; importance of, 3, 4, 33, 49, 201–3; neoliberal restructuring and, 38
research methods, 29–32; countertrafficking efforts, 178n3; employment agencies, 113n9; intersubjectivity, 33; interview formats, 29–30, 53n11, 57n13, 113; IOM research, 6, 29, 182n6; multisited ethnography, 5–6, 9, 12–13, 14–15, 30, 208; research motivations, 31–32
Ries, Nancy, 59, 91
Rivkin-Fish, Michele, 195
Rogers, Douglas, 21, 23, 24n21
Romania, 26, 78–79, 83–84
Romanian (language), 77–78, 82, 83
Rubin, Gayle, 212
rurality, 85–86, 87–92, 96, 146, 196
Russia, 38, 76, 77, 97
Russia, as migration target, 202; Gagauz Russian identity and, 79–80, 85; Gagauz transnationalism and, 12; labor value in, 66, 77, 145–46; for men, 2, 83–84, 89–90; migration costs, 50n
Russian language, 77–83, 93–94, 95, 96

Sassen, Saskia, 6, 22, 35, 39
secularism, 11; among Turkish elite, 115, 213; Turkish perceptions of Moldovan domestics, 26–27, 105–6, 122–23, 127

sexuality: ambition stereotypes and, 210; Gagauz women as liberal, 160, 167; home community criticisms of mothers and, 46, 62; police harassment and, 165; "sexscapes" concept and, 170; sexualization of domestic workers, 104, 106, 110, 126–27, 130, 131–32, 156–57, 161. *See also* natashas
sex work: advancement and, 43n, 139–40; diversity in, 94n16, 111, 141, 168–70; forced, 150, 168, 212; increase in, 39; "sexscapes" concept and, 167
Shami, Seteney, 211
shuttle-trading. *See* tourist-trading
Silverstein, Paul, 13n13
sités, 115–16
Smith, Adrian, 25, 42, 212
social disorder, blaming of commuter mothers for, 33, 175; compared with migrant fathers, 46–47, 64; home community criticisms, 54, 62, 63–65, 66, 68, 73–74, 172, 201, 210; in IOM discourses, 172–73, 192, 194–95, 198, 200, 205
social field concept: descriptions of social field of transnational labor, 5–6, 8, 14; strengths of concept, 9–10, 11–12, 15–16, 22, 27–28
socialist moralities, persistence of, 25, 207–8; *blat* relations experience and, 41, 142–43, 147, 154; negative perceptions of migrant domestic labor and, 48, 68–69, 146–47; physical labor, value of, 66, 68, 85, 91–92, 146; women as wage earners, 7. *See also* worker-mother discourse
Soviet Union/Soviet era, 41, 58–59, 79. *See also* socialist moralities, persistence of
Stenning, Alison, 25, 42, 212

stereotypes of Moldovan women: as "driven," 106, 126–27, 129, 130, 138, 158, 210; high value as domestics and, 19, 26–27, 99–100, 103, 105–6, 109–10, 112–13, 119–20, 122–23, 125, 139, 209–10. *See also* natashas

Taiwan, 104, 105, 139
Taylor, Savitri, 202n14
Tempo (magazine), 112–13, 122, 123, 124
tourist-trading, 41–42, 93–94, 110–11, 169, 179
trade, 90–91, 93–95, 141, 146
trafficking, 149–50, 155, 176; as common concern, 4–5, 178–79, 211; definitions, 183–84n9, 186, 187; retrafficking, 4, 187. *See also* countertrafficking campaigns; International Organization for Migration
transnationalism: as analytical frame, 10–12, 75–76, 98; diversity/particularities and, 24–25, 27; motherhood discourses and, 45, 46–47, 69–70, 71; multisited research and, 12–13, 14–15; neoliberal adjustments and, 33–34; transnational family, 33, 46, 64, 74, 202n14. *See also under* social field concept
trust assessment, 15; demonstrations of affection from employer to employee, 139–40, 142, 147, 153, 170; information about work opportunities, 50n; Turkish perceptions of Moldovan women, 99–100, 103, 110, 120
Turkey: Europe and, 24, 26; feminist movement in, 117; as postsocialist state, 20–21; visa practices, 101–2, 123–25, 151; wages in, 3, 93, 102, 113, 114. *See also* legal migration; secularism

Turkey, as migration target, 86; entry costs, 50n; gender and, 83–84; language similarities and, 11, 83, 84–85; trends, 2–3, 203–4
Turkey, Gagauz negative perceptions of, 19, 26; criticism of commuter mothers and, 62–63, 65, 66, 76, 77; influence on commuter mothers' narratives, 67, 68, 75, 97; Turkish men, 82–83; Turkish women, 158–60
Turkish employers: bad employer descriptions, 147–51; demand for migrant domestic workers, 21, 100–107, 110, 111, 126, 132–33; as elites, 113–14, 115–16, 128–29; good employers, importance of, 140, 142–54; history of villagers as domestics, 117–19; research methods and, 30, 31–32; tension/conflict with domestic workers, 127–32, 154–60, 171–72. *See also* modernity, as goal of employers; trust assessment

Ukraine, 3n3, 26, 49n9, 79, 83
undocumented labor, difficulties from: counter strategies, 167, 171; deportation, 137–38; employer views, 126; good employers and, 140, 151; legal migration difficulties, 124–25; migration costs/risks, 24, 72; police harassment, 3, 136, 165–66, 169; work conditions and, 58, 138–39, 143–44, 149–50, 172
unemployment in Moldova, 181, 186, 187n10, 194, 199–200, 201, 202, 203
United States: countertrafficking funding and, 175, 176–77, 178–79, 180, 183; elite Turks and, 115, 116; as migration destination, 76, 95; Moldova and, 26

uplift and upward mobility, 42–43; desperate mother narratives and, 3, 18, 46–47, 69, 70, 71; diverse interpretations of, 37, 76, 86–87, 92, 98; examples of, 35, 59–62, 63, 87–90; IOM discourse and, 193; jealousy and, 91; justification for migrant work and, 16, 36, 50, 209; socialist moralities and, 48
urbanity, 85–86, 92–96, 100–101
Uygun, Banu Nilgün, 22, 108–9, 111, 167, 169–70

Verdery, Katherine, 20, 41

wages: in Moldova, 1, 2, 49, 53–54, 57, 93, 200; in Turkey, 3, 93, 102, 113, 114
Washington Post (newspaper), 176
wedding expenses, 54, 57, 63, 87, 210
whiteness/Westernness of Moldovan domestics: assumptions as sex trafficking victims, 5, 22, 141, 168, 212; positive perceptions of Moldovan domestics and, 122, 125; sexualization of Moldovan domestics and, 127, 161
wine industry, Moldovan, 38n2
Wong, Madeleine, 202n14
worker-mother discourse: IOM migration management and, 205; justifications for migrant work and, 37, 50, 68–69, 74, 91–92, 146; migrant opinions of Turkish women and, 154; neoliberal values and, 19, 214; relative value of motherhood in, 58–59, 70n17; socialist values and, 3–4, 18–19, 56, 58–59, 61–62, 68–69, 70–71, 207–8, 214

Yükseker, Deniz, 110, 111, 166, 169

Zimmerman, Mary, 48

Printed and bound by CPI Group (UK) Ltd, Croydon, CR0 4YY
22/03/2026

14847708-0001